# Applied Ecology

## A Nontechnical Approach

# Applied

A NONTECHNICAL APPROACH

# ECOLOGY

ALDEN D. HINCKLEY

MACMILLAN PUBLISHING CO., INC.
NEW YORK
COLLIER MACMILLAN PUBLISHERS
LONDON

Printed in the United States of America



Macmillan Publishing Co., Inc.
866 Third Avenue, New York, New York 10022

Collier Macmillan Canada, Ltd.

Library of Congress Cataloging in Publication Data

Hinckley, Alden Dexter.
Applied ecology.

Includes index.
1. Human ecology. 2. Environmental protection.
3. Conservation of natural resources. I. Title.
GF47.H56 301.31 75-6804
ISBN 0-02-354551-8

Printing: 1 2 3 4 5 6 7 8 Year: 6 7 8 9 0 1 2

# Preface

This book is based on a course entitled "Ecology and Man" that I taught at the University of Virginia in Charlottesville. The primary goal is to show students unfamiliar with the natural sciences how the science of ecology can help solve problems associated with human population increase, resource depletion, pollution, and all forms of technological impact on the environment. This is not a book on basic ecology, for only a few of many principles are explained. Nor is it focused exclusively on human ecology, because the environmental relationships of many other organisms are discussed.

*Applied Ecology* is designed for versatility. It can be used by instructors with diverse professional interests including population control, resource management, or pollution abatement. It should also be useful in many different programs of environmental education at universities, junior colleges, and certain high schools. With supplementary materials, it could also be used in a home study course on ecology for the citizen.

In tone, *Applied Ecology* can be described as having a calm and rational, but sometimes satirical, approach to serious environmental problems. I have tried to avoid the extremes of hysteria or dullness. Furthermore, I have omitted very important but highly subjective material, especially the aesthetic basis of environmental judgments and the political strategies required to solve national or international environmental problems. Apologies for such omissions may not be necessary because the scope of the book has been stretched to the utmost. I simply hope that enough different topics are included to show how ecological knowledge can be combined with information from many other disciplines as we work toward lasting solutions of environmental problems.

I would particularly like to thank my former colleagues in the Department of Environmental Sciences at the University of Virginia, Dennis W. Barnes, Ronald B. Hanawalt, George W. Hornberger, Mahlon G. Kelly, William E. Odum, S. Fred Singer, Stephen Skjei, and Joseph C. Zieman. They provided ideas, chapter reviews, and spirited criticism. I also feel indebted to many authors, especially those whose texts I have used in conjunction with the

"Ecology and Man" course and its descendants. In this book, Raymond F. Dasmann, Paul R. Ehrlich, and Richard H. Wagner will see ample evidence of their inspiration. I owe a special debt to the late Marston Bates, who wrote many excellent nontechnical books and articles on applied ecology. In the hope that this text continues his tradition, I dedicate it to his memory.

A. D. H.

# Contents

## PART I OVERVIEW



## PART II LAND

## PART V ALTERNATIVES

# OVERVIEW

# 1

# The History and Scope of Ecology

## Key Concepts

- Ecology
- Relationships
- Interdisciplinary approach
- Observation
- Classification
- Environment
- Natural history
- Utilization
- Extraction
- Pollution
- Conservation
- Preservation
- Profession of ecology

*Ecology* is essentially the study of *relationships,* either those involving interactions between organisms or those embodied in physical and chemical processes affecting the survival of living creatures. Environmental biology is a simple synonym for ecology, yet it should be emphasized that ecologists, in their attempt to understand relationships, must draw on the knowledge and techniques of many scientific disciplines. Biological sciences contributing to ecology include genetics, physiology, and ethology. Environmental sciences especially useful to ecology include geochemistry, hydrology, and meteorology. To attack the very large and complex problems of pollution assessment or resource management, ecologists must work on teams that include not only specialists with other biological or environmental expertise but also researchers with socioeconomic competence (Figure 1–1).

To use a theatrical analogy, the science of ecology is now a "star." *Interdisciplinary*, relevant, and lively, ecology has come to the center of the environmental stage. After many years in supporting roles, it is unaccustomed to stardom and must beware lest, bemused by public acclaim, it forget that there are many other actors in the play. The audience should also be able to appreciate the performances of other actors and to recognize the contributions made by those who "built the sets, provided the music, and worked the spotlights." There will be other plays on other stages that may deserve, and get, more public attention in years to come, but it is hoped that this book will help all those concerned with environmental quality to a better understanding of the role played by ecology in describing and, hopefully, solving environmental problems. Ecological principles can inform and inspire us in our search for ways in which to work for a better world.

**Figure 1–1.**
*Ecology and other sciences*

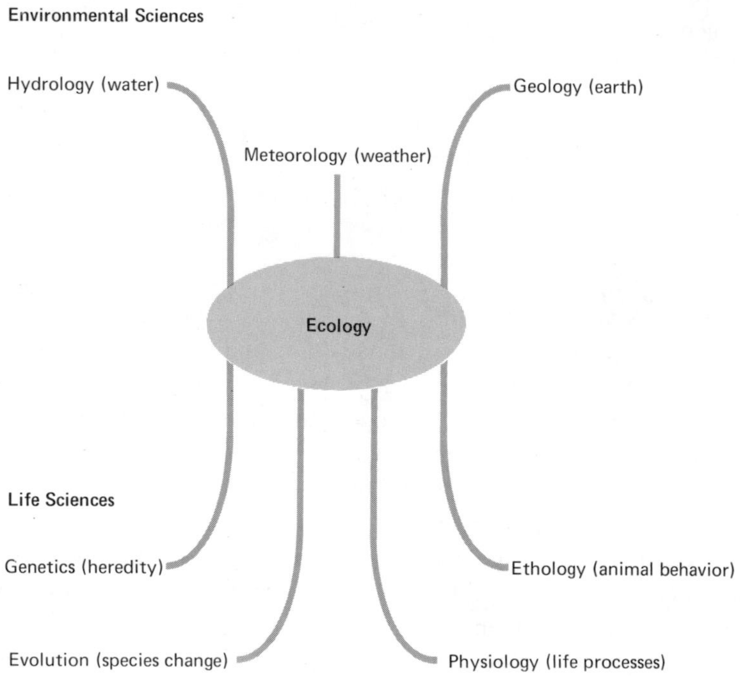

Environmental Sciences
Hydrology (water)
Geology (earth)
Meteorology (weather)
Ecology
Life Sciences
Genetics (heredity)
Ethology (animal behavior)
Evolution (species change)
Physiology (life processes)

## OBSERVATION

As Eugene Odum points out in the introduction to his excellent but massive third edition of *Fundamentals of Ecology,*[1] "The writings of Hippocrates, Aristotle, and other philosophers of the Greek period contain material which is clearly ecological in nature. However, the Greeks literally did not have a word for it." Aristotle (384–322 B.C.) described many natural phenomena, both animate and inanimate, relying on firsthand observation to a large extent, although he can be faulted for accepting "travelers' tales" uncritically.[2] Aristotle was so good, however, that subsequent generations of scholars completely neglected to use their own eyes and spent futile lives arguing "from authority."

Not until the time of Linnaeus (1707–1778) did another major breakthrough take place. This gentle doctor set about classifying the species of plants, animals, even minerals, that he collected or received from others. His *classification* has been much modified, yet he provided the framework for a description of the living world in a systematic way. Communication between scientists of different nations was facilitated by a common use of the Greek-Latin binominals, although that communication has broken down when specialists disagree over the classification of certain organisms. Linnaeus did miss one vital point by assuming that species had been created separately and had remained immutable.

It took a nonpreaching parson by the name of Charles Darwin (1809–1882) to see that creation is an on-going process. Species have evolved and are evolving; the parents most successful in competing for requisites and dealing with the changing physical-chemical environment pass the secrets of their success to their offspring. For most species, this transmission is genetic but Darwin did not understand the mechanism of inheritance.[3] It is only in this century that the full complexity of the code transmitted by the successful individuals and populations to subsequent generations has been recognized and analyzed (Figure 1–2).

During the latter part of the nineteenth century many curious observers were exploring their *environment*. Some, such as Jean Henri Fabre (1823–1915), were satisfied with investigations in a backyard full of insects. Others, such as John Burroughs (1837–1921), traveled widely throughout North America, Europe, and tropical islands.[4] Whatever the scale and scope of their efforts, these naturalists, through their writings, interested others in the study of nature, preparing the way for the development of

**Figure 1–2.**
*Darwin, who gathered evidence of evolution* (Courtesy Library of Congress)

ecology as a science. Coined by the German biologist Ernst Haeckel (1834–1919) in 1869, the word *ecology* has been used little, even in biological writings, until this century.[5] *Natural history* was always the preferred phrase for descriptions of natural phenomena.

The phrase *natural history* continues to be used to this day, sometimes referring to a component of the elementary school curriculum and sometimes to a hobby pursued, often in the form of bird watching, by young boys and old ladies. Actually, natural history is still the foundation of all environmental sciences. With its tradition of accurate, firsthand observation, natural history provides an empirical link with reality. The observations can be improved in quantity and quality by modern techniques of monitoring and analysis, yet the original interest in "what makes nature tick" is still there.

## UTILIZATION

To describe this component of ecology, it is not necessary to single out any individual scientists or writers. In a very real sense, we are all interested in the utilization of the environment. What we can get out of it, especially food, has been a constant concern. Well back in prehistory, the *extraction* of fuel, usually in the form of firewood, began to take on importance. However, only in this century, with the rapid rise of industry, automobiles and cities, have the problems associated with fossil fuel utilization and urban waste concentration come to the fore. (See Chapters 18 through 21.) An ecologist is saddened by the realization that most people did not know they had an environment until it became dirty!

Either dumping waste into the environment, or taking energy out of it, requires some understanding of ecology. The basic strategy of farming involves favoring one species of plant while reducing weeds (which compete with the crop for light, water, and nutrients) and pests (which compete with us for the privilege of eating the crop). A good farmer applies many ecological principles in the management of his acres (Chapters 8 through 11). Predicting the impact of new inventions or large-scale engineering works also demands ecological insights, as government and industry have learned when they have tried to implement programs for the prevention or reduction of *pollution* (Chapters 23 and 26). Finally, the medical profession has become aware of the correlation between an individual's good health and the quality of his environment, which is leading to new concepts of preventive medicine (Chapter 22).

Very early in the history of man, the dangers of resource depletion were recognized. The renewing silt brought by the flooding of the river Nile took on a religious significance. In our unbelieving time, however, men dare to thwart this natural process by building the high dam at Aswam and thus deprive the lower Nile and the Mediterranean Sea of needed nutrients. Unfortunately, there are many other cases in which man has shortsightedly destroyed a resource, even if he recognized that it is dangerous for harvest rates to exceed replacement rates (Chapters 6, 7, 14, and 15).

All the information derived from human efforts to control and use the environment is of potential value to ecologists. Like detectives, they can visit the scene of the crime, examine the evidence, identify the culprits, and suggest ways for the prevention of similar crimes (Chapters 24 and 25).

## CONSERVATION

Concern about human population growth and the consequent depletion of food, fuel, and other resources is the basis for an uneasy alliance between those who merely want to observe nature and those who would like to use her riches. Ecologists feel very strongly that some areas of wilderness should be preserved because it is only in such "Edens" that the full complexity of evolved interrelationships can be studied and analyzed. In fact, many ecologists are reluctant to work in situations where the disturbing factors of man, his machines, and his poisons intrude. Yet other ecologists have been dragged out of the woods and into areas much modified by the impact of civilization.

The different concepts of conservation are best exemplified by the great dispute between John Muir (1838–1914) and Gifford Pinchot (1865–1946) over the fate of American forests. Muir felt that they should be preserved in a pristine state, but Pinchot argued that unused land is wasted land. The utilization view seems to have prevailed in parks, because even though logging, hunting, and other "extractive industries" are excluded, the parks still suffer the impact of intensive recreational development. However, large areas have been set aside as "wilderness" with limits set on all human incursions, including backpacker traffic (Figures 1–3 and 1–4).

The conservation movement took on new dimensions in 1962 with the publication of *Silent Spring*, by Rachel Carson (1907–1964).[6] With the appearance of this book, such organizations as the Audubon Society were made aware that the establishment of wildlife sanctuaries did not necessarily insure the *preservation* of species. Persistent pesticides could all too

**Figure 1–3.**
*John Muir, proponent of preservation* (Courtesy Library of Congress)

easily invade such sanctuaries and kill or sterilize birds, especially those feeding high in the food chain (for example, an osprey eats fish that feed on smaller organisms that graze on algae contaminated with DDT). The sad fate of certain birds served as a warning to us because we also dine high in food chains, when we can afford to do so. The recognition that many living things were being contaminated by man-made chemicals led to a refocusing of ecological research, defining and illuminating the links between human health protection, preservation of living resources, and pollution abatement (Figure 1–5).

## THE PROFESSION OF ECOLOGY

As a formal profession, ecology is young and small. The Ecological Society of America was founded in 1915. By 1917, it had 307 members and by 1973, the membership total was 5,148.[7] To be sure, some practicing ecologists have not joined, either because they do not like the dues or they do not believe in organizations. Then again, some of the members are not

**Figure 1–4.**
*Gifford Pinchot, advocate of utilization* (Courtesy Library of Congress)

active in ecological research, but are engaged in various combinations of teaching and administration. Therefore, 4,500 would be a fair estimate of the ecological task force active (or available) in the United States. In such countries as Australia, Japan, the Soviet Union, and the United Kingdom, ecologists are present in numbers sufficient to support one or more profes-

**Figure 1–5.**
*Transfer of pollutant (DDT) through a simplified food chain*

sional journals for the publication of their research results. However, there are large areas of the globe, especially in the tropics, where no ecological research is being done on a continuing basis and very little ecological information has been accumulated in publications.

Despite the development of educational programs reflecting environmental concern, it is unlikely that the number of ecologists will increase dramatically during the coming decade. To become a professional ecologist, a young man or a young woman interested in living organisms and their environmental relationships must obtain a good undergraduate education in a scientific discipline, usually biology, and then spend four to seven more years earning a Ph.D. by demonstrating the ability to do independent research on an original problem. It would be unwise to circumvent this thorough training with a crash program. Ecologists are needed but they cannot be produced through accelerated education.

There are enough well-trained ecologists now available to show how ecological principles apply to the description of problems associated with technological impacts, resource depletion, and changes in human population distribution and abundance. They can serve on research teams studying natural relationships and finding ways in which we can use our environment without degrading it. They can also work with those in government and industry who are trying to protect or improve our environment. Finally, and perhaps most important of all, ecologists can help develop educational programs for students of all ages who want to gain a better understanding of the interrelationships between man, other organisms, and the environment we all must share.

## SUMMARY

Ecology is defined, with emphasis on its key position as both an environmental and a biological science. The origins of modern ecology are traced to the observations of natural historians, the needs of practical men, and the concerns of both groups for conservation. In this chapter the idea has been introduced that ecological principles can be applied to the description of many environmental problems. However, the need for cooperation between ecologists, other professionals, and all concerned citizens is stressed if we are to solve our problems.

### Discussion Questions

1. Why did people not know they had an environment until it became "dirty"?
2. What are the contrasting attitudes toward resource conservation exemplified by John Muir and Gifford Pinchot?
3. In what ways is ecology like the star of a popular show?

## Suggested Projects

1. Ask your friends what word they associate with ecology. Record the percentage who say "pollution."
2. Check the indices of a magazine or newspaper for the last seven years to determine whether "ecology" or "environment" references have peaked out.
3. Find out how many (if any) ecologists live in your community and what sort of research they do.

## Notes

1. Eugene P. Odum, *Fundamentals of Ecology* (Philadelphia: Saunders, 1971.) As the author indicates in his preface, this is really three books in one. In its entirety it can be used for a graduate course in ecology, portions can be used for undergraduate instruction, and Chapters 1 through 4 and 9, 15, 16, and 21 review principles of ecology for concerned citizens, nonscience majors, and specialists in other fields.
2. Richard McKeon, ed., *The Basic Works of Aristotle* (New York: Random, 1941). Good examples of Aristotle's nature lore can be found in the selections from *Historia Animalium* translated by D'Arcy Wentworth Thompson and presented on pp. 633–640.
3. Charles Darwin, *On the Origin of Species* (London: J. Murray, 1859 and many later editions). Ironically, Darwin inclined toward the now discredited theory that acquired characteristics can be inherited.
4. Donald W. Cox, *Pioneers of Ecology* (Maplewood, N.J.: Hammond, 1971). Although aimed primarily at high school students, this book has valuable vignettes of many early naturalists and conservationists, including Alexander Wilson, John James Audubon, Henry David Thoreau, George Perkins Marsh, John Burroughs, John Muir, Gifford Pinchot, and Rachel Carson.
5. "'Ecology': A Clarification," a letter from R. P. McIntosh in *Science* **188,** 1975, p. 1258.
6. Rachel Carson, *Silent Spring,* Boston: Houghton, 1962.
7. "Directory of Members," *Bulletin of Ecological Society of America,* Durham, N.C., **54** (1973), 75 pp.

# 2

# Ecological Abstractions

## Key Concepts

Biosphere
"Spaceship Earth"
Biomass
Biomes
Life zones
Ecosystems
Biogeochemical cycling
Communities
Food web
Niche
Habitat
Populations
Limiting factor
Carrying capacity

To see the world as an ecologist sees it, a discussion of ecological abstractions is necessary. Biosphere, biome, ecosystem, community and population—are the abstract concepts rooted in reality. They lack the concrete reality of the individual deer or oak tree, yet they are useful abstractions in that they provide a means of describing, comparing, and analyzing phenomena at similar levels of complexity.

It should be remembered that these abstractions, essentially figments, are flexible and can be used in different contexts by various authors. So when a term is encountered, seek a paragraph where it is used in conjunction with a specific example. Only then will you know how the author links the word to the real world.

This particular hierarchy of abstractions can be thought of as a set of boxes within boxes. Briefly, many populations of different species together form a community; a community and its proximate physical-chemical environment can be considered together as an ecosystem; related ecosystems occupying a similar climatic zone across a continent (or, perhaps, along an ocean shore) can be called a biome; and, finally, the layer of life on land and in the oceans can be called the biosphere (Figure 2–1).

## BIOSPHERE

Let's start with the largest abstraction first. In more than one way the biosphere is a concept of the space age.[1] Ecologists may begrudge the vast

**Figure 2–1.**
*Levels of ecological organization*

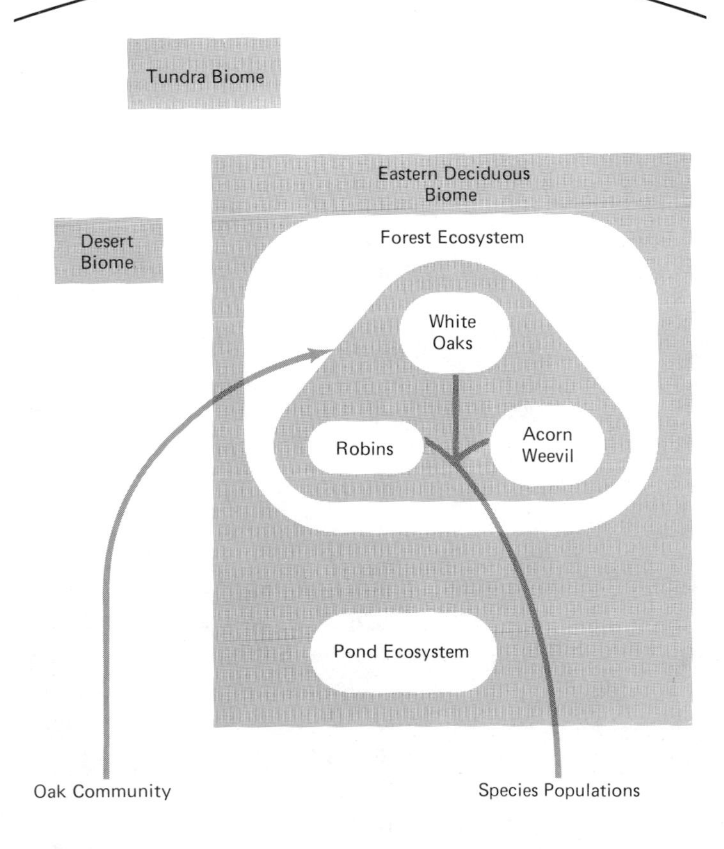

sums spent in reaching a lifeless moon, yet they are the first to admit that the magnificant photos and TV imagery of terra seen from space have helped millions realize the finite nature of our planet; because 70 percent of it is ocean, perhaps it should be called aqua, yet much of the 30 percent above water is too dry for life, either because the water is frozen or has evaporated (Figure 2–2).

The *"Spaceship Earth"* analogy can be carried farther. Not only does the planet have a finite capacity, but also the survival of its human passengers depends on the proper functioning of a complex life-support system that recycles waste material, releases oxygen, and provides food. This aspect was dramatically illustrated by the near tragedy of Apollo 13 in 1970. James A. Lovell, Fred W. Hoise, and John L. Swigart (coincidentally, all "Juniors") had to jury rig a system to scrub carbon dioxide ($CO_2$) out of the air they breathed, and were told by ground control not to dump overboard any liquid or solid waste for fear that their safe trajectory home would be deflected. One astronaut also learned the true meaning of energy depletion as he shivered in the 48°F temperature of the powerless command module.

There is a danger, as with most analogies, that the spaceship concept will be carried too far. On a real spaceship, all the passengers have equal access to the supplies and each makes a similar contribution to waste. Yet, one of the harshest realities of the real world is the maldistribution of wealth, resources, and technologies within and among nations. If we return to the biosphere image, this patchiness of resources is quite apparent. Constrained by extremes of cold or heat, or lack of energy and nutrients, the layer of life can be very thin indeed.

Measured in *biomass* (weight of living organisms per unit of area or volume), the biosphere probably reaches its greatest density in the forests of the world. In the ocean, even in the euphotic zone (the upper layer penetrated by light), biomass nowhere approaches the terrestrial densities; conversely, however, the euphotic zone is never as lifeless as a desert or a glacier.

At the inner bounds of the biosphere there are creatures living in the lightless depths of caves and oceans, dependent on debris and visitors from upper regions. The outer limits might well be set by a high-flying bird, although there is a "parabiosphere" consisting of such dormant stages as fungal spores. On land, the "highest life" is presumably found on Himalayan mountain slopes where lichens and spiders survive, the spiders subsisting on insects blown up from the valleys far below. Various factors (cold,

**Figure 2–2.**
*Terra seen from outer space* (NASA photo)

winds, higher ultraviolet radiation, and less oxygen) combine to prevent an upward expansion of the biosphere, but the lower limits seem more simply related to lack of solar light and heat (Figure 2–3).

## BIOMES

Given the continental gradients of hot to cold from the equator to the poles, and rainy to arid from east to west, it is not surprising to see zones of life reflecting the stresses imposed by the gradients. Although it is custom-

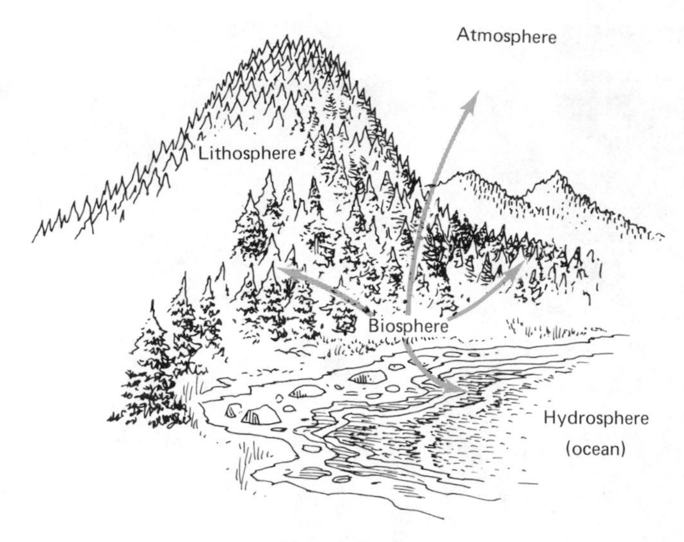


**Figure 2–3.**
*Biosphere interfacing with atmosphere, hydrosphere, and lithosphere*

ary to characterize each zone by the dominant form of vegetation, with a casual reference to some of the larger mammals, it is important to remember that myriad species of microorganisms, insects, and other creatures have also evolved to exist under the same climatic constraints.[2]

For brevity, only seven major terrestrial biomes will be described:

1. Desert: low precipitation, sparse vegetation, and cryptic animals well versed in water rationing. Some deserts can get quite cold, so the absence of moisture rather than presence of heat is the common characteristic (Figure 2–4).
2. Grasslands: somewhat more rainfall than deserts, yet not enough for trees for grow. The stresses of periodic fires and grazing help maintain the dominance of grass.
3. Savanna: open stands of trees interspersed with grass; hot and sometimes wet. This, of course, evokes images of the big game in East Africa.
4. Tropical rain forest: hot and wet, the most complex of all the biomes with multitiered canopies of leaves, the top layer being the foliage of slow-growing giants, their trunks and branches festooned with epiphytes (for example, orchids) and lianas (vines). This biome

may have the longest history and, should exploitation of the tropics continue apace, the shortest future.

5. Temperate deciduous forest: dominated by trees such as oaks and maples that shed their leaves in the fall. This is the biome familiar to most Americans and Europeans because it is where they live.
6. Coniferous (or taiga): a huge belt of needle-leafed trees stretching across Canada, Scandanavia, and the Soviet Union. These areas are cool and moist with various combinations of pine, hemlock, spruce, and fir.
7. Tundra: the coldest biome. The tundra has a layer of lichens, mosses, and sedges on permafrost (ground permanently frozen with only the top few inches thawing in the summer months); it is the land of mosquitoes and caribou.

Much modern ecological research is being organized at the biome level. Many of the contributions by the United States to the International Biological Program (IBP), a five-year worldwide effort, were made by teams working in the deciduous, coniferous, grassland, and desert biomes of the contiguous states as well as in the tundra of Alaska and the tropical forest of Hawaii. The results of such studies can be compared with similar work being done elsewhere. This can be especially useful in attempting to predict the impact of oil on tundra or in assessing the potential productivity of undeveloped grasslands and forest.

In many ways, the *life zones* encountered going up a high mountain resemble the biomes traversed going from the equator toward a pole. The mountain may be ringed with successive bands of deciduous trees, conifers, grass, and even tundra. Yet, going down from the shore to the ocean depths, the zonation is quite different, starting with coastal marshes in temperate regions and mangrove swamps in the tropics (Figure 2–5).

## ECOSYSTEMS

Not only is the *ecosystem* central to the hierarchy of ecological abstractions, it is also the focus of many large and interesting projects being conducted by ecologists and other scientists in various parts of the world. This is the largest working unit that can be studied conveniently (but not always easily) by a research team, and the IBP emphasized the comparison of ecosystems within a biome.

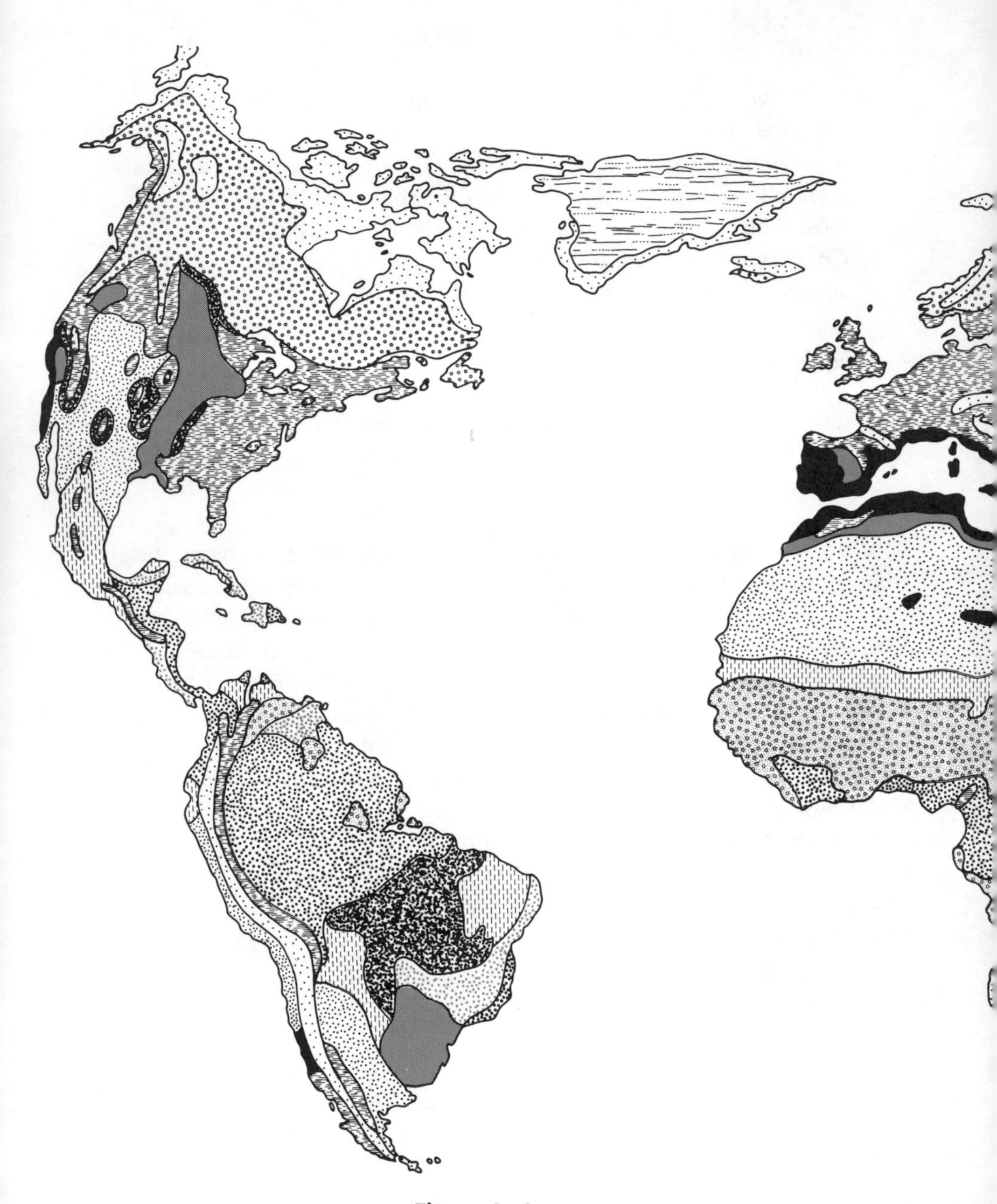

**Figure 2–4.**
*World biome map* [Courtesy R. H. Whittaker *Communities and Ecosystems,* 2nd. ed. (New York: Macmillan, 1975)]

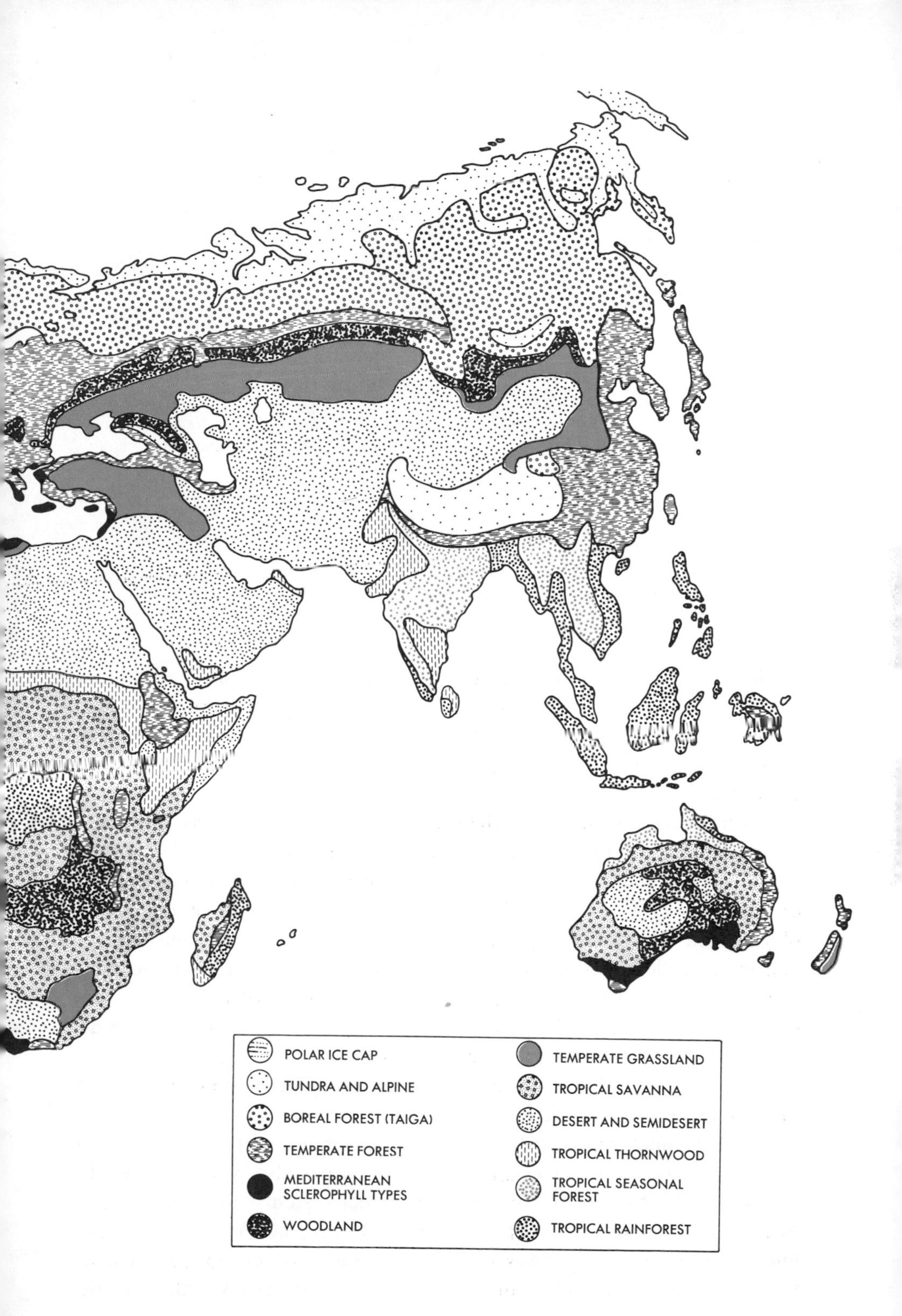
POLAR ICE CAP
TUNDRA AND ALPINE
BOREAL FOREST (TAIGA)
TEMPERATE FOREST
MEDITERRANEAN SCLEROPHYLL TYPES
WOODLAND
TEMPERATE GRASSLAND
TROPICAL SAVANNA
DESERT AND SEMIDESERT
TROPICAL THORNWOOD
TROPICAL SEASONAL FOREST
TROPICAL RAINFOREST

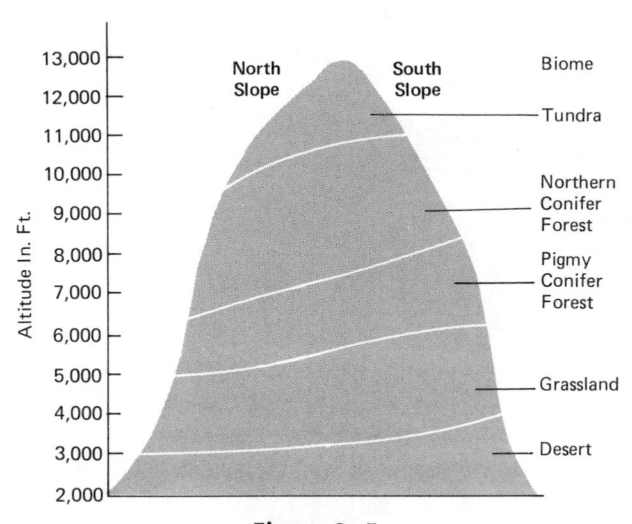


**Figure 2–5.**
*Life zones on mountain*

The ecosystem under scrutiny could be a pond, a field, or a portion of a forest; it is, perhaps, the most flexible of all the ecological abstractions, as it has no standard size dimensions. If containerized and isolated from the rest of the world (for example, an aquarium or terrarium), the term preferred to ecosystem is *microcosm.*

Whatever the bounds set on the ecosystem, a favored analytic approach is input and output: how much sunlight, dust, and rainfall enters; how much energy fixed in organic form is produced. It is also possible to measure the exchange of $CO_2$, $O_2$, and dissolved nutrients. A group of organisms playing a similar community role (to be discussed in the next unit) can be considered collectively as a compartment. Such data can be overwhelming in sheer volume, yet be stored in some small corner of a modern computer's memory bank. In fact, the growth of the computer has made ecosystem analysis practical, permitting the storage of data, as well as speeding its summation. (A discussion of the computer and environmental model making will be deferred until Chapter 24.)

Although much research has dealt with the movement of chemicals in ecosystems undisturbed by human activities, it has also proved profitable to study such *"biogeochemical cycling"* in ecosystems subject to experimental manipulation. Under the direction of George M. Woodwell, a high-intensity radiation source was installed in a securely fenced Long Island forest and exposed above ground for twenty hours each day with dramatic effects on the structure, function, and species composition of the forest.[4] In another case, one New Hampshire watershed, after careful preliminary studies by F. H. Bormann and G. F. Likens, was stripped of its vegetation by winter cutting and summer herbicide treatment and then was compared with similar watersheds to evaluate the true importance of forest cover in retaining water and nutrients.[5]

Further discussion of ecosystems is not needed at this point, because Chapter 5 is devoted specifically to terrestrial ecosystems and Chapter 13 to aquatic ecosystems. In Chapter 19, the ecosystem concept is used to describe urban problems.

## COMMUNITIES

Although community studies focus on the interactions of organisms, excluding effects of the physical-chemical environment, the level of complexity is still very high. Not only is it necessary to know who's who in the community, but also one must find out who is eating who.[6] In listing the plants and animals in a community, the ecologist pays homage to Linnaeus—for without a system of naming and classifying organisms, it would be impossible to describe and discuss interrelationships. A systematist who identifies a bug by comparing it with labeled museum specimens supports the efforts of the ecologist who collected the bug in a far-off forest; the ecologist reciprocates when he collects some new bug, never before known to science (systematists delight in plugging new species into the Linnaean classification).

*Food* is the key word in many phrases used to describe communities: food chain, food web, food pyramid. An idealized *food web* appears in Figure 2–6.

Green plants (also known as autotrophs), through photosynthesis, capture solar energy and fix it in the form of edible calories (carbohydrates). These are consumed by plant eaters, ranging from the mite to the elephant, and they, in turn, support various predators and parasites. All plants and animals contribute waste (and, upon death, their whole biomass) to the pool of organic material on which the detritivores subsist. Things get complicated when a carnivore eats both herbivores and detritivores, but it is often possible to speak of fairly distinct food chains linked by either herbivores or detritivores. Whatever the living links may be, the facts of death and decay remain, with the assurance that nutrients will be released to foster new plant growth and, thus, keep the web alive.

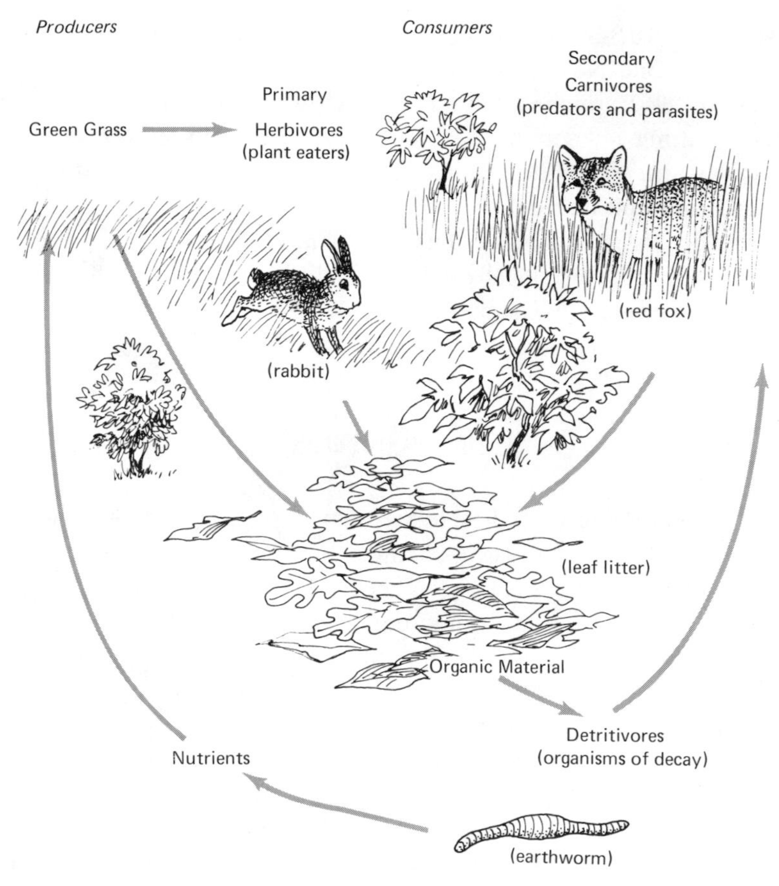


**Figure 2–6.**
*Simple food web*

The exact position of an organism in the food web has been referred to by ecologists and evolutionists as its *niche*. This is not to be confused with *habitat,* which is the place it lives, not the job it does. For example, a deer and skunk may share the same oak-forest habitat, but the deer browses on leaves and acorns while the skunk digs for beetle grubs and turtle eggs, two contrasting life-styles! Niche is a useful term and will appear again in discussions of food production and wildlife preservation.

One final phrase used in describing community structure is the food pyramid, shown in Figure 2–7 for the same relationships that appeared in the web under the guise of the herbivore food chain.

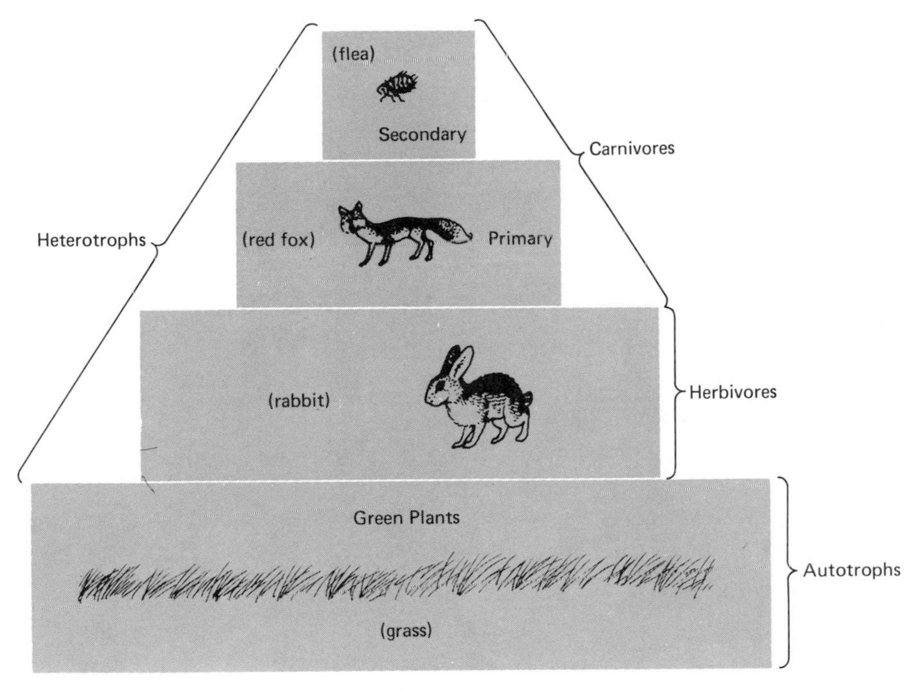


**Figure 2–7.**
*Simple food pyramid*

This model is helpful because the size of each step is roughly proportional to the biomass of organisms occupying that trophic level, thus emphasizing the inherent inefficiency of energy transfer from green plant to "top-dog" predator. In the interest of simplicity, some authors give the impression that this transfer always involves 10 percent from the level below ("conforming to Lindeman's 10 percent law"), but the conversion efficiency for a metabolically sophisticated mammal, bird, or octopus may be higher; for an insect, which needs the water in green plants more than it needs the food, the efficiency may be much less.

## POPULATIONS

At the level of populations, ecological abstractions finally link up with reality. Even here, however, the population is surrounded by an intellectual fence because it is seldom possible to study all the individuals in a particular species. Therefore, the population ecologists must be content with samples taken from the population in a given area, using, if possible, topographic features or other natural borders to delineate the area, or simply setting arbitrary bounds.

Ecology at the population level (autecology) contrasts with research at higher levels of complexity (synecology), but the explanation of population fluctuations remains elusive. The influence of weather, other organisms, and the availability of food and shelter (or, for plant populations, suitable combinations of nutrients, water, and soil) must be considered in the search for the causes of a population spurt or decline. Yet, as will be shown in later chapters, such correlations are vital to the successful management of a species, be it food, wildlife, or pest. In many of his efforts, the ecologist tries to look at the world from the viewpoint of the population he is studying so that he can see what it needs and fears.

All populations are groups of individuals, young and old, weak and strong. They collectively share some characteristics that also can be studied in individuals: growth, structure, and metabolism. Yet groups also have attributes that are unique to the population level and that determine the density of the population (per unit area, or relative to some essential component of its environment). These are expressed as rates: natality (birth rates), mortality (death rates), and migration (immigration or emigration rates) during a specified time period. Once again, input-output analysis is appropriate because births and immigrants enlarge the population while deaths and emigrants reduce it. Every successful population, when studied during a fair portion of its range, is found to be regulated by various intrinsic and extrinsic mechanisms that serve to insure that it neither dwindles to extinction nor eats itself out of house and home. These mechanisms can be called homeostatic (analogous to temperature regulators in warm-blooded animals) or feedbacks (similar to the cybernetic controls that prevent a computer model, or a machine, from running wild).

Perhaps a short history of a hypothetical population would clarify the operation of natural checks and balances. A new subdivision is built, trees are planted and, after some years, the area is colonized by robins. This initial immigration is accomplished by youngsters displaced from other areas; they, in turn, establish territories that the males defend against trespassers, a good example of a genetically-controlled behavior pattern that profoundly affects population density. Year by year, the robin population grows, but its growth is limited—not by its depletion of earth worms, but by the finite number of trees suitable for nesting. This, of course, may be partly determined by the number of neighborhood cats, lean and hungry enough to climb trees, molesting the nest builders or catching their fledglings. Still, the robin population maintains its numbers, replacing catastrophic losses from late frosts in the northern spring or insecticide poisoning during its Florida overwintering. It may even produce a surplus, these individuals colonizing yet another subdivision and starting the cycle again.

Several phrases are useful in describing population phenomena. The availability of some requisites (for example, nesting trees for robins, or dissolved phosphates for fresh-water algae) may be the *limiting factor* in the environment of a specific population, setting a ceiling on its growth. If the population does grow to a point where it starts to deplete essential requisites and degrade its environment, it can be said to have exceeded the *carrying capacity* of the environment. No species can endure long above the carrying capacity; drastic reduction, or even localized extinction, is the usual consequence.

Although a deliberate effort is made to avoid the vast subjects of human evolution and ecology, emphasizing instead the application of ecological concepts in the description of problems, it will be necessary to show in the next chapter how man has created many ecological problems by temporarily evading the natural processes that regulate all populations.

## SUMMARY

Abstractions are concepts rooted in reality, and abstractions that describe different levels of organization are especially important in ecology. A population is a group of organisms belonging to the same species; several interacting populations form a community; and when the community is considered together with the physical-chemical factors affecting it, we are at the ecosystem level. The next level is the biome—related ecosystems found in a similar climatic zone—and the most complex is the biosphere—on our planet the layer of life interacting with the atmosphere, the hydrosphere, and the lithosphere.

### Discussion Questions

1. How can an abstraction be useful in discussing natural relationships?
2. What are the limits of life?
3. Can you think of any other biomes in addition to the seven listed?
4. Why are green plants essential to any community?
5. How is a natural population regulated?

## Suggested Projects

**1.** Find out as much as you can about the biome in which you live.
**2.** Take a field trip to a well-defined ecosystem (for example, a pond or wood lot) and identify some of the more important autotrophs, herbivores, carnivores, detritivores, and physical-chemical characteristics.
**3.** Follow the fluctuations of a population's density during a period of time.

## Notes

1. *Biosphere,* a special issue of the *Scientific American,* (Sept. 1970) and later published in book form (San Francisco: Freeman, 1970) has useful, but fairly technical, articles, mostly on the movement of energy and chemicals in the biosphere.
2. Good descriptions of terrestrial biomes can be found in Eugene P. Odum, *Fundamentals of Ecology* (Philadelphia: Saunders, 1971) and Peter Farb's *Ecology* (New York: Time-Life, 1969).
3. Marston Bates, *The Forest and the Sea* (New York: Vintage, Random, 1960, pp. 15–27) makes some wonderful comparisons between the tropical rain forest and the coral reef. He also suggests that the shallow tropical seas and the ocean depths can be considered distinct biomes (p. 131).
4. The ecology forest at Brookhaven National Laboratory has been described by George M. Woodwell, "Ecological Effects of Radiation," *Scientific American,* **208:**40–49 (1963).
5. The Hubbard brook experiment has been the subject of several technical papers and one semipopular account: F. H. Bormann and G. E. Likens, "The Nutrient Cycles of an Ecosystem," *Scientific American,* **223:**92–101 (1970).
6. In Chapter 10 of *The Forest and the Sea,* Bates, op. cit., has an excellent discussion of the biological community, considering such topics as symbiosis, key-industry animals, and the distinction between predation and parasitism.

# 3

# Human Population Growth and Concentration

## Key Concepts

- Population explosion
- Death control
- Birth control
- Control of environment
- Malthusianism
- Neo-Malthusianism
- Natural selection
- Growth stresses
- Motivation
- Family limitation
- Concentration effects
- Urban implosion

The human species is in the midst of its third *population explosion*. This is certainly the biggest and loudest, but it is interesting and profitable to identify those factors common to all three periods of rapid human increase.

The first surge of population appears to have been associated with a breakthrough in weapons technology, nothing so elegant as a bow and arrow, but, rather, a throwing stick that served to launch a spear at high speed from a safe distance toward such large and thick-hided prey as the mastodon. In addition, fire may have played several roles during this period of progress some fifty thousand years ago. After man learned how to start fires, he could burn the grasslands, driving large game into marshlands or over cliffs. When he started to use fire to cook the meat from successful hunts, he greatly reduced the chance of infecting himself with the parasites that burden most mammals. His diet may have become much less vegetarian,[1] and the increased intake of animal proteins presumably lowered both prenatal and infant mortality. Although there were no census takers in those days, archeological evidence indicates that after these discoveries, humans dispersed throughout the Eurasian land mass, spilling over to Australia and the Americas some eighteen thousand years ago (Figures 3–1 and 3–2).

Man continued to chase, or gather, food for many thousands of years. Only when some bands settled down to domesticate certain plants and animals did man's standard of living, and numbers, start to rise again. The settling process is by no means complete because the urge to hunt remains strong, although the camera can be substituted for the gun. However, most of our food comes from cultigens, plants or animals brought under man's control several thousand years ago. Early agriculture seems to have prospered in two distinct environments in which the soil fertility was renewed without much intervention by man: in the valleys of the great rivers, (Nile, Tigris, Euphrates, Indus, Ganges, Yangtze, Hwang Ho and Mekong) and on islands (such as Honshu or Java) on which replenishment was accomplished by repeated volcanic eruptions. In both situations, it was possible for human populations to achieve and maintain high densities (several hundred per square mile) without any of the benefits of modern civilization. It could be argued that some civilizations, especially the Mayan of Central America, reached high population densities in less fertile regions, but actually they may have collapsed because of soil depletion.

The most recent, and last, explosion has been superimposed on the earlier ones; populous valleys and islands have become even more densely

**Figure 3–1.**

*Three periods of human population increase* (from "The Human Population" by Edward S. Deevey, Jr. Copyright © Sept. 1960 by *Scientific American, Inc.* All rights reserved.)

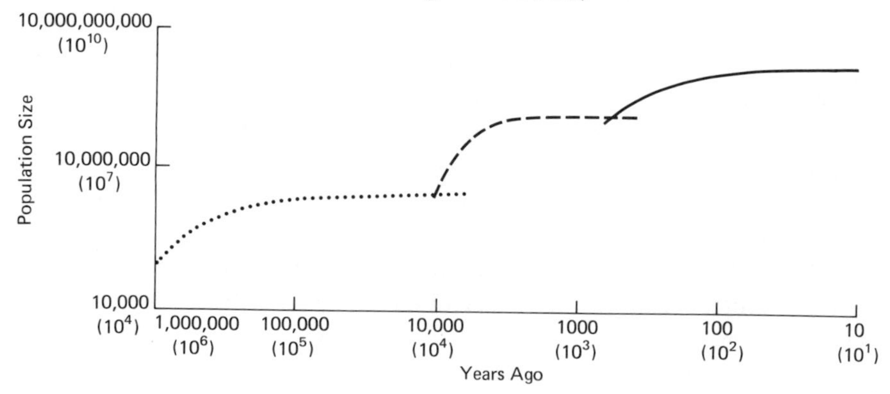

**Figure 3–2.**
*Primitive but effective hunters*

inhabited. Technologies to increase food production have joined with campaigns to reduce disease in a very effective (perhaps too effective) fashion. Especially since they learned how to apply genetic principles, plant and animal breeders have been able to produce new domesticated varieties, more efficient in converting solar energy into the calories we like to eat. Food production also has been boosted by bringing new lands under cultivation and by intensive application of fertilizers to old lands depleted of nutrients. Our cultigens have been well protected against organisms that otherwise would consume our food before it reached the dinner table.

We also have done a pretty good job of protecting ourselves, using immunization, water purification, disease vector control, and, increasingly, health education to reduce the frequency of epidemics. Most of these innovations have been accepted readily by all nations. People seldom knowingly pass up a chance to increase life expectancy for themselves and for their children (Figure 3–3).

That brings us to the crux of the population problem: *death control* is accepted much more readily than *birth control*. Children are variously regarded as old-age security, evidence of virility, objects of devotion, cheap labor, future soldiers (or believers) and/or potential consumers. In a prehistoric society, failure to bear as many children as possible could contribute to the extinction of the tribe and rigorous taboos must have

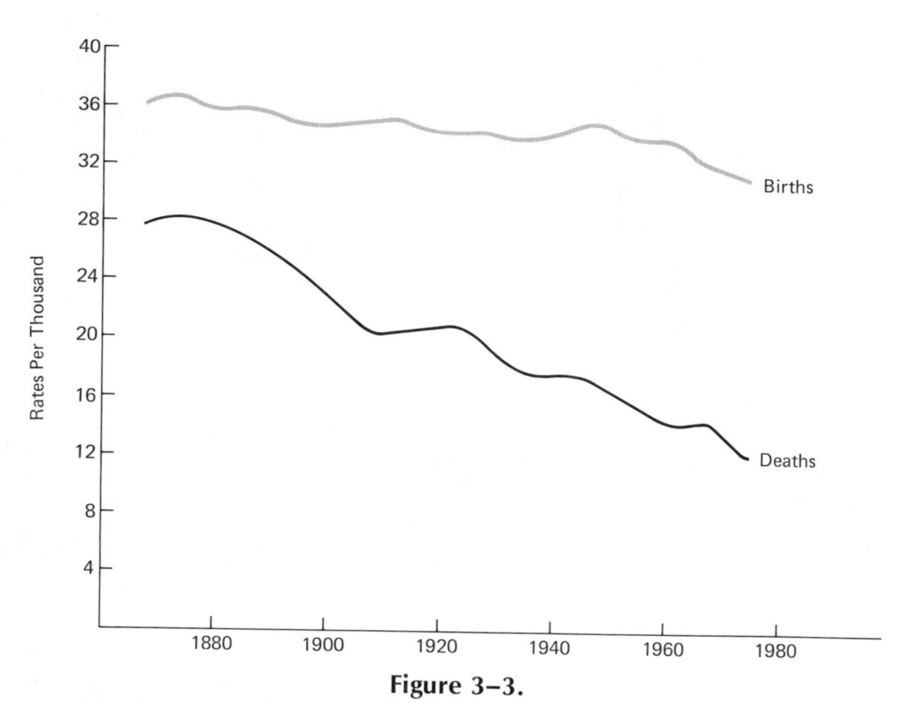


**Figure 3–3.**
*Death rates decline but birth rates remain unchanged–population explosion (hypothetical country)*

discouraged attempts to reduce fertility. In modern civilization, the mores are far more elaborate, yet the social pressure is still toward parenthood.

What do these successive surges, or population growth, have in common? Each involves increased human *control of the environment* shared with other organisms. Some species, cultigens, are encouraged; other species, pests and pathogens, are suppressed. Each set of innovations effectively broadens the human resource base, thereby increasing the carrying capacity of the environment for our species. However, increased control is not synonymous with decreased dependence. Man remains enmeshed in a web of ecological processes that supports him and, once he recognizes its existence, should restrain him.

## MALTHUS AND HIS CHILDREN

Although he knew little of the first two population explosions, Thomas Robert Malthus (1766–1834) heard the third one coming. His main mistake was expecting it to come sooner than it did. However, he was right in recognizing that the human species, like all living species, has the potential to out-strip any finite resource (the doctrine of *Malthusianism*). He was particularly concerned that we would expand right up to the limits of our food supply, to be checked only by "extreme poverty, bad nursing of children, great towns, excesses of all kinds, the whole train of common diseases and epidemics, wars, plague" and, ultimately, "famine."[2] To free man from the misery of such checks, Malthus proposed deferment of marriage and chaste conduct, because he did not believe that birth control was moral (Figure 3–4).

The "gloomy curate's" conclusions and suggestions were not well received when he published his First (1798) and Second (1803) Essays, nor have they ever won universal acclaim. His diagnosis of social ills ran counter to the revolutionary, optimistic, and expansionistic currents of the time, and his prescription was not heeded (if heard) by the lusty masses. Some economists have now accepted the Malthusian doctrine with modifications *(neo-Malthusianism)*, but most reject it, claiming that the application of technology, the substitution of new resources for those depleted, and the redistribution of wealth will permit both the economy and the population to grow for many years to come, with per capita prosperity maintained or even increased.

Still, Malthus's ideas were accepted and applied in a different area by Darwin. "Surplus progeny" became an essential part of evolutionary theory because only by the elimination of offspring could *natural selection* occur. This concept is often misunderstood; it is not "survival of the fittest," it is the survival of those individuals adapted to the prevailing patterns of food, shelter, competition, and so on. The champion characteristics of one generation may be selected against in a subsequent generation if there has been a change in the environment and there are new rules for the game of life.

The sad fate of surplus sprats in an overcrowded oyster bed evokes no sympathy from man. Yet, we do take care of our own and are generally unwilling to let natural selection start working on the human species again. Enjoying the comforts of our technological civilization, we know that few of us could survive on our own in the wilderness. There have been some misguided attempts to apply evolutionary theory to competition between nations or races, with the feeling that the best group will, and should, win out and perpetuate its numbers and values. Such "social Darwinism" fails to recognize the full diversity of talent in the human species or the transitory nature of "best." (See Chapter 27.) There is no rational ranking of human groups.

**Figure 3–4.**
*Malthus, the gloomy but far sighted curate* (Courtesy Library of Congress)

The modern ecologist has a view of the present population explosion which puts his vantage point somewhere between those of Malthus and Darwin. He recognizes that all species have great potential for increase, yet he knows that many have evolved intrinsic mechanisms which lessen the chances of habitat destruction. Territoriality, delayed breeding and reduced sizes of clutches or litters have been observed in various animals. The ecologist does not argue that famine and disease are the only natural checks on human population growth. Rather he contends that family limitation by any effective means is also "natural" in that the precedent has already been set by other (perhaps wiser) species.

The ecologist and economist often have divergent views of human population growth despite the fact that their professional titles have a common origin (*oikos,* Greek for house or dwelling). An ecologist concerns himself with the exchange of nutrients or energy; an economist with money and gross national product (GNP). They are worlds apart when discussing balance, one thinking balance of nature, the other balance of trade. No wonder the ecologist is more concerned about growth; he has seen its dire consequences in other species freed from regulation. The economist cannot find anything inherently wrong in growth of populations because additions, first as consumers then as workers-taxpayers-consumers, increase the GNP and that's a "good thing" isn't it?[3] (See Chapter 25 for further discussion of these divergent viewpoints.)

## EFFECTS OF RAPID GROWTH

As Paul R. Ehrlich and many other authors have shown, rapid *growth* places *stresses* on any resource, facility or service that grows less rapidly.[4] In many developing countries with recently reduced death rates and continuing high birth rates, the proportion of the population under fifteen is 40 percent. This dependency load effectively frustrates attempts to improve the educational system; schools can not be built or teachers trained quickly enough to keep up with the need, so illiteracy remains. Attempts may be made to reach the illiterate majority with village TV sets tuned to satellites overhead, but lack of reading ability will continue to thwart programs to improve agriculture, industry, and health or political institutions.

Even the affluent nations find it hard to raise enough taxes to support adequate public services. So it must be much more difficult for government leaders in a country of children and farmers. Aid programs, unilateral (United States) or multilateral (United Nations), cannot possibly compensate for the fact that virtually no surplus income is available in a country of consumers living at or near the subsistence level. To be sure, there may be poverty in a sparse, slowly growing population, but there the potential for resource development and increased per capita productivity remains. This is not so when all efforts must be devoted to getting food sufficient for survival (Figure 3–5).

Perhaps the most ominous aspect of the population explosion is that it may lead to an even more lethal explosion—that of a thermonuclear (H-bomb) war. Mankind has long engaged in fratricidal wars. Even when hunting bands roamed over vast plains, they fought over water holes or stolen brides. Now rockets are ready and aimed. The command to fire may come more easily to a leader who believes his nation can afford to lose half its population. As long as the bombs remain poised, the possibility of a third (and *final*) world war, and a "permanent solution" to the population problem, must haunt us all.[5]

Because the population bomb has already gone off, it is inappropriate to talk of defusing it; however, efforts are being made to dampen the explosion. Safer and more effective birth-control techniques are essential. We still do not know quite how the "loop" works; in fact, we know more about the reproductive physiology of cattle than of humans. Knowledge of means to limit family size must be quickly and widely disseminated, bypassing

**Figure 3–5.**
*Decline in per capita food*

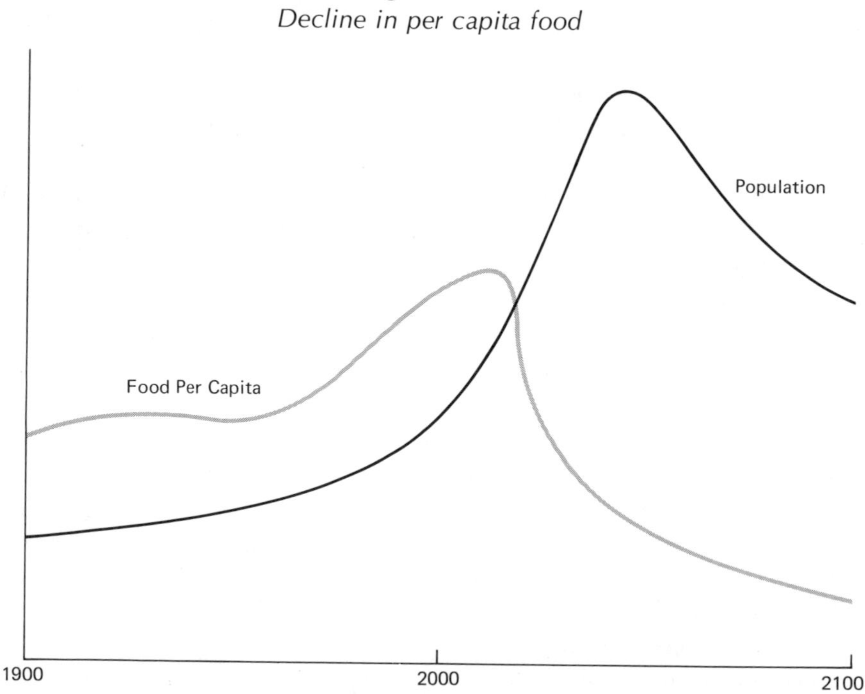

conventional educational institutions when they fail to cooperate. However, knowledge without *motivation* will not reduce the number of children in a completed family, so the pressure of society must shift from enforcement of parenthood to encouragement of *family limitation.* Motivating benefits could include lower taxes, more social security, and wider alternatives to motherhood, truly liberating women to use their talents outside the home.

Sadly, many countries are finding it impossible to develop programs that can catch up with, and slow, population growth. It is very hard to train paramedical personnel in numbers sufficient to intercept all potential overproducers, and "careers for women" is hardly apt to be popular when men are unemployed or underemployed. However, we know that birth-control techniques available forty years ago were effective enough to slow population growth when the economic depression provided sufficient motivation. We can only hope that positive rewards for small families will be as effective as economic penalties.

Some authors, under the guise of tough-mindedness, suggest that we let nature take its course. "Those who overpopulate will perish—so what?" they say. This view if inhumane, immoral, and counterproductive. As Roger Revelle[6] recommends, we must continue to improve health care until parents are sure that each one of their two or three children has a very good chance of reaching maturity. Then, and only then, will the perpetuation of a family name, and all that entails in most societies, no longer be dependent on the production of a brood large enough to compensate for infant and other premature mortality.

## EFFECTS OF EXCESSIVE CONCENTRATION

Many writers, Ehrlich included, partially confuse the effects of growth and concentration. It is true that, for most species, distribution and abundance can be regarded as two sides of the same coin.[7] It is also true that, for the human species, the same technological advances that foster the population explosion also contribute to the *urban implosion.* However, it is possible for a slowly growing nation to experience a spectacular internal migration from farm to city. This has been most noticeable in developed countries as farming has shifted from labor-intensive family operations to large corporations (or collective farms) that use chemicals, machines, and "animal factories" to feed city dwellers. In the United States, the patterns of migration have been quite intricate, with nonwhite ex-farm labor moving to the inner city while whites move to suburban developments, actually creating two sets of ghettos.

In developing countries, urban growth is following patterns that differ from those in the United States. For peasants coming to Calcutta or São Paulo, it is flight from rural poverty to urban misery. They do not settle in the inner city but create peripheral slums, "do-it-yourself" developments. A common set of goals unites all those who move to cities in developed or developing countries. They seek jobs or, at least, food and services not available on their home farms. The fulfillment of their hopes and expectations remains a politically explosive issue in all urbanizing countries.

An ecologist recognizes the many social, economic, and political dimensions of urban problems. His main contribution to urban studies is the concept of the city as a man-made ecosystem that draws its support from distant mines, farms, and watersheds and dumps its waste gases, nutrients, and heat, with the result that natural ecosystems near the city or contributing to its support are degraded or disrupted. The concept of a city as an ecosystem will be expanded in Chapter 19. However, some aspects of urban impacts on natural ecosystems (and human nervous systems) will be considered under the heading "Overcrowding" in the next chapter.

## SUMMARY

As we have gained greater control over the environment, our population has increased with a consequent stress on resources and services that grow less rapidly than population. This was considered a serious problem by Malthus and his intellectual descendants but has been regarded as a challenge to human ingenuity by others.

The same technological advances have made possible both urban concentration and over-all growth. However, the stresses associated with excessive concentration and with rapid growth can be quite different.

### Discussion Questions

1. How have we, the human species, gained greater control over the environment?
2. In what ways has our control of the environment contributed to population increase?
3. Compare growth effects (the population explosion) with concentration effects (the urban implosion).

**4.** Do you think that (a) the human species is increasing too rapidly? (b) your nation, region, or city is growing too fast? or (c) you should limit the size of your family to help prevent population problems?

## Suggested Projects

**1.** Use some census records to make a line graph of population change in your country and in your home community since 1850.
**2.** Ask ten friends (not in this course) if they know anything about Thomas Malthus, Malthusianism, or neo-Malthusianism.
**3.** Find out as much as you can about the population opinions of those in positions of responsibility (government, business, and church leaders). Do they regard growth and/or concentration as good, bad, or insignificant?

## Notes

1. The idea that man is descended from a meat-eating "killer ape" is dismissed on both anatomical and archeological grounds by Marvin Harris, "You Are What They Ate," *Natural History,* **81:**24–25 (Aug.–Sept. 1972).
2. Quoted in J. O. Hertzler, *The Crisis in World Population* (Lincoln: University of Nebraska Press, 1958), p. 97; this is a very useful book with a sociological viewpoint.
3. A concise and readable summation of the ecological view that mankind's growth must be slowed now to avoid a world of Malthusian misery is presented in D. Meadows et al., *The Limits to Growth* (New York: Potomac Associates, Universe Books, 1972). Their models and conclusions have been strongly criticized in H. S. D. Cole et al., *Models of Doom* (New York: Universe Books, 1973).
4. Many effects, some highly hypothetical, of rapid population growth are discussed in Paul R. Ehrlich, *The Population Bomb* (New York: Ballantine, 1968), a popular paperback, and in Paul R. and Anne H. Ehrlich, *Population, Resources, Environment,* 2nd ed. (San Francisco: Freeman, 1972), a lively college text.
5. Perhaps the most disturbingly effective account of the human species destroying itself through nuclear war is found in Neville Shute, *On the Beach* (New York: Morrow, 1957).
6. This point was stressed in a talk, "What Must Be Done to Solve the Population Problem" given at the Brookhaven National Laboratory,

Upton, Long Island, New York, on April 24, 1969 (one of three George P. Pegram Lectures presented by Dr. Revelle.)

7. Relationships between population density and dispersion are explored in depth in H. G. Adrewartha and L. C. Birch, *The Distribution and Abundance of Animals* (Chicago: U. of Chicago, 1954).

# 4

# The Impact of Man and His Technology

## Key Concepts

- Technology
- Impact on environment
- Overexploitation
- Megafaunas
- Overhunting
- Sustained yield
- Overfarming
- Overgrazing
- Chemical application
- Overcrowding
- Sense of territory

In many ways, the three types of impacts discussed in this chapter are echoes of the three population explosions. The *technologies* that made growth possible have, almost inevitably, been overused, first to the detriment of other species but ultimately to the deprivation of our own. Barry Commoner, in his stimulating books and articles,[1] has emphasized the *impact* of recent shifts in technologies; in this chapter, however, will show that we have been *overexploiting* for a long, long time.

## OVERHUNTING

It may be hard to believe, but primitive hunters, armed with fire and shafted weapons, apparently were able to exterminate many large species of mammals. The aggregation of certain species at water holes during prolonged periods of drought undoubtedly contributed to the hunter's "success." Climatic changes may have also put the large mammals at a disadvantage by reducing their food supply or increasing their overwintering mortality. However, human hunters armed with new techniques seem to have delivered the final blow. Evidence, circumstantial but convincing, includes the extinction of *megafaunas* (large animals, especially large mammals) on four continents: 40 percent in Africa, 50,000 to 40,000 "BP" (before present), 70 percent in North America 15,000 to 10,000 BP, and high percentages in South America and Australia more recently; all these correlate with the cultural advance or immigration of man[2] (Figure 4–1).

A domino effect may have been involved in the extinctions. According to the Krantz hypothesis, human hunting actually helped the American bison by removing large, postreproductive members of the population. As the bison herds increased, they displaced other species (camels and horses), depriving specialized predators (such as the camel-eating cats) of their prey.[3] Human interactions with the sabertooth may have included competition and mutual predation, the tiger ultimately losing out.

Related phenomena include the extinctions of large flightless birds soon

**Figure 4–1.**
*Overkill by Paleoindians in the Americas* (Courtesy Paul S. Martin)

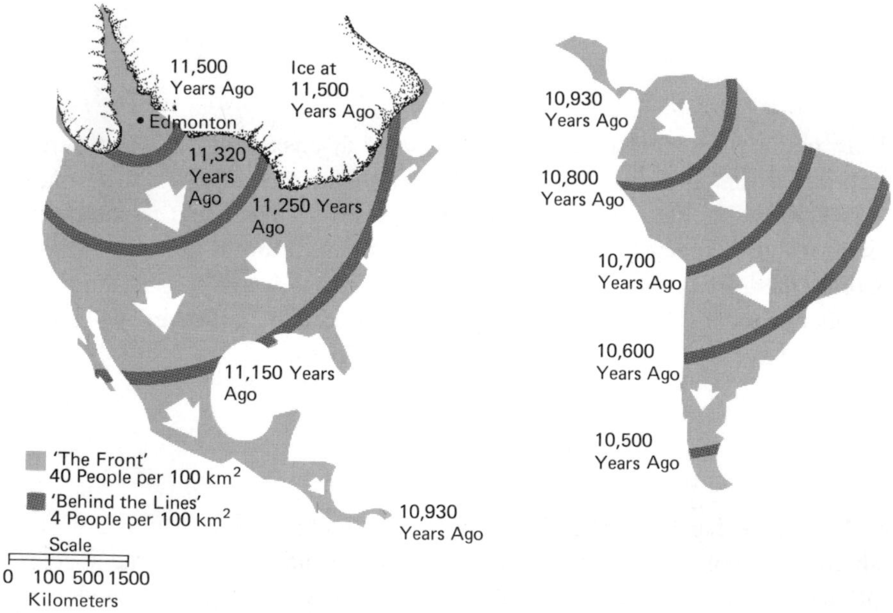

after the arrival of man. Polynesian immigration more than one thousand years ago proved lethal to the fabled roc *(Aepyronis maximus)* of Madagascar and the giant moas of New Zealand. However, Polynesians cannot be blamed for the extinction of the dodo, a large pigeonlike bird destroyed on Mauritius by Dutch sailors during the short period 1638 to 1680.

**Figure 4–2.**
*Modern whaler* (Courtesy Japanese Embassy)

Although the dodo was clubbed to extinction, further advances in weaponry were needed to wipe out the passenger pigeon. In the early 1800s, this species formed large colonies throughout the forests of the eastern United States. A combination of deforestation and shooting reduced numbers below the density needed for a breeding aggregation. For this edible pest, fattened on a farmer's grain, there was no safety in numbers because it was decimated from billions to one in fewer than one hundred years.

There is ample evidence that overhunting continues. Populations of large cats are being wiped out by hunters and poachers. Even the vast expanse of the oceans provides little security for the great whales. To quote Ehrlich:

> Technological "space-age" advances have greatly aided the whalers in their overexploitation. Ship-based helicopters locate whales and then guide killer boats to the quarry. The killer boats hunt by sonar, killing the quarry with an explosive harpoon attached to a nylon line with an 18-ton strength. The dead whale is inflated with compressed air so it will not sink, and a radio beacon is attached to the catch so that the towboat can find it and tow it to the factory ship, where it is rapidly processed[4] (Figure 4–2 on page 43).

You might think that the whaling countries, especially Japan and the Soviet Union, would be willing to harvest whales on a *sustained-yield* basis—taking only the number replaced by natural recruitment. Although this would prolong the useful life of their specialized capital equipment, the lure of immediate maximum profit has proved overwhelming to both Communist and capitalist, with the result that most large-whale species, and many finfish, are being overhunted.[5]

## OVERFARMING

Just as it is possible to deplete an animal population more rapidly than it is replenished, so also it is possible to extract nutrients and humus from the soil more rapidly than they can be restored. This can be observed even in the lush tropical forests where the most primitive form of slash-and-burn agriculture is still practiced. The farmer makes a clearing in the forest by cutting down, drying, and burning most of the trees. He then plants seeds or tubers under the nutrient-rich ashes. One, two, or possibly three good harvests follow; then he must move to another part of the forest to start all over again. As long as population pressure does not force the reutilization of the abandoned plot before several decades have passed, this system works reasonably well. It works because the tropical forest slowly mines nutrients from the soil, bringing them up into the biomass where they will be available once again. If settled agriculture is attempted in this environment, many problems develop; for example, the rain washes nutrients down into a lateritic hard pan where they become unavailable to crops and the soil loses its organic component, turning bricklike when dry and eroding when wet.

Soil exhaustion also has occurred in many temperate regions. In 1799, after some decades of tobacco growing, Albermarle County, Virginia, was described as a "scene of desolation that baffles description—farm after farm . . . worn out, washed, and gullied, so that scarcely an acre could be found in a place fit for cultivation."[6] Overfarming also can involve expansion into zones marginally suitable for agriculture. This happened in the United States creating the Dust Bowl in the arid grasslands, and it happened again when the Soviet Union embarked on its ill-fated scheme to till the "virgin lands." *Overgrazing* is still another example—recurring in the Middle East, the western United States, India, Africa, and Australia—whenever goats, sheep, or cattle are permitted to multiply beyond the carrying capacity of forage vegetation on the range. The zones used for grazing are even drier than those marginally suitable for cultivation. As Raymond F. Dasmann has pointed out, "a range properly stocked for a high rainfall year may be dangerously overstocked if drought follows" and "there is a strong temptation to try and hold excessive numbers of livestock in the hopes that better conditions will return. Damage always results."[7] (See Figure 4–3 a, b, and c.)

Range damage caused by overgrazing includes soil erosion and the proliferation of weedy species not favored by the grazers. The weeds, in turn, contribute to outbreaks of rodents and jack rabbits. A number of efforts have been made to correct the balance by introducing weed-eating insects, the most successful being the colonization of a cactus-eating caterpillar (*Cactoblastis cactorum* from South America) to consume the prickly pear in Australia and leaf-eating beetles (*Chrysolina* spp. from Europe) to control Klamath weed in the Pacific Northwest. It has also been suggested that the niches left open by the Pleistocene extinction of large mammals in North America be filled with carefully screened introductions of African antelopes that could graze on such unlikely fare as mesquite and creosote bush, both species having expanded as forage favored by cattle decreased.[8] This would be adding the equivalent of ten to twenty million head of cattle to the fifty million already at home on the range without any reduction in the range's carrying capacity.

Overfarming can take forms other than soil exhaustion, exploitation of

a

b

**Figure 4–3.**
*Overgrazed range land* (U.S.D.A., Forest Service) **a.** *Exclusion experiment* (K. W. Parker) **b.** *Starving cattle* (K. W. Parker) **c.** *Erosion* (D. F. Costello)

c

**Figure 4–3.** *(Continued)*

marginal land, and overgrazing. When acreage available for agriculture is reduced by absolute shortage (as in Japan) or by soil-bank subsidies (as in the United States), *chemicals* are intensively *applied* to boost production per acre. The problems associated with intensive and extensive use of agricultural chemicals will be discussed in Chapter 9. Briefly, however, the overuse of pesticides can lead to the evolution of superpests, the elimination of natural enemies, and the contamination of food chains, while the excessive application of fertilizers can contaminate drinking water and contribute to algal blooms.

## OVERCROWDING

Many of the impacts associated with the aggregations of people, machines, and their respective emissions are discussed in Chapters 19, 20, and 21. From an ecological viewpoint, these impacts can be considered the force that displaces natural ecosystems and maintains a man-made ecosystem. The role of energy from fossil fuels and other sources in supporting the transformation will be analyzed in the pivotal Chapter 12.

At this point, however, it is appropriate to consider the possibility that crowding, in and of itself, is detrimental to the human species. Here the ecologist must use, with great care, observations made by ethologists (students of animal behavior), sociologists, and anthropologists. Many animal species, especially when confined in cages, exhibit physiological and psychological pathologies as the frequency of contact with conspecific individuals increases (specifically, they bump into each other). John B. Calhoun has described some of the quirks of crowded rodents: for example, cannibalism, homosexuality, and apathy.[9] Other studies have shown that male odors can cause fetal reabsorption and earlier sexual maturation in females of the same species, phenomena that would seem to have opposite effects on population increase.

The critical question with these animal studies is their applicability to the human species. To what extent do we perceive the city as a crowded cage and react accordingly? The Japanese, who have a long history of high density on their central islands, have made many social and psychological adjustments to crowding, tolerating people packing in subways and houses far more readily than Americans would. Is there any reason why Americans cannot make similar accommodations to density as they forget the "wide open spaces" they once enjoyed? Certain individuals may feel the need to be surrounded by a people-free zone, and they may want to own land and/or a house, but there is little evidence from the social sciences that we are inherently territorial, no matter how often bellicose leaders may play on patriotic feelings. But perhaps we need a *sense of territory* so that humans of many cultures will not continue to tolerate crowding in a degraded urban environment and will reduce their fecundity to the replacement rate.[10]

## SUMMARY

The technological innovations that expanded our resource base and permitted our population to grow and/or concentrate have been carried too far, with resultant overexploitation of hunted species, farm land, range land, and, possibly, urban living space. These echoes of the three population explosions may be damaging first to other species, but eventually they also will harm us if they cause species extinction, resource exhaustion, and hazards to human health.

## Discussion Questions

1. What is technology and how is it related to scientific knowledge?
2. Describe (a) some of the cultural and economic factors that encourage the overuse or misuse of technology and (b) some of the restraints that can prevent abuse.
3. How can the environmental impacts of technology be magnified in or near urban concentrations?

## Suggested Projects

1. Prepare a small-scale impact assessment describing, for example, exactly the environmental changes that occur when a house is built or a garden is planted.
2. Survey your community for signs of runaway technology.
3. Ask at least ten people what they consider to be an uncomfortable degree of crowding.
4. Read tonight's newspaper and see if there are any stories on technological impacts (pollution, for example).

## Notes

1. See Barry Commoner, *Science and Survival* (New York: Viking Compass, 1963); and *The Closing Circle* (New York: Knopf, 1971); the latter first appeared as articles in *The New Yorker*.
2. Pleistocene overkill was first hypothesized in Paul S. Martin and H. E. Wright, Jr., eds., *Pleistocene Extinctions The Search for a Cause*. (New Haven: Yale University Press, and London, 1967).
3. Grover S. Krantz stated his hypothesis in "Human Activities and Megafaunal Extinctions," *American Scientist*, **58:**164–170 (1970). It was attacked, mainly for mathematical reasons, in John D. Buffington, "Predation, Competition, and Pleistocene Megafauna Extinction," *BioScience* **21:**167–170 (1971).
4. Paul R. and Anne H. Ehrlich, *Population, Resources, Environment*, 2nd ed. (San Francisco: Freeman, 1972), p. 131.

5. S. J. Holt, "The Food Resources of the Ocean," *Scientific American,* **221:**178–194 (1969) indicates that fourteen of thirty major fish "stocks are certainly or probably in danger of being badly overfished" (p. 190).
6. From a letter by John H. Craven to "Farmer's Register" in Avery O. Craven, *Soil Exhaustion As a Factor in the Agricultural History of Virginia and Maryland, 1606–1860,* Studies in the Social Sciences, **13,** (Urbana: University of Illinois, 1925); also quoted in William Vogt, *Road to Survival* (New York: Sloane, 1948), p. 116.
7. Raymond F. Dasmann, *Environmental Conservation,* 3rd ed. (New York: Wiley, 1972, pp. 254–255), is one of the best-balanced texts on conservation, covering a wide range of subjects with examples drawn from many countries.
8. See Paul S. Martin, "Pleistocene Niches for Alien Animals," *BioScience,* **201:**218–222 (1970).
9. John B. Calhoun, "Population Density and Social Pathology," *Scientific American,* **206:**139–146 (1962), and subsequent papers.
10. For a very good, but rambling, discourse on the human condition, see René Dubos, *So Human an Animal* (New York: Scribners, 1968). See pp. 153–160 for comments on crowding and its possible effects.

# Summary of Part I

Ecology is the science of interrelationships, and ecologists study relationships between organisms as well as the interactions of organisms with their physical-chemical environment. As a science, ecology is quite young, yet it has roots deep in the observations made by natural historians and by practical men wresting a living from their surroundings. Facts from other sciences, biological and environmental, are also of great value in developing ecological concepts, especially those pertaining to the five levels of organization: populations, communities, ecosystems, biomes, and the biosphere, abstractions that have been quite useful in describing the living world and changes in that world caused by human activity.

Most forms of environmental degradation, especially pollution and resource depletion, can be explained in terms of human population increase and overuse of the technological innovations that made the increase possible. Improved hunting weapons increased the meat supply but contributed to the extinction of the hunted species; the development of agriculture increased the average intake of calories but accelerated soil erosion; and the modern combination of machines and medicine gave us still greater control over the environment, extracting resources and reducing hazards, but led to the concentrated dumping of waste products. Population changes (growth, movement, and concentration) have been part of each phase. However, the environmental impacts come from population *plus* technology, this being most obvious in the urban implosion that created modern cities.

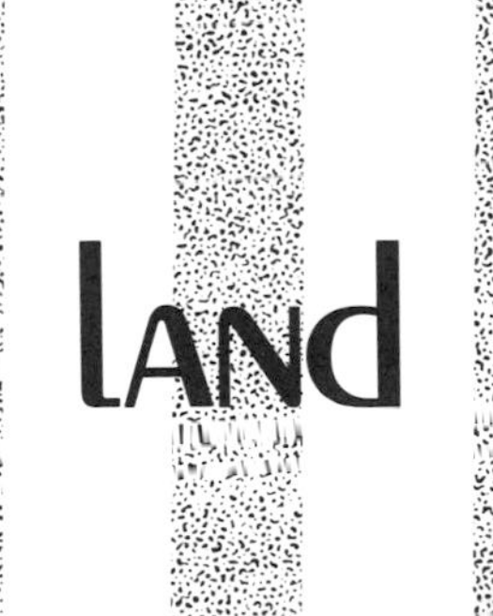
LAND

# 5

# Terrestrial Ecosystems

## Key Concepts

- Evolution
- Coevolution
- Adaptation
- Convergence
- Succession
- Diversity
- Climax

The distinction between terrestrial and aquatic ecosystems is artificial and somewhat arbitrary. All life is ultimately dependent on water, rock-derived nutrients dissolved in the water, vital gases ($CO_2$ for green plants and $O_2$ for animals), and on energy from the sun. However, terrestrial communities are unique aggregations of organisms that have evolved to cope with varying temperatures and intermittent precipitation. Think of the conditions prevailing in a tropical forest, a Chilean desert, and on Antarctic peninsulas. Dry land can be very dry indeed, with less than 1 inch of precipitation each year, or it can be inundated by an inch of rain each day. Midcontinental temperatures can range from −60°F. to 120°F. Even a small pond amidst the prairies would not go through such a wide annual fluctuation, because surface ice would insulate it during the winter and surface evaporation would cool it during the summer. The physical-chemical environment of the ocean is far from homogenous, but its variations are less extreme than those characteristic of fresh-water or terrestrial ecosystems.

## EVOLUTION

To understand terrestrial ecosystems, it might help to go back in time to see just how life was able to leave the oceans. In a sense, the oceans threw out a protective mantle that made possible life on land. Phytoplankton in the seas produced oxygen that, at the outer limits of the atmosphere, was ionized to form a layer of ozone, screening out ultraviolet radiation that had, until then, killed organisms at or near the ocean surface. With the screen emplaced one billion years ago, further increases in phytoplankton biomass and oxygen production were possible. Gradually, multicelled animals evolved from single-celled forms. Some 400 million years ago, the first land plants emerged, soon followed by the ambitious arthropods ancestral to insects[1] (Figure 5–1).

Insects and land plants have continued to evolve together, a long and uneasy association marked by ploy and counterploy. Those varieties of plants equipped with spiny leaves or toxic alkaloids may, for a while, avoid defoliation by caterpillars or other chewing insects. Eventually, however, some insect strain will evolve a means to circumvent the spines or detoxify the poison.[2] As will be shown in Chapter 10, we often have helped the insects by removing a wild plant's protection in our efforts to make it palatable.

Not all the plant-insect relationships are antagonistic. With the appearance of flowering plants and social insects some 100 million years ago, the intricate dependence between pollinator and "pollinatee" began. Bees have specialized combs on their legs that transport pollen back to the hive, yet there is enough spillage at collecting stops to insure the successful cross-fertilization of flowers. Other pollinators may extract a higher price for their services. A butterfly may transfer some pollen, but its caterpillars can feed on the same plant species, reducing the photosynthetic surface of the plant and lessening its chances of setting seeds and surviving competition with other plant species. Perhaps the most intricate relationship is that of the yucca plants and the *Pronuba* moth in the American Southwest. The moth pollinates yucca flowers, but its caterpillars eat some of the yucca seeds[3] (Figure 5–2).

Turning from the *coevolution* of plants and insects, let us consider some examples of adaptations to physical conditions prevailing on land. A forest canopy sets the stage for what can be described as a fight for light. Various strategies have been developed. Some plants (epiphytes) develop from seeds lodged in forks high in a tree; others (lianas) cling to trunks and branches, climbing toward the light. Still others are fast-growing spindly

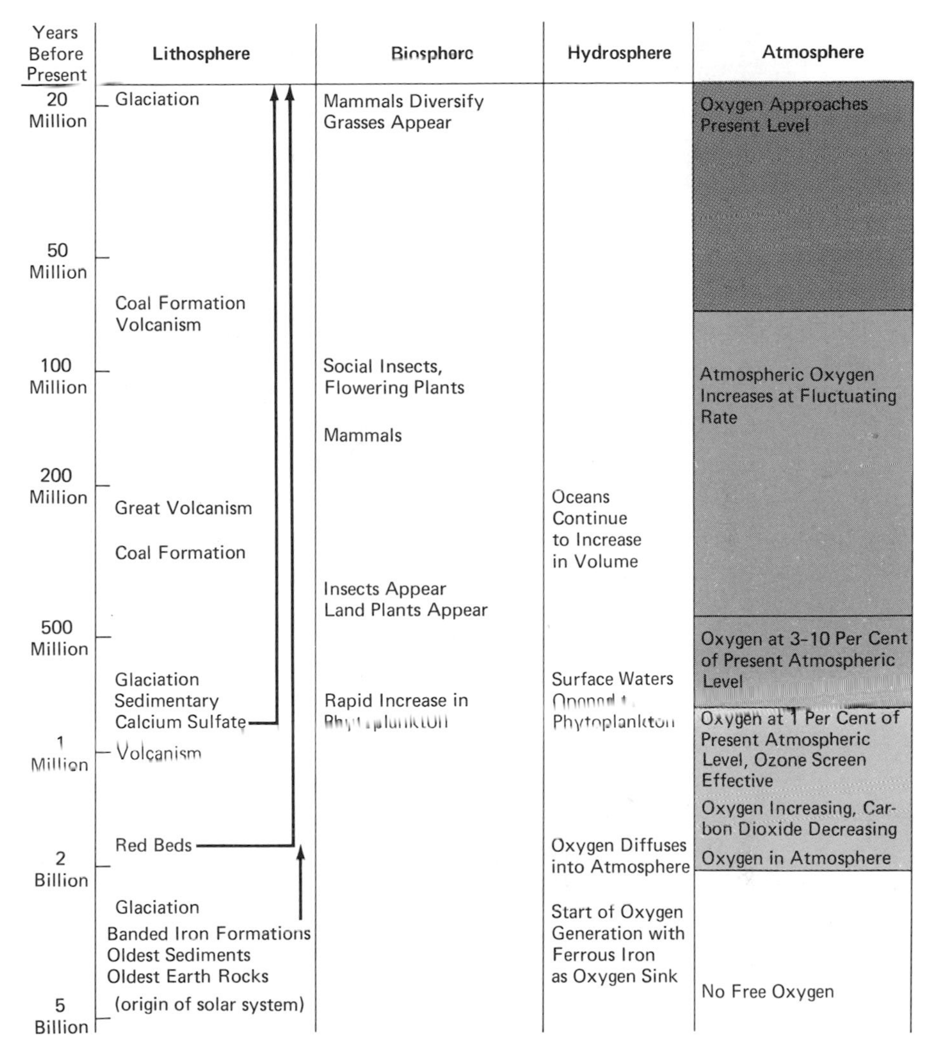


**Figure 5–1.**

*Development of the atmosphere and biosphere* (from "The Oxygen Cycle" by Preston Clered and Aharon Gibot. Copyright © Sept. 1970 by *Scientific American,* Inc. All rights reserved.)

trees that spring up in clearings created by the toppling of a forest giant. Some do not strive upward but make do with the light that filters through to the forest floor. In a tropical forest, as many as five strata of vegetation variously adapted to the dimming gradient of light can be recognized. In the deciduous woodlands, the understories of dogwood or blueberries and the

**Figure 5–2.**
*Honey bee collecting nectar on alfalfa blossom (note pollen packed on leg)* (U.S.D.A. photo)

ground covers of mosses and ferns represent well-defined strata determined by the availability of light [4].

Animal *adaptations* to the grasslands environment provide another array of evolutionary paths to a common goal. Marsupials in Australia and placental mammals elsewhere have remarkably similar groups of herbivores and carnivores. Through *convergent* evolution, many of the animals have become similar in form. There are antelopelike grazers both in North America and in Africa; and rabbitlike, molelike, and wolflike creatures in

Australia, Africa, and North America. To avoid excessive predation, the grass eaters have evolved talents for running or borrowing.

In deserts, the common patterns of adaptation are also apparent. New World cacti and the spiny euphorbs of Africa both have developed stem photosynthesis, tissues to store water, and waxy coatings to help retain the water. Many desert plants have deep roots reaching down to the water table and some secrete inhibitory chemicals that prevent the germination or growth of plants near enough to be potential competitors for water. Desert animals have their packages of tricks for survival, burrowing to escape the noonday sun, metabolizing water from dry seeds, and cutting down on water loss with impermeable body covering or through concentration of excreta.

All these examples serve to show how the communities of plants and animals in terrestrial ecosystems have evolved to coexist, utilize requisites, and survive the rigors of their physical-chemical environment. When we tinker with terrestrial ecosystems, we seldom recognize all the consequences of our actions, a blissful ignorance that can lead to blunders.

## SUCCESSION

One sequence of phenomena well studied in many terrestrial ecosystems, especially those within the deciduous biome, is referred to by ecologists as succession. Two major groups of autotropic succession, with communities of green plants replacing one another in more or less predictable sequences, have been recognized. These are, not too surprisingly, called primary and secondary. Primary succession starts with a new flood plain or a fresh lava flow and secondary succession begins on a burnt hillside or an abandoned farm. The latter type, also known as old-field succession, has been exten-

**Figure 5–3.**
*Old-field succession*

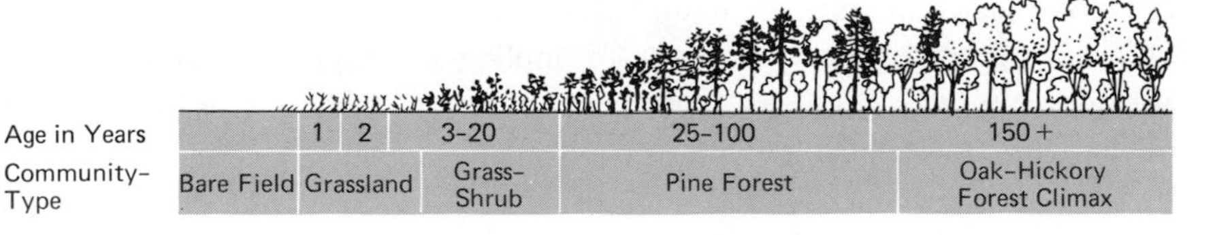

sively investigated in the eastern part of the United States because so many East Coast farmers headed west during the last century (and into cities during this one) (Figure 5–3).

The normal sequence of old-field succession is weeds, grass, shrubs, conifers, and oaks. Like most norms this is subject to many equally natural variations, determined by soil conditions and proximity of seed sources. A field isolated from conifers and surrounded by locusts may have locusts replacing both the shrub and conifer stages. On moist soil, maples may do far better than oaks, replacing them in the final, or *climax,* stage. Repeated fires may create an environment in which only certain fire-adapted pines can survive (in the next chapter the use of fire in forestry will be discussed). There is no one, inevitable sequence, but general patterns emerge. During a period of 100 to 150 years, the vegetation increases in height, biomass, respiration, and structural complexity. Changes in species diversity may not be quite so straightforward, with many species of weeds and grasses being replaced by a few species of fast-growing pine. *Diversity* increases again with the development of strata and various microhabitats in the climax forest.

With primary succession, the pioneer vegetation is determined largely by the nature of the soil substrate. A lava flow is ever so gradually colonized by lichens and, in fissures, by ferns. On new sand dunes along the shores of Lake Michigan, pioneers include grasses and willow, cherry, and cottonwood trees.[5] Still other species may be successful on a rocky landslide or on a recently drained bog. It should be remembered that these brief descriptions of primary and secondary autotrophic succession have not mentioned the animals associated with each vegetational stage. Insects, nesting birds, and many other animals have habitat preferences linking them to one stage; however, the greatest diversity within the animal community is attained in the climax forest.

Successional patterns can also be observed in newly created microhabitats. These—a mushroom, a fallen tree, or a carcass—provide food and shelter for unique assemblages of animals and organisms of decay as long as they exist as distinct entities. A log may be penetrated by fungal myceliae, then colonized by termites, and finally riddled with millipeds. Even a human corpse falls into this ecological category. One of the least attractive assignments given to an entomologist well versed in the ecologies of flies is to determine, through a sampling of maggots, just how long someone has been dead. All these patterns, unassociated with living green plants, can be classified as heterotrophic.

## EXPLOITATION

The next six chapters will deal with the exploitation of terrestrial ecosystems: the extraction of renewable resources—timber, trophies, or food—and human incursions into forests for recreational activity. Either form almost inevitably has some effect on the diversity and stability of the ecosystem. Human management of terrestrial ecosystems often involves fostering certain successional stages: early ones for food production, various others for wildlife preservation, and the fast-growing trees of mid-succession for timber production. Therefore, a recurrent theme will be the use of ecological understanding to soften human impacts. "Do nothing" is rejected; "do what must be done, but do it wisely" is espoused.

## SUMMARY

Terrestrial ecosystems, although sharing many basic characteristics with aquatic ecosystems, can be regarded as unique end-products of long evolutionary periods because they contain organisms that have evolved under different ranges of temperature, precipitation, and other fluctuating factors. Thus, the plants and animals in a terrestrial ecosystem have various adaptations that permit them to survive the variations in their environment, to draw on resources, and to coexist. However, the species composition of terrestrial ecosystems often changes over the years, this being most noticeable on new or open ground. Pioneer species invade the area, they are replaced by waves of other species, and a mature ecosystem gradually develops. This process is called succession. Ecosystem management often is directed toward the preservation of a successional stage.

### Discussion Questions

1. Compare and contrast terrestrial and aquatic ecosystems.
2. How does a species adapt to the challenges and opportunities presented by other organisms and the diversity of the physical-chemical environment?
3. What is succession? Distinguish (a) primary from secondary succession, and (b) autotrophic from heterotrophic.

## Suggested Projects

**1.** Establish or visit a small weather station (rain gauge, maximum-minimum thermometer, and, possibly, a hygrograph for recording humidity) in order to observe the local fluctuations affecting terrestrial organisms.

**2.** Take a field trip to an old field and identify some of the plants and animals that have invaded it since cultivation ceased.

## Notes

1. P. Cloud and A. Givor, "The Oxygen Cycle," *Biosphere* (San Francisco: Freeman, 1970), pp. 59–68.
2. Paul R. Ehrlich and P. H. Raven, "Butterflies and Plants," *Scientific American* **2**:104–113 (1967).
3. Marston Bates, *The Forest and the Sea* (New York: Vintage, Random, 1960), p. 153.
4. R. H. Whittaker, *Communities and Ecosystems,* 2nd ed. (New York: Macmillan, 1975), p. 66.
5. Eugene P. Odum, *Fundamentals of Ecology,* 3rd ed. (Philadelphia: Saunders, 1971), pp. 258–259.

# 6

# Forest Utilization

## Key Concepts

- Inventory
- Multiple use
- Clearcutting
- Sustained yield
- Cost-benefit ratio
- Preemptive, controlled burns
- Fire-maintained niche
- National parks
- Conservation organizations

Humans are strangely ambivalent in their feelings about forests. We are terrified at the thought of being lost in a wilderness, beset by savages and animals, yet we enjoy trees and will travel many miles to view fall foliage.[1] To the American suburbanite, trees have assumed a status not unlike the sacred groves worshiped by ancient druids. Developers are finding it worthwhile to put up houses amidst trees, rather than bulldoze them out of the way. Forestry schools and departments are being forced to develop programs on suburban forestry, dealing with the tricky problems of leaf disposal, gypsy moth control, and the inherent incompatibility of trees and aboveground wiring.[2] Thus, the interactions between man and forest continue. The singlemindedness of the slash-and-burn farmer or the cut-and-run timber baron has been replaced in many countries by policies, not always wisely implemented, of conservation and multiple use (Figure 6–1).

**Figure 6–1.**
*Suburban forest in Reston, Virginia* (U.S.D.A., Forest Service photo by P. Steucke)

## FOREST INVENTORY

The point at which a grove of trees becomes a forest is not always clear. Differences in definition have led to varying estimates of forest cover in the United States and other countries. Using minimums of 1 acre in area and 120 feet in width, the current estimate for the forty-eight contiguous United States is 32 percent, down from approximately 50 percent four centuries ago. The reduction has been even greater in many other countries. Despite some recent efforts at reafforestation, centuries of overexploitation have left many parts of Asia virtually treeless. Only 18 percent of India and 9 percent of China can be described as wooded.[3]

The United States still has the fourth largest forest, as shown in this short Table 6-1:[4]

**TABLE 6–1.**

| | Forested Area (thousand acres) | Total Area (%) |
|---|---|---|
| USSR | 2,273,000 | 41 |
| Brazil | 978,000 | 56 |
| Canada | 832,000 | 34 |
| US (contiguous) | 621,000 | 32 |
| Alaska | 200,000 | 54 |
| Hawaii | 1,200 | 29 |
| US (total) | 822,200 | 36 |

It is possible that Americans may have even more trees than were present at the time of Columbus, because the average size per tree has almost certainly been reduced through centuries of cutting and recutting. Only 72,000 square miles of virgin timber suitable (but, hopefully, not available) for harvest now remain.

Another way in which forest resources can be assessed is on a per capita basis. By that standard, each citizen of the United States has about 4 acres of forest. You think that might satisfy the most ardent tree lover, but two basic problems—one ecological and one sociological—reduce the utility of "nature's 4 acres." Trees grow slowly, especially as they near maturity, so relatively small quantities of wood can be harvested from a near-climax forest, assuming you cut it only at a rate equal to replacement (see the discussion of sustained yield later in this chapter). Furthermore, our urbanized society values forests mainly as a destination for recreation, and 4 acres without a campsite, picnic table, or nature trail may be regarded as worthless. In 1960, only ⅕-acre per capita was available "in national parks, monuments, recreation areas, state parks, and in national forests used primarily for recreation,"[5] many of which are located far from population centers (Figure 6–2).

Forest resources can be measured many other ways. The regional forest atlases of the United States Department of Agriculture (USDA) Forest Service include maps indicating species composition, administrative con-

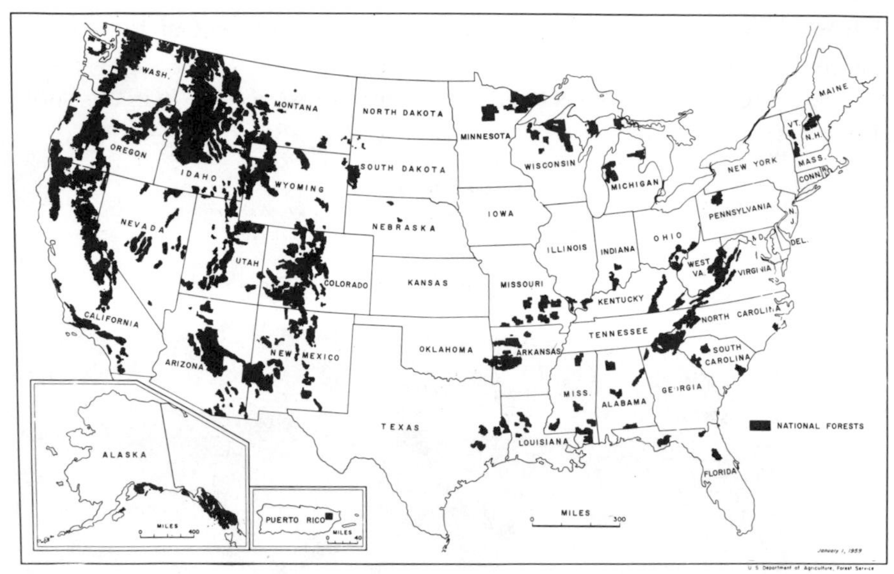


**Figure 6–2.**
*National forest of the United States* (U.S.D.A., Forest Service)

trol, meteorological hazards, as well as incidences of forest fires, pests, and diseases.[6] Although there have been many recent improvements in sampling and evaluation, forest assessment is still far from being an exact science. Much of the concern about timber shortages has been based on underestimates of standing timber or overestimates of projected losses and harvests. Ecological studies conducted in the deciduous and coniferous biomes should provide more accurate estimates of biomass, growth, and potential yield.

## MULTIPLE USE

One way of looking at a forest is as just so many trees waiting to be made into houses and newspapers. This view is still held by many timber farmers and old-style foresters. However, the Forest Service of the USDA[7] and many modern forestry schools are expounding the doctrine that timber harvest is only one way in which forests can be used. They also serve as sites for recreation and as habitats for wildlife. Forest cover reduces erosion and run-off in hilly areas, although forest soils can be saturated by heavy rains, with subsequent run-off causing floods downstream. In some western areas, cattle have been permitted to graze amidst the trees, but this practice is now discouraged because the cattle prevent forest regeneration by trampling or chewing young trees. Anyway, forage in a wooded area is not nearly as good as it is in improved pastures. One final use, which an ecologist considers especially important, is for research and education. Forest ecosystems have a great potential for activities ranging from elementary school nature study to sophisticated forms of environmental monitoring.

In theory, multiple use permits a finite resource to be used wisely by many different groups. In practice, it does not always work well because users have conflicting goals. The timber farmer wants to get maximum yield per acre, cutting large patches of trees as soon as their growth slows, and replanting the *clear-cut* land with a new crop. Campers and hunters both enjoy a diverse woodland with varied scenery and wildlife. However, campers do not want to become moving targets, so hunting seasons are those during which camping and hiking activities are minimal. If a watershed is forest covered, those in charge of a municipal water supply may be concerned about any activity. They do not want clear cutting because of the increased siltation in their reservoirs (see Chapters 11 and 15). Nor do they want camping, because fecal contamination or forest fires might reduce the quality of their water supply (Figure 6–3).

If the forest is large enough, conflicting uses can be segregated one from another, some areas being designated for commercial forestry, others for camping, and still others as wilderness or watershed. In smaller public forests, particularly those near urban areas, the multiple-use concept breaks down completely, with recreational activity taking first priority. It will be very interesting to see if the millions of small, privately owned parcels of woodlands can be better managed. Too small for efficient management as timber or game farms, too isolated to be commercial campsites, it is likely that these will remain backwoods for some time to come (Figure 6-4).

## MANAGEMENT

With the problems of multiple use in mind, you can guess that forest management has become increasingly difficult.[8] To maintain a forest in perpetuity, there should be a balance between new growth and the amounts of wood removed by pests, disease, fire, and harvest. This *sustained-yield* concept is applied in many national and private forest areas, but it does not

a

b

**Figure 6–3.**
*Clear-cutting of forest and subsequent recovery* (U.S.D.A., Forest Service)

c

d

**Figure 6–3.** *(Continued)*

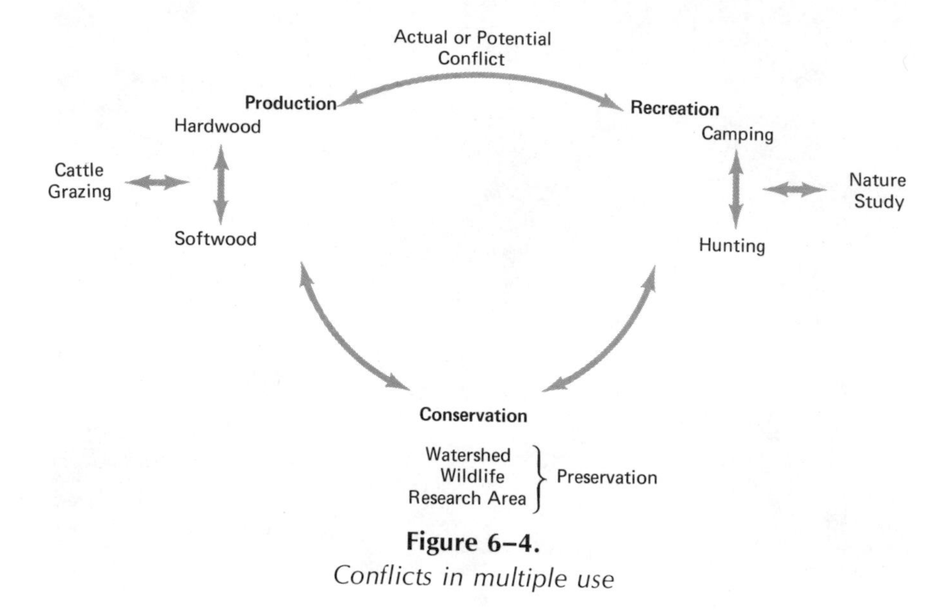


**Figure 6–4.**
*Conflicts in multiple use*

look as good in practice as it might. Huge blocks of slow-growing conifers in the Pacific Northwest are being replaced by fast-growing seedlings of the same or different species. Of course, care is taken to leave a belt of giant trees along the roadside so the scenery appears unaltered. In the Southeast, many areas of pines are clear-cut every twenty to thirty years in order to provide a steady supply of pulp for our paper-shuffling society. Perhaps the greatest dangers in both the Northwest and Southeast are that a conifer monoculture will encourage outbreaks of pest species (for example, tussock moth) or gradually lower the quality of forest soils. Similar problems beset the timber industry in Germany during the last century and "after 1918, there was a swing . . . back toward a more natural type of forest."[9]

Even the well-managed European forests yield only 31 cubic feet per acre (2.2m$^3$ha) each year. Approximate yields for the United States are 13 cubic feet and, for the slower growing Canadian conifers, 4.6 cubic feet per acre per year.[10] Although many useful products can be made from wood, their market value is not great and cash income from forest lands is often less than fifty dollars per acre per year. This hard economic fact has important ecological considerations, because it means that those responsible for the management of forests, public or private, cannot afford to spend very much on control of pests and diseases. This has encouraged the forestry profession to use chemicals sparingly and to seek cheap, safe, and effective biological controls whenever possible. Now that "the age of ecology has dawned,'' foresters can claim that their record is not badly besmirched by the chemical overkill mistakes of the agriculturalists. Perhaps they were working wisely with nature, but the suspicion lingers that the foresters would have used insecticides and herbicides more freely if they had not been restrained by *cost-benefit ratios*.

Another ecological aspect of forest management concerns the use and prevention of fires. Yes, use and prevention, for despite the frequent admonitions of Smokey the Bear, fire has become an important tool of the forester seeking to encourage the growth of certain conifers.[11] Because forest fires at the wrong time and place can be both destructive and dangerous, the forest service and state divisions of forestry spend much time and money trying to persuade people not to start forest fires through carelessness with cigarettes or campfires. This investment has apparently paid off, although the authorities have had less success dealing with arsonists who cause most of the fires in the Southeast. In the Far West, lightning is the principal cause of forest fires, and the scientists of ''Project Skyfire'' are studying patterns of susceptibility that may improve both predictions and prevention (Figure 6-5).

The reasoning behind the use of fire in forest management is similar to

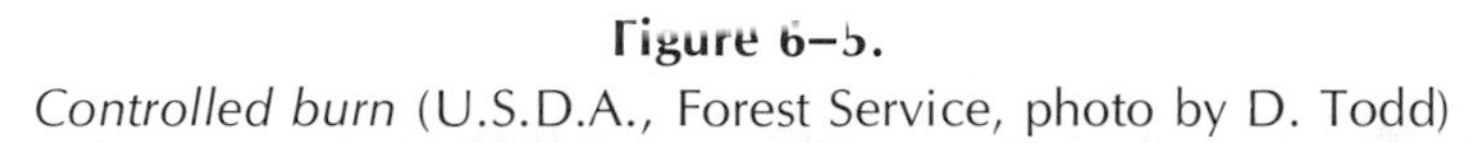

**Figure 6–5.**
*Controlled burn* (U.S.D.A., Forest Service, photo by D. Todd)

that justifying immunization in medicine. It is better to have a smallpox vaccination than the disease itself, and it is better to have an easily contained ground fire than a wildfire leaping from crown to crown, destroying thousands of trees. *Preemptive* burning at three- to five-year intervals removes the debris that accumulates under conifers, thus preventing the creation of a tinderbox situation. It also fosters seed germination and seedling survival of such pine species as longleaf and ponderosa. *Controlled burns* are used in many parts of the United States, helping perpetuate communities associated with sequoias, jack pine, and the shrubby chaparral.

This last aspect is discussed by Richard H. Wagner in his book under the heading "*Fire-maintained Niches.*"[12] Many species of plants and animals are recognized as members of subclimax communities subject to repeated fires. Elimination of fires would effectively doom these species to extinction. Therefore, such unlikely allies as the Audubon Society and the local firemen join together to set fire to the woods. Patches of jack pine, 40 acres or more, are burnt in north-central Michigan. Pine cones burst open, scattering seeds that germinate in the barren soil and produce a young forest of jack pines, the lowly habitat suitable for breeding pairs of Kirtland's warbler. This species leads a precarious existence, spending its winters on 4,400 square miles of the Bahamas and its summers in 850 square miles of the jack pine region.

The California condor is even less secure. It must hunt for carrion in an increasingly urbanized portion of southern California, its principal home being Los Padres National Forest, part of the Los Angeles watershed. The remaining forty to sixty condors need burnt openings in the chaparral where they can spot dead animals, land, feed, and take off again. Controlled fires can also be useful in protecting property and human life, because the proximity of dense, dry chaparral endangers the sprawling suburbs of Los Angeles.

The National Park Service may soon have to revise its policy on forest fires. Some areas under its control have been so well protected from fire that they have lost the diversity of early successional stages. If enough dead wood has accumulated in these *national parks,* a huge ecological short circuit may occur, with a holocaust suddenly releasing stored nutrients and solar energy. This happened in 1947 when much of the forest at Acadia National Park on Mt. Desert Island, Maine, was destroyed. It could also happen in Shenandoah National Park, Virginia, and in several of the western parks. Preemptive burns require skill, manpower, and money, but they may be a necessary part of forest—and park—management.

Forests used primarily for recreation have other management problems. So many people have been visiting parks that noise, litter, and trampled vegetation have become major concerns of those trying to preserve the ecosystem. Tighter controls of vehicles and hikers are needed, restricting access to certain wilderness areas. Although this would seem to impair the very freedom urbanites are seeking in their forest visits, wise regulation is essential if future generations are to have any chance of enjoying forests, or any other finite resource. Many *conservation organizations* are working toward the ideal combination of utilization and preservation. You can help by actively supporting one or more of the following groups:

American Forestry Association
Conservation Foundation
Friends of the Earth
National Audubon Society
National Parks Association
Nature Conservancy
Wilderness Society

## SUMMARY

Wise management and prudent utilization of forests require careful inventories of forest resources and detailed understanding of the processes involved in the development and maintenance of forest ecosystems. With such information, it is possible to decide which combinations of production, recreation, and conservation are compatible in a forested area, also recognizing certain situations where such multiple use is impractical. Furthermore, it is possible to select the strategies and tools that will create or preserve the forest types appropriate for a pattern of utilization: for example, identifying forests where burns can help increase pulp production and other sites where efforts to exlude fires can be justified on grounds of safety, uniqueness, or preservation of climax ecosystems.

### Discussion Questions

**1.** If you were in charge of a forested area, which use would you most strongly encourage and which would you forbid:
(a) clear-cutting
(b) camping

(c) hunting
(d) ecological research
(e) watershed?

**2.** In what ways is fire useful and in what ways is it damaging in forests?
**3.** How can forested areas be preserved or even expanded?
**4.** Discuss the relationships between sustained yield and cost-benefit ratios in forest management.

## Suggested Projects

**1.** Visit the nearest forest after finding out as much as you can about its age, species composition, and management.
**2.** If possible, go to a similar forested area that has been burnt and record some of the differences observed.
**3.** Invite a member of one of the groups listed on p. 73 to come to your class to describe the goals of his organization.

## Notes

1. This theme is explored in Rutherford Platt, *The Great American Forest* (Englewood Cliffs, N.J.: Prentice-Hall, 1971).
2. Steps in this direction have been taken by the Connecticut Agricultural Experiment Station. See P. E. Waggoner and J. D. Ovington, "Proceedings of the Lockwood Conference on the Suburban Forest and Ecology," *Connecticut Agricultural Experiment Station Bulletin,* **652** (1962), 102 pp., and by the Yale School of Forestry.
3. J. Dorst, *Before Nature Dies* (Boston: Houghton, 1970), p. 139.
4. Based on World Table 3 "Land Resources," in G. D. Hudson, ed., *Encyclopaedia Britannica, World Atlas* (Chicago: Benton, 1961).
5. R. Revelle and H. H. Landsberg, eds. *America's Changing Environment* (Boston: Beacon, 1970), p. 114.
6. For example, T. C. Nelson and W. M. Zillgitt, "A Forest Atlas of the South" (Washington, D.C.: USDA Forest Service, 1969), 27 pp.
7. "Multiple Use, The National Forests and Your Family" (Washington, D.C.: USDA Forest Service, P.A. no. 423, March 1961).
8. G. Hill, "National Forests: Timber Men vs. Conservationists," *New York Times,* 15 November 1971.
9. Raymond F. Dasmann, *Environmental Conservation,* 3rd ed. (New York: Wiley, 1972), p. 239.

10. Based on data in Dasmann, ibid., pp. 236–237.
11. See these articles: C. F. Cooper "The Ecology of Fire," *Scientific American,* **204**(4):150–160 (1961); and V. Johnston "The Ecology of Fire," *Audubon,* **72**(5):76–119 (1970). (The Johnston article later was published as a chapter in her book, *Sierra Nevada* (Boston: Houghton, 1970).
12. Richard H. Wagner, *Environment and Man* (New York: Norton, 1971), pp. 89–92.

# 7
# Wildlife Preservation

## Key Concepts

Preservation
Vulnerability
Narrow niche
Habitat restoration
Captive rearing
Public involvement
Management
Ecological-political compromise
Wildlife habitat
Disease reservoir

The problems of wildlife *preservation* fall into two main categories. Most publicized, and rightly so, is the one concerned with endangered species. However, another set of problems surrounds the management of wildlife (and fish) species common enough to be shot, caught, or harvested in any other way. The ability of man to transfer a species from hunted, to endangered, to extinct categories has been amply demonstrated during the past fifty thousand years. Recall the phenomena of overkill discussed in Chapter 4. Nevertheless, wildlife management also involves policies and practices designed to prevent a species from destroying its own habitat. This is, of course, most apt to be necessary when and where man has excluded the great canine and feline predators assuming the title "sole proprietor and top predator." Before considering the management of game species, such as deer, let's focus on the more dramatic plight of species so rare that they may become extinct.[1]

## ENDANGERED SPECIES

One of the last questions that might have been asked by the last dodo is "How did I get myself in this fix?" For a dodo, that would have been a very intelligent question, because his species embodied many characteristics of *vulnerability*. The dodo was large, flightless, isolated, edible, and presumably had a reproductive rate so low that it could not replace the losses inflicted by club-wielding Dutch sailors. Other species now endangered may not share all the dodo's failings, but many of them are both specialized in their feeding habits (they have a *narrow niche*) and restricted in their range. During the last two decades, a new threat has been superimposed on patterns of weakness already present. Agricultural and industrial chemicals have entered the food chain, causing reproductive failure in bird populations already hard-pressed and declining.

Ecologists, as champions of endangered species, sometimes overstate the case for preservation. The world's food web will not collapse when the last ivorybill (woodpecker) expires. Other creatures, perhaps less spectacular, will utilize the logs and grubs left by the ivorybill. No, the real justification for saving a species is both rational and ethical. We have no right to destroy a species, especially without even understanding how it came to be and how it works. Every species is a unique package of genetic adaptations. By studying its strengths and weaknesses we can better define its niche and our own. From a utilization viewpoint, the destruction of species also would seem unwise. Perhaps we have no use for the Devil's Hole pupfish, but some future generation may want to base an entire protein industry on fish preadapted to warm, brackish water. Potential knowledge and possible utility are dual justifications for preservation. The intellectual and the practical should find at least one argument convincing.

What strategy can we use to preserve endangered species? Because each finds itself in a unique predicament, its specific salvation must also be unique. Yet, certain general principles apply to most cases. First, there is no place like the home habitat. To preserve the species, we must save its environment, insuring that all its essential requisites (food, shelter, and the like) are maintained. Sometimes this involves excluding man, his domestic animals, or even exotic weeds. *Habitat restoration* can also involve planting native vegetation, constructing ponds, or reducing pollution.

A second principle is not to collect a species to extinction. Zoos, museums, and certain private citizens are enchanted by rarity and there is a very real danger that every individual in a rare species will end up in a cage or a glass display case. This is not to say that zoos and other institutions cannot make prudent collections, especially when the home habitat is threatened with total destruction and there is a chance that the species will breed in captivity. Successful mating, gestation, and rearing of the young in zoos can be very difficult, as shown by the much-publicized, but unproductive, romances of giant pandas in the United Kingdom and the United States. Still, there have been some successes with *captive rearing* when the animals are given a good diet, plenty of space, and left alone—an example of which is the bald eagle at the Pautuxent Wildlife Research Center in Maryland. However, it should be remembered that the objective is *wildlife* preservation. If the species is reared in cages for many generations, it will become just another domesticated pet. Whenever and wherever a suitable habitat can be found, the species should be released into the wild.

A final guiding principle is to get the *public involved.* Wildlife preservation is too important to be left to scientists. Here zoos, TV programs, and schools can make vital contributions showing the plight of rare species and what can be done to save them. Never underestimate the power of concerned kids writing their congressmen on behalf of the sea otter. Laws protecting endangered species and their habitats are needed for everything from eagles to tigers. We can severely punish those ranchers caught using helicopters as gunships to shoot down our national bird, but we can do little to prevent a Bangladesh citizen from killing tigers. Still, banning importation of tiger pelts or coats made with tiger fur does cut off one market, making tiger killing somewhat less profitable.

Some case histories of endangered species and protection will help to illustrate the application of preservation principles. Each ivorybill requires 6 square miles of uncut forest, with standing tree trunks that have been dead for at least three years and are inhabited by large beetle grubs. As lumbermen have moved into the last virgin timberlands of North America, the swamp forests of South Carolina, Florida, Louisiana, and Texas, the ivorybill populations have dwindled to the verge of extinction. To be sure, a tape recording of the ivorybill's call was played—and answered—in one swampy forest, but the call may have been the lament of a lonely spinster. The last hope for this species is the preservation of large, uncut forests such as the Big Thicket in Texas (Figure 7–1 a, b).

Another example of a species being endangered by the destruction of a requisite essential to its survival is the black-footed ferret.[2] This relative of the mink and weasel subsists on a steady diet of prairie dogs. Unfortunately, extensive poisoning campaigns have been launched against "dog

a

b

**Figure 7–1.**
**a.** *Young Ivory-bill woodpecker, Mar. 6., 1938, Singer Tract, La.* (James T. Tanner from National Audubon Society) **b.** *Black-footed ferret* (U.S. Dept. of Interior, Fish and Wildlife Service, Photographer: L. C. Goldman)

towns'' throughout the plains states, largely on the unproven assumption that 32 prairie dogs equal one sheep, and 256 equal one steer, in grass consumption. Actually, the prairie dog is a member of the weed and short-grass community that symptomizes overgrazing. Ranchers hate to admit this and raise another objection to dog towns, claiming that holes made by badgers digging out the dogs are ''widow makers,'' endangering the lives of cowboys galloping across the plain. Whatever the justification for dropping oats laced with 1080 (sodium fluoroacetate) down dog-town burrows, the black-footed ferret has suffered and may now have a total population somewhere in the range of forty to eighty. Even if it does not eat a poisoned prairie dog, it may starve after the dog town is wiped out. Any chances of black-footed ferret survival are based on the wildlife research center at Pautuxent—and a bomb range in South Dakota! Six young ferrets were taken from South Dakota to Pautuxent for an attempt at breeding them in captivity. Despite immunization, four females died of distemper, leaving the researchers with a difficult decision: whether to risk trapping mates for the two surviving males. In South Dakota, the Defense Department has assumed the role of ferret protector because it maintains a 42,000-acre bomb range, with 3,000 acres containing thirty dog towns off-limits to both poisoning and bombing. If the Pautuxent breeding program is successful, the ferret can be recolonized in other protected areas, such as the Badlands National Monument in South Dakota, which may contain more than one thousand dog towns.[3]

A final case history deals with attempts to preserve the native birds of Hawaii.[4] The Polynesians who colonized the archipelago a thousand years ago had little direct effect on the native flora and fauna, although other waves of Polynesians apparently wiped out the fabled roc of Madagascar and the giant moas of New Zealand. The Hawaiians caught the unique and beautiful honey creepers, plucking their feathers to make royal garments, then releasing them, deprived of dignity but not of life. The first Hawaiians did introduce the dog, the pig, the chicken, and, accidentally, a small rat; however, later introductions by Asian, European, and American settlers were far more damaging. Goats, cattle, and deer exerted varying degrees of grazing pressure on the native vegetation. Birds infected with fowl pox or avian malaria served as a reservoir for mosquito transmission to native birds that had little or no resistance to the exotic pathogens. Other birds were released in the lowlands only to penetrate the highland forests where they competed with native birds for food. Even some creatures introduced to control agricultural pests got out of hand, invading the forests and reducing native insect populations to such a low level that native birds dependent on the insects could not survive. On all the large islands except Kauai, the mongoose was introduced under the misapprehension that it would control rats. Unfortunately, it works the day shift and rats are active at night, so the mongoose, although it killed some rats imprudent enough to venture forth during the day, destroyed several species of ground-nesting birds. The ultimate catastrophe for many other species was the destruction of their forest home. Lowlands were cleared for sugar cane, pineapples, and cattle; highlands for fruit trees, pines, and eucalyptus. Altogether twenty-four of the seventy species (or subspecies) of birds known in Hawaii were driven to extinction and another twenty-seven are endangered (including one just discovered in a high valley on Maui in 1973), leaving only nineteen reasonably secure.[5]

To preserve the survivors, a complex program of import bans, captive rearing, habitat restoration, and sanctuary designation must be developed. Almost every year exotic species of birds escape (or are released) and become established in Hawaii. Insects are accidentally introduced by boat and plane; others are deliberately reared and released to attack weeds or pests, usually with little evaluation of their effect on target or other species. Game animals such as the axis deer are imported or moved from one island to another. From past mistakes, it would seem wise to ban, or at least more closely regulate, all such importations if the native fauna and flora are to be protected.

Some excellent work has been done rearing the nene (Hawaiian goose), reduced to fifty by 1945. After finding the combination of climate and vegetation conducive to breeding, it was possible to increase the population to five hundred, established in suitable habitats on Hawaii and Maui. Four areas, totaling more than 44,000 acres have been set aside as sanctuaries for the nene.[6] A similar program for the propagation of the koloa (Hawaiian duck) is under way, and others may be started for the honeycreepers as more is learned about their care and feeding (Figure 7–2).

Even if rearing is successful, releases may be doomed unless habitats are restored and protected. Only the Alakai swamp on Kauai's Mt. Waialeale and the forest on the outer, windward slope of Haleakala crater of Maui can be considered relatively undisturbed wilderness areas. A subject of much debate in Hawaii is the degree of federal control needed to protect native birds.[7] The low, small islands northwest of Kauai were designated as the Hawaiian Islands National Wildlife Refuge by Teddy Roosevelt in 1909, but the Alakai swamp is less protected by isolation or law, although it was

**Figure 7–2.**
*Nene Goose in Hawaii Volcanoes National Park. Once common on the islands of Hawaii and Maui, this species of goose was seldom seen in its native haunts. With the help of man this bird is gradually increasing its numbers and is no longer classed as a nearly extinct species.* (U.S. Dept. of the Interior, National Park Service photo)

made a state wilderness area in 1964. The most recent efforts have been directed toward expansion of the Hawaii Volcanoes National Park (established in 1916) and Haleakala National Park (established in 1960). In 1971, Kipahulu Valley, a haven of the Maui parrotbill, the nukupu'u, and the crested honey creeper, was added to the Haleakala National Park,[8] and the recent discovery of a new species in the Hana rain forest shows how important it is that other valleys be brought under protection.

## MANAGED SPECIES

Wildlife *management* is usually thought to concern birds and mammals hunted as game. However, similar applications are found in the management of fresh-water, estuarine, and marine species of shellfish and finfish. There are other groups of animals presently being collected with little concern for their perpetuation. Even biologists stand guilty in this respect, because they have depleted wild populations of frogs[9] and many denizens in West Coast tide pools in the name of teaching and research.

The laws governing wildlife management programs represent a *compromise between ecological ideals and political realities*. Hunting seasons should, theoretically, avoid breeding periods and permit the harvesting of animals that might not survive the winter anyway. In selecting hunting seasons and locations various human uses of the habitat must be considered so that the safety of campers or hikers is not jeopardized. Other laws, through a combination of licensing requirements and bag or creel limits, are supposed to regulate the harvesting, but such variables as the sportsman's skill, enthusiasm, and honesty make a "fine tuning" of the harvest difficult.

Measures to foster wildlife populations can be as simple and acceptable as the provision of old Christmas trees for shelter or as controversial as "varmint" control. Are the wolves of Canada and northern Michigan competing with hunters for the privilege of killing deer? Perhaps the wolves are merely culling the herds of sickly and old individuals, reducing the danger of overbrowsing and increasing the average trophy size. To quote the late Aldo Leopold,

> I have lived to see state after state extirpate its wolves. I have watched the face of many a newly wolfless mountain, and seen the south-facing slopes wrinkle with a maze of new deer trails. I have seen every edible bush and seedling browsed, first to anaemic desuetude, and then to death. I have seen every edible tree defoliated to the height of a saddlehorn.
>
> I now suspect that just as a deer herd lives in mortal fear of its wolves, so does a mountain live in mortal fear of its deer.[10]

Similarly, West Coast fishermen regard the sea otter as a pesky competitor, but it seems more likely the sea otter is protecting an important fish habitat by feeding on the sea urchins that threaten kelp beds.

Almost as clouded in controversy are programs to introduce, rear, and release fish and game species. These operations can be very tricky, even when they involve no more than moving a native species from one habitat to another. With exotic species, government agencies are even more likely to find themselves locked into a continual restocking program. Ring-necked pheasant in South Dakota or coho salmon in Lake Michigan simply cannot maintain wild populations and need help from the hatcheries. Cost-benefit studies in this area are much needed. Many a hunter pays three dollars for a license and gets a brace of pheasants that cost ten dollars to rear (Figure 7–3).

Before giving you three short case histories of managed species, one more general concept should be delineated: wasteland is not a good habitat for wildlife. Land-use planning (see Chapter 26, "Resource Allocation") traditionally has relegated wildlife to rocky, barren and/or mountainous

**Figure 7–3.**
*Ring-necked pheasant* (U.S.D.A.-F.S. photo)

terrain useful for little else. Wild species, like domesticated varieties, thrive best in *habitats* with fertile soil and healthy vegetation. If we truly value our wildlife, a shift in land-use priorities is in order.

The first example of management is, almost inevitably, based on the maintenance of a deer herd, this being the most important game animal in many states.[11] However, the population in this case is not hunted currently. Not that it would provide much venison, or a good trophy, because the average weight of the adult is 50 pounds.[12] This is the Key deer, a dwarf race of the white-tailed deer, found only on Big Pine Key, Florida and nearby islands. Back from the brink of extinction, they now number six hundred and are near the carrying capacity of their habitat, as shown by the fact that they have started eating such unlikely fare as the bougainvillea in the ranger's garden. Management includes the preservation of their habitat from housing subdivision and nursing back to health individuals hit by autos. A policy decision not to export any Key deer to zoos was calculated shrewdly to preserve their uniqueness as a wild population and a tourist attraction. Soon, however, some harvesting, dead or alive, may be necessary to protect the herd and its habitat because the automobile is such an inefficient predator (Figure 7–4).

An even more spectacular recovery from near-extinction has been achieved in the Soviet Union. The saiga antelope, down to one thousand in 1920, now numbers two million. Admittedly, they are sparsely scattered over 4 million square miles of steppes (Eurasian prairies), but three hundred thousand are shot each year, producing "6,000 tons of good meat, fat, leather, and horn"[13] and the herds are still increasing, indicating that even more could be harvested on a sustained-yield basis. The migratory habits of the saiga have kept it from destroying its food supply, and because it eats many plants that cattle will not consume, it is presumably compatible with cattle (unless it serves as a reservoir for some pathogen endangering the cattle).

The *disease reservoir* problem is just one of many besetting antelope farming in East Africa. To protect cattle herds from the trypanosome (a protozoan transmitted by tsetse flies) that causes bovine sleeping sickness, antelope herds have been eradicated in many districts. Although protein production per unit for antelope is seven times that for scrub cattle, the Masai tribesmen can use only cattle to buy brides and achieve status. Further complications derive from an African ambivalence toward wildlife. Many of the leaders in East Africa recognize the value of antelope, elephants, lions, and other spectacular animals in national parks because the animals attract free-spending tourists. Yet, the parks can also be viewed as

**Figure 7–4.**
*Key deer* (Bureau of Fisheries and Wildlife, Photo by W. H. Julian)

vestiges of colonialism. There may even be a deep feeling that the preservation of wildlife encourages the totemism and tribalism so dangerous to a new country in search of a national identity. Nonetheless, it should be possible to work out a program that will insure a steady supply of both dollars and meat. This may involve game cropping in parks and other areas where habitat destruction from excessive grazing and trampling has been observed. Part of the program should include efforts to reduce the numbers of cattle while upgrading their quality. Some tinkering with tribal mores may be necessary, but a redefinition of bride price to include consideration of cattle quality might be possible. Also, campaigns based on slogans such as "Preserve the Parks and Feed the People" may be needed to convince East Africans, especially those living in cities, that their wildlife heritage is of great value.

## SUMMARY

We are apt to be interested in two groups of wildlife species, those that are very rare and those that are common enough to be hunted as game. For species in both groups, an understanding of their environmental needs is essential. Preservation of an endangered species requires public support for the appropriate combination of habitat protection and captive rearing. Management of a game species involves ecological-political compromise with the objective of a population large enough to satisfy hunters but not so large that habitat degradation results. Case histories illustrate some of the complications in actual attempts to preserve the black-footed ferret, the ivorybill, Hawaiian honey creepers, the Key deer, the saiga antelope, and African game animals.

## Discussion Questions

1. To what extent do our "uses" of wildlife parallel those of forest resources in the conservation, recreation, and production categories?
2. How would you justify the preservation of the dodo to a hungry sailor?
3. What are the main differences between an endangered species and a game species?
4. Discuss your attitudes, and the attitudes of those you know, toward hunting.

## Suggested Projects

1. Find out if there are any wildlife specialists in your community; if so, ask one to tell your class about his work.
2. Write to your governmental representatives on behalf of an endangered or overhunted species (for example, the blue whale).
3. Provide feeders in winter and nest boxes in summer for those species of birds that you enjoy watching.

## Notes

1. Two good books on wildlife preservation are Jean Dorst, *Before Nature Dies* (Boston: Houghton, 1970); and James Fisher, *Wildlife Crisis* (New York: Cowles, 1970). A simplified, but accurate, source of information on wildlife in the broadest sense (including many insects) is Maurice Burton and Robert Burton, eds., *International Wildlife Encyclopedia,* 20 vols. (New York: Marshall Cavendish Corporation, 1970).
2. See John Madsen, "Dark Days in Dogtown," *Audubon,* **70**:32–43 (1968).
3. Faith McNulty's short, effective account of the black-footed ferret

tragedy appeared in *The New Yorker* in 1970 and was published as a paperback, *Must They Die?* (New York: Audubon-Ballantine, 1971).

4. G. Laycock "The Hawaiian Islands of Birds," *Audubon,* **72**:44–61 (1970).
5. These numbers vary, depending on who is doing the counting, because it is not always clear whether extinct forms were distinct species or just races on other islands. The statistics used here are from Warren King, "Hawaii: Haven for Endangered Species?" *National Parks,* **45**:9–13 (1971); for the addition of the species recently discovered on Maui, see James D. Jacobi and Tonnie Casey, "New Species of Bird Discovered on Maui, Hawaii," *The Elepaio,* **34**:83–84 (1974). (This mimeographed journal of the Hawaii Audubon Society is a very useful source of information on current conservation efforts in Hawaii.)
6. Harry A. Goodwin, "The Endangered Species Conservation Program for Hawaii," *The Elepaio,* **34**:23–27 (1972); and Ronald L. Walker, "1972 Report of Nene Restoration Program by State Department of Land and Natural Resources," *The Elepaio,* **34**:123–128 and 135–142 (1974).
7. Andrew J. Berger, "The Present Status of the Birds of Hawaii," *Pacific Science,* **24** (1970); reprinted in *The Elepaio,* **31**:41–47 and 51–58 (1970).
8. King, loc. cit.
9. E. S. Gibbs, G. W. Nace, and M. B. Emmons, "The Live Frog is Almost Dead," *BioScience,* **21**:1027–1034 (1971).
10. Aldo Leopold, "Thinking Like a Mountain," *A Sand County Almanac* (New York: Oxford U. P., 1949), pp. 130 and 132.
11. W. Dasmann, *If Deer Are to Survive, How to Meet Food and Cover Needs* (Harrisburg, Pa.: Stockpole, 1971); and W. P. Taylor, *Deer of North America* (Harrisburg, Pa.: Stockpole, 1956). Both of these books were sponsored by the Wildlife Management Institute.
12. H. S. Zim, *A Guide to Everglades National Park and the Nearby Florida Keys* (New York: Golden Press, 1960) p. 21.
13. Dorst, op. cit., p. 304.

# 8

# Food Production

## Key Concepts

- Monoculture
- Domestication
- Cultigens
- Production strategy
- Importation strategy
- Genetic engineering
- Ghost acreage
- Population equivalents
- Deficiency disease
- Adequate diet
- Quality improvement
- Production increase
- Green revolution

In discussing utilization of forests and preservation of wildlife, we were describing terrestrial ecosystems that had been modified only slightly by man and his technology. Now we will consider those that have been changed greatly, often to the point where a pure culture of one food species in an early successional stage is the agricultural goal. Such *monoculture* is, of course, the antithesis of the climax forest, with its diverse community of plants and animals achieved after 100 to 150 years of successional development. Monoculture is not inherently evil, but all those whose food supplies depend on the perpetuation of monocultures (and that includes most of mankind) must recognize the ecological price they are paying.

## DOMESTICATION

The history of agriculture includes a series of steps leading to increased control over certain species of plants and animals. This is one of the ways, and a very important way, in which man has modified his environment to

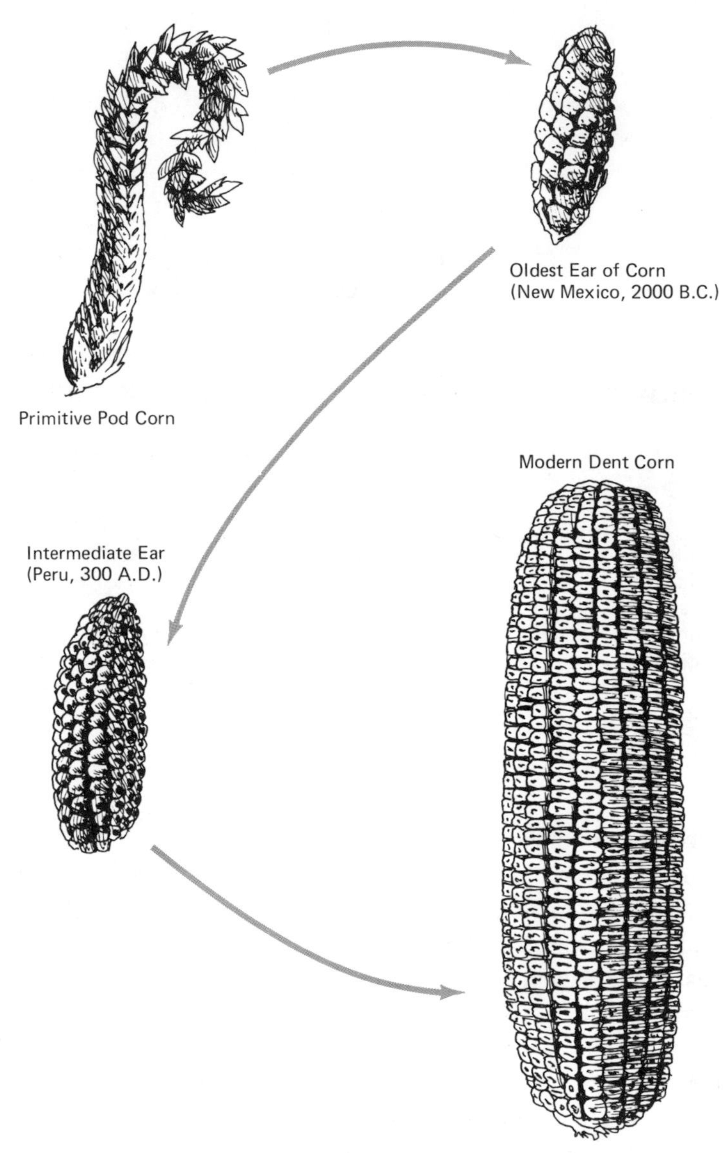


**Figure 8–1.**
*Domestication of a grain crop* (adapted from "The Mystery of Corn" by Paul C. Mangelsdorf, July, 1950, *Scientific American*)

his own advantage. Domestication is the process, and those organisms that have become enmeshed in the process are *cultigens*. Both external and internal changes have occurred because the cultigens have genetic characteristics and environments quite different from those of their ancestors (Figure 8–1).

A scale of domestication can be visualized by comparing organisms much changed by man with those so little changed that they are virtually indistinguishable from their wild relatives. Corn (maize) is a hybridized freak far different from its ancestral grasses, but wild rice is unchanged from prehistoric times, still being harvested in the Lake states by Indians who beat the grains into their canoes. Similarly, the factory chicken, penned with thousands of her kind, never seeing the sky or eating a bug, is quite a different bird than the turkey, which can still forage for acorns in woods even if it starts its life on a game farm. Other contrasting pairs include trees (apple versus guava), fish (carp versus eel), and mammals (cattle versus antelope). (See Table 8–1.) Calibrating the scale of domestication is not easy, but a critical point—where the cultigen "can't go home again"—is recognizable. Up until that point, the cultigen's dependence on man is not strong enough to preclude a return to the wild. Many horticultural varieties have demonstrated this by escaping from gardens, sometimes losing status and becoming weeds. Domestic animals also can go feral, as shown by cats, dogs, and horses in various parts of the United States. However, for hybrid corn and the factory chicken, the point of no return has been passed; they are completely dependent on us for their perpetuation. An interesting question poses itself in this vein: Have we become completely dependent on our cultigens? Most of us may have lost the ability to live directly off the land, foraging for fruits, roots, and grubs as did our distant ancestors. If suddenly we were forced to do so, the survival of those who did not own a copy of Euell Gibbon's "Stalking the Wild Asparagus" would be in grave jeopardy[1] (Figure 8–2).

**TABLE 8–1. Degrees of Domestication**

| | Grain Crops | Fruit Trees | Poultry | Cattle |
|---|---|---|---|---|
| Wild, but taken by man | wild rice | guava | wild turkey | antelope |
| Can still survive on own in the wild | barley | apple | pigeon | feral cattle |
| Completely tame | hybrid corn | navel orange | factory chicken | dairy cow |

a

**Figure 8–2.**
**a.** *Fox grape, wild species* **b.** *Cardinal grape, hybrid cultigen* (U.S.D.A. photos)

## STRATEGIES

This brings us to the two basic strategies by which modern man feeds himself. One, a *strategy of production,* is basically ecological; the other, a *strategy of importation,* is essentially economic. Without the continuation

b

**Figure 8 –2.** *(Continued)*

of and improvements in both, it is unlikely that our present standards of living and eating can be maintained.

Food production involves the provision of requisites—energy, nutrients, and water—to our cultigens and the protection of those cultigens from organisms that directly attack them or indirectly harm they by competing for requisites. The form of energy provided depends on the needs of the cultigen: for a green plant, sunlight or a reasonable facsimile; for cattle, fodder; and for mushrooms, detritus. Among the elements essential for life, nitrogen is especially important because it is the precursor of amino acids which, in turn, must be present in our diet for normal development and repair of brain and muscle. Many other elements, two dozen all told, are essential, some being needed only in trace amounts but doing a vital job in an enzyme system[2] (Figure 8–3).

In recent years, *genetic engineering* of cultigens has greatly increased their efficiency in converting energy and nutrients into edible calories. Examples include rice varieties that, after fertilizer applications, respond with vigorous growth and ignore day-length cues, maturing in four months instead of eight. (These will be discussed later in this chapter in "The Green Revolution".) Also a product of artificial selection is the factory chicken, converting 1 pound of grain, and an indeterminate amount of water, into 1 pound of drumstick. Some serious questions have been asked regarding the advisibility of adding hormones and antibiotics to chicken feed, or cattle fodder, in order to accelerate growth. Rapid turnover, more efficient use of production facilities, and lower prices for animal protein are the benefits, but the price may include hormone-induced cancers and antibiotic-resistant bacteria in humans.[3]

Technology, especially chemical technology, also has been applied to protect cultigens. We have used chemical weapons to kill the weeds competing with crops for requisites; to inhibit the growth of parasitic and pathogenic organisms; and to kill, sterilize, or repel pests. In the next chapter, the numerous failings of our present weapons will be detailed. The basic principle of chemical control, however, is not condemned and, in Chapter 10, various ways in which chemicals can be used wisely in conjunction with other techniques to control pests, without fouling the biosphere, will be discussed.

Because few Americans or Europeans live on farms and feed themselves, importation of food is a daily necessity for most communities. We have come to take for granted the availability of California vegetables, Florida oranges, Kansas beef, and Georgia chicken in New England supermarkets. What we may not realize is that entire nations have become dependent on a dual strategy of food importation: trade and fishing. Japan is, perhaps, the best (or worst) example, growing only 23 percent of its food and getting the rest by sending out huge fishing fleets to harvest the seas and by trading transistor radios for Thai rice. With 100 million people on a group of mountainous islands—in area 10 percent smaller than the state of California (whose population in 1970 was about twenty million)—it is not surprising that the Japanese are far from self-sufficient. It is, nonetheless, one more symptom of overpopulation, and a departure from the ecological ideal of living well below the carrying capacity. Georg Borgstrom, a geographer, discusses many aspects of this problem in his interesting and important book, *The Hungry Planet,* introducing the term *"ghost acreage"* to show

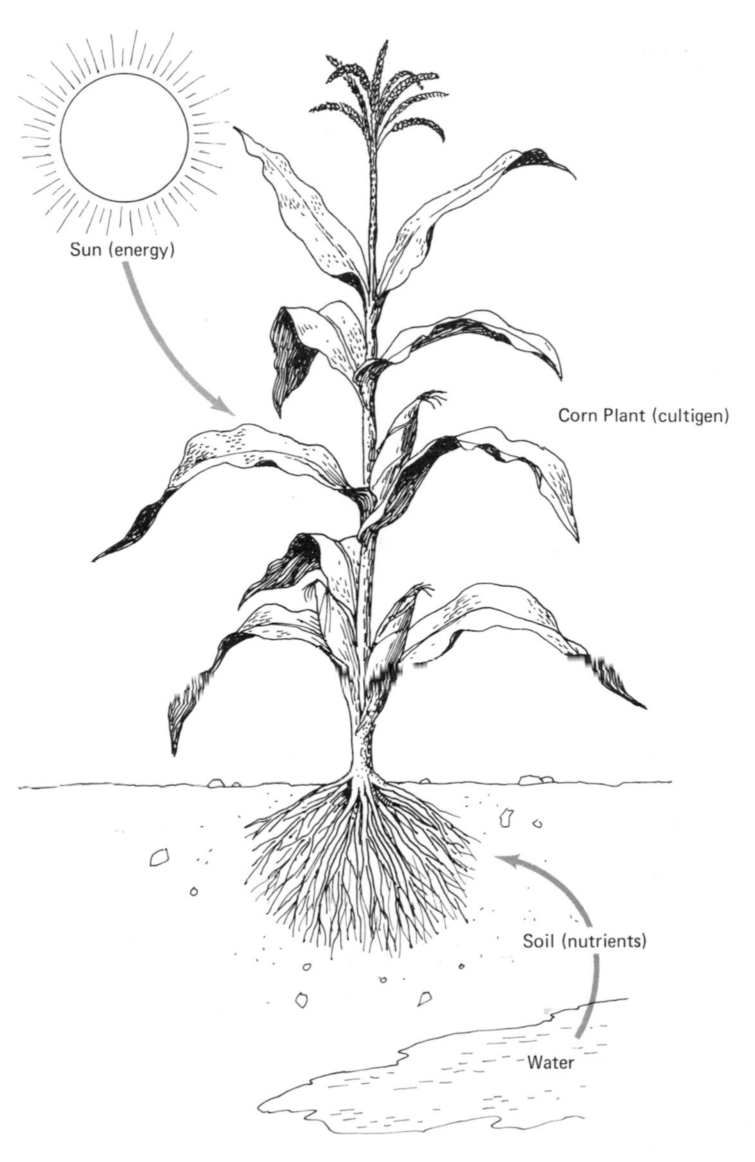


**Figure 8–3.**
*Food production requisites*

how much land would be needed by various nations to produce the food now obtained through trade or by oceanic fishing. He also shows the vast acreage given over to the production of animal protein in both developed and some developing nations, using *"population equivalents"* to estimate the combined impacts of human and livestock populations[4] (Figure 8–4).

## NUTRITION

One of Borgstrom's gravest concerns is that the Food and Agriculture Organization of the United Nations (FAO) has been measuring the nourishment of mankind only in calories per capita. This can be very misleading, even dangerous, because it can lull leaders into believing that their people have enough food when, in reality, they are malnourished.

There are many *deficiency diseases,* some caused by lack of vitamins, others by lack of minerals, but the most serious one now confronting mankind is caused by insufficient protein. Children whose diet does not include enough protein, especially animal protein (milk or its equivalent), which contains essential amino acids, cannot attain their full physical or mental potential. No matter how well fed they may be during their adult years, they remain stunted and retarded. Symptoms of protein deficiency are widespread and go by various names, kwashiorkor in West Africa and "sugar baby" in Jamaica; but the actual toll, measured in terms of human degradation, is unknown.

Determining and providing *adequate diets* require not only the special competence of those in departments of home economics but also the expertise of physiologists and ecologists. Individual requirements vary greatly, depending on age, activity, environmental conditions, and genetic heritage. For example, a small, sedentary woman may need no more than 1,500 calories (KCAL) per day; if she consumes more, she starts bulging in the wrong places. However, a lumberman chopping trees from dawn to dusk in a cold climate may need 8,000 calories to keep going. Despite this range of requirements, it is worthwhile to consider that elusive nutritional ideal: a balanced diet for an average person. We will assume that this person weighs 70 kilograms (154 pounds) and is getting enough fruits, vegetables, or supplementary pills to provide needed vitamins and minerals. Then what does he need in the three main categories: protein, fat, and carbohydrate (starches and sugars)? Remembering that, burnt by the body, each gram of fat yields 9 calories and each gram of protein or carbohydrate

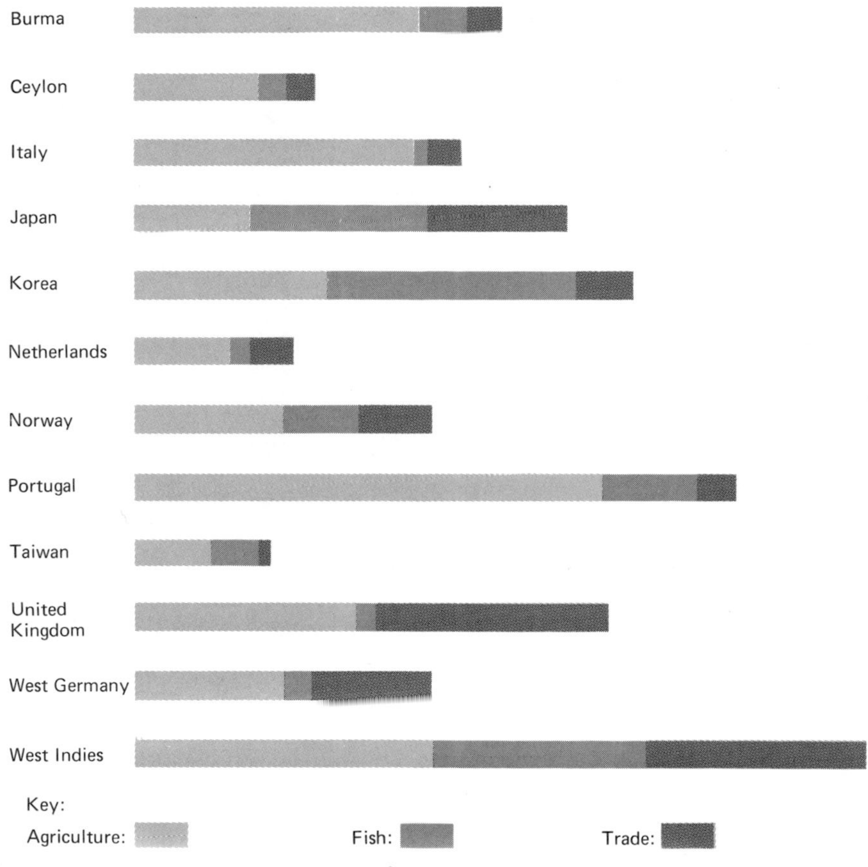


**Figure 8–4.**

*Real and ghost acreage* [after "The Hungry Planet" (Second Revised Edition) by Georg Borgstrom (Copyright © Georg Borgstrom 1965, 1967, 1972)]

can produce 4 calories, it is possible to estimate the energy provided by a diet with low, but adequate, levels of protein[5] (Figure 8–5).

## IMPROVEMENT

To provide even an adequate diet for most humans, programs for the improvement of agriculture must aim for both increased production and better *quality*. Because humans are reluctant to add new foods to their diet, the best procedure may involve improving the nutritional value of a familiar

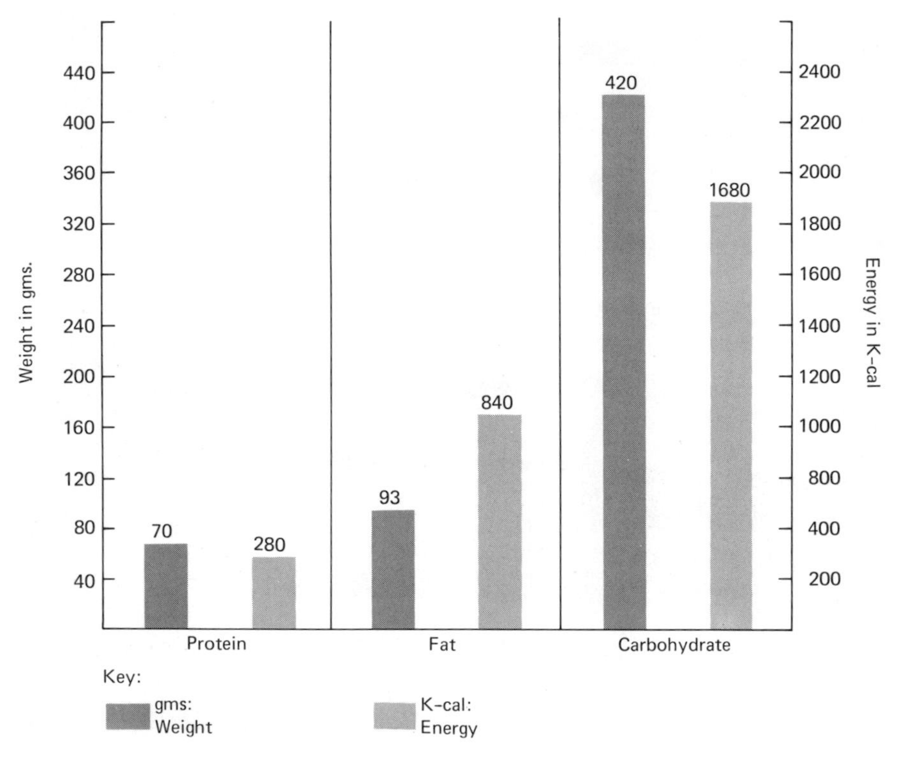


**Figure 8–5.**
*An adequate diet*

food. The starchy staple of many Africans is corn meal. By developing varieties of corn that contain more amino acids, especially lysine, yet retain suitable milling characteristics and an acceptable flavor, it should be possible to reduce the incidence of kwashiorkor[6] (Figure 8–6).

If protein-hungry people can be persuaded to try something new, many other options are available. Leguminous (bean) crops not only add nitrogen to the soil (with the help of symbiotic bacteria in root nodules), but they also can be a good source of vegetable protein. Soybeans can even be fabricated into synthetic milk or meats. Research is now under way to produce protein from bacterial cultures, but this single-celled protein (SCP) is apt to meet consumer resistance unless its humble origin is thoroughly disguised. More acceptable, perhaps, are the various fish-protein concentrates (FPC), derived from otherwise inedible fish and now available in

**Figure 8–6.**
*Soybean plant, a typical legume* (U.S.D.A. photo)

odorless forms as substitutes for, or additives to, milk and flour.[7] It has been said that man's greatest benefactor is "he who makes two blades of grass where one grew before" but "a chicken (or its equivalent) in every pot" may be a better goal.

Increased *quantities* of food can be obtained through the expansion of agricultural acreage or higher yields per acre. Such improvements will come at greater and greater costs—to the economy and to the environment. Acreage expansion has been achieved by reclamation of ruined soil (the Tennessee Valley Authority did much of this) and by impounding, draining, and desalting coastal shallows (the polders of the Netherlands). Arid lands have been brought into production through irrigation, sometimes with disastrous ecological consequences, as in the case of the High Dam at Aswam in Egypt where the price of progress included reduced fishing in the Mediterranean and increased schistosomiasis (caused by a parasitic worm that develops in the snails that thrive in the irrigated area).[8] One other irrigation technique is based on the use of tube wells. For a while, these may actually wash salt out of the crop root zone, but eventually salt can reach the water table or the water may be depleted (Figure 8–7).

Perhaps the ultimate in irrigation, now too expensive for production of

**Figure 8–7.**
*Irrigation* (U.S.D.A. photo)

anything other than luxury crops, is hydroponics. Soil is not needed because the plant roots dangle in troughs with a flowing nutrient solution. Sunlight or, where electricity is cheap, "grow lamps" provide the energy for photosynthetic fixation. If the plants are grown in air-tight buildings, there is the further possibility of growth stimulation by increasing the $CO_2$ concentration.

Another possibility is the development of a detritus agriculture. Right now we have mushroom caves, but Eugene Odum envisions an agriculture based on essentially unpalatable, pest-free plants that are converted "into edible products by microbial and chemical enrichment in food factories." He also suggests further development of aquaculture, using shellfish or finfish to convert detritus into high-quality protein.[9]

The most recent efforts to increase yields per acre have been based on chemical applications to field crops: fertilizers to feed them and biocides to protect them. These programs are closely linked to genetic engineering, crop varieties being selected for fertilizer response, rapid growth, and easy harvest. This package of applied technology has such significance to mankind that it merits a separate discussion.

## THE GREEN REVOLUTION

As recounted by Lester R. Brown in *Seeds of Change,* this quiet revolution started late in 1944 when "a group of four young Americans assembled in the hills outside Mexico City." Their mission was the application of American know-how to the problems of grain production in Mexico. Sponsored by the Rockefeller Foundation and led by Dr. George Harrar, the research team achieved its goals. Wheat production increased threefold and corn twofold, changing Mexico from a hungry country to a food exporter. More important to the average Mexican was a 40 percent increase in his food intake.[10] Because this diet included both tortillas (maize pancakes) and frijoles (beans), dietary imbalance did not occur. Unfortunately, this has not always been true in later phases of the green revolution. Much of mankind subsists on "empty calories."

The Ford Foundation joined forces with the Rockefeller Foundation to found, in 1962, the International Rice Research Institute (IRRI) at Los Banos in the Philippines near the University Philippine College of Agriculture at Laguna. Using modern techniques of crossbreeding, researchers at IRRI developed a number of high-yielding varieties adapted to local environmental conditions. A happy combination of characteristics contributed to the productivity of these varieties. They responded to fertilizer applications by growing vigorously but, despite the weight of their seed heads, they did not topple over (lodge) before harvest because their stems were short and sturdy. Some even ignored the cues of changing day length (photoperiod) and reached maturity in four months, permitting farmers to grow two, or sometimes three, crops each year. In flavor and cooking characteristics, these varieties did not always quite please traditional tastes, but they were so bountiful that they soon achieved popularity in many Asian countries.

Unfortunately, the green revolution is a technological package deal of which new varieties are but one part. A Filipino ready to try out IR-8 on a 100- by 100-foot demonstration plot is given 2 pounds of seed, 42 pounds of fertilizer and, just in case he needs it, 6 pounds of pesticide. If impressed by the results, he buys enough the next year for his whole farm but finds that he has increased his investment elevenfold, from eight to eighty-eight dollars per acre. Naturally, he wants to protect his investment, so he rents a sprayer to coat his rice with insecticide when he sees planthoppers or stem borers. If water is short in supply, he buys or rents a pump to irrigate his fields and, if the monsoon comes while he is harvesting, he must rent a dryer and find storage space to protect his grain. Obviously, this escalation of technology is easy only for the educated, enterprising, and already affluent. Marginal farmers are driven off their land and find themselves fighting for employment on large farms or in cities. Such economic displacement is common wherever rice yields have gone up—and rice prices down.

What are some other costs of the green revolution? A far too starchy diet, caused in some areas by pesticides killing fish in rice paddies and thus depriving the rural populace of accessible and vital animal protein. The appearance of virulent pathogens and superpests, thriving on the new varieties and resistant to chemical controls, may be next. Just as wheat importations from the United States to India during the 1960s supported continued growth of the Indian population and let their government dilly-dally on implementing family-limitation programs, so also has the green revolution temporarily and artificially raised the carrying capacity of India and other countries.

## SUMMARY

For food production, we have controlled certain terrestrial ecosystems, simplifying them to monocultures of domesticated species that we provide with both requisites and protection. However, few human populations can subsist on food available in their immediate environment and most must rely, to some degree, on importation. The ecological strategy of production and the economic strategy of importation should combine to create a diet adequate in calories, protein, vitamins, and minerals, the animal protein supply for children being essential for normal physical and mental growth. Improvement of food production should include new genctic varieties and novel sources for better quality and increased quantity. Expansion of agricultural acreage is still possible, but the costs of vast reclamation, clearing, or irrigation projects can be very high if they are not ecologically prudent.

## Discussion Questions

1. In what ways have we increased our control over cultigens and their environments?
2. Compare the two strategies on which we rely to get our food.
3. Why is protein such an important part of our diet?
4. How can we increase food production without degrading our environment?
5. Has the green revolution bought time for the development of world population control or has it just increased the magnitude of the problem?

## Suggested Projects

1. Keep records of your daily food consumption, estimating the number of calories you get from proteins, fats, and carbohydrates.
2. If possible, visit a farm and take enough photographs to make a photo essay on food production.
3. Find out the amounts and kinds of food imported and exported by your state or country (such information can be obtained from almanacs or similar references).

## Notes

1. See Euell Gibbons, *Stalking the Wild Asparagus* (New York: McKay, 1962); *Stalking the Blue-Eyed Scallop* (New York: McKay, 1964); and his article "Stalking Wild Foods on a Desert Isle," *National Geographic,* **142**(1):46–63 (July 1972).
2. Fluorine, silicon, tin, and vanadium are recent additions to the list. See

Earl Frieden, "The Chemical Elements of Life," *Scientific American,* **227**:52–60 (1972).

3. The possibility of a resistant strain transferring its resistance to other bacteria is discussed in Kevin Shea, "Blunted Weapons," *Environment,* **12**:28–35,41 (Jan.–Feb. 1970); it was reprinted in S. Novick and D. Cottrell, eds. *Our World in Peril: An Environment Reader* (Greenwich, Conn.: Fawcett Premier, 1971), pp. 310–320.
4. Georg Borgstrom, *The Hungry Planet* (London-N.Y.: Collier-Macmillan, 1967).
5. N. W. Pirie, *Food Resources, Conventional and Novel* (Baltimore: Penguin, 1969).
6. Dale D. Harpstead, "High-Lysine Corn," *Scientific American,* **225**:34–42 (Aug. 1971), describes research along these lines.
7. Pirie, loc cit.
8. See this excellent article on the Egyptian tragedy: Claire Sterling, "The Aswan Disaster," *National Parks,* **45**:10–13 (1971).
9. Eugene P. Odum, "The Strategy of Ecosystem Development," *Science,* **164**:262–270 (1969); reprinted with modifications, in R. L. Smith, *The Ecology of Man: An Ecosystem Approach* (New York: Harper, 1970), pp. 28–38.
10. Lester R. Brown, *Seeds of Change: The Green Revolution and Development in the 1970s* (New York: Praeger, 1970), p. 3.

# 9

# Agricultural Chemicals

## Key Concepts

- Fertilizers
- Biocides
- Side effects
- Broad-spectrum insecticides
- Persistence
- Mammalian toxicity
- Mode of action
- Resistant strains
- Food-chain concentration
- Teratogens
- Ecocide
- Defoliation
- Nitrite poisoning
- Fertilizer runoff

The slogan of modern agriculture might well be "better living through chemistry." Various *fertilizer* combinations of nitrogen, phosphorous, and potassium (N, P, K) are applied to the soil, a process that must be repeated often because some of the nutrients are removed when crops are harvested and much of the rest washes down into the soil beyond the root zone, sometimes as far as the water table. Fertilization is the term used, but the same word describes the union of sperm and egg. Plant feeding is no better because green plants derive energy from the sun and $CO_2$ from the air, so nutrients dissolved in water form only part of their diet. Perhaps a new phrase, plant nutrification, could be used, but the world may not be ready for another clumsy neologism.

Semantic fuzziness also plagues discussions of *biocides*. Many chemical companies object to the broad toxicity implied by the word biocide, preferring to emphasize the target organisms and dismissing any harm to innocent bystanders as a "*side effect.*" Medical doctors and pharmaceutical firms like that weasel phrase, too, using it whenever a patient becomes noticeably sicker after ingesting medicine. Perhaps the target classification is the easiest—and it does emphasize what we are trying to do. Briefly, biocides are listed in Table 9–1.

In this chapter, toxicological and ecological problems associated with insecticides, rodenticides, herbicides, and fertilizers will be discussed.

## INSECTICIDES

A small dose of chemistry is necessary at this point. Insecticides generally fall into three large chemical families: (1) inorganic (noncarbon compounds), (2) natural-organic (derived from plants) and (3) synthetic-organic, this last being further divided into three subfamilies:

chlorinated hydrocarbons: DDT, BHC, dieldrin, mirex
organophosphates: malathion, DDVP, parathion
carbamates: carbaryl ("Sevin"), zectran.

The natural organics include pyrethrin (extracted from a daisylike plant) and nicotine (extracted from tobacco and marketed as a potent brew called Black Leaf 40). Inorganics, once widely used, include lead arsenate (Figure 9–1 a, b, and c).

Most of these insecticides, in any chemical category, are *"broad-spectrum,"* killing anything from mosquitos to crabs. In fact, they are supposed to be that way, because the manufacturer wants to produce a multipurpose poison that can be used by a wide range of customers, from health

**TABLE 9–1.**

Pesticides

insecticides: kill insects
acaricides: kill mites
nematocides: kill roundworms
rodenticides: kill mice, rats, and other rodents
fungicides: kill (or inhibit) fungi
weedicides: kill weeds because weeds are just plants out of place, weedicides often are sold under the honest label of herbicides, emphasizing that they kill many kinds of plants.

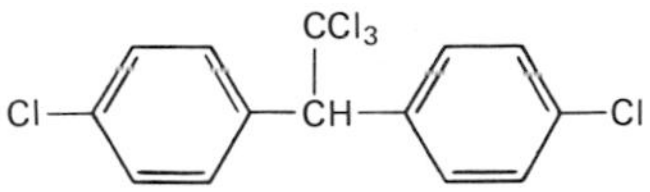

$C_{14}H_9Cl_5$

DDT

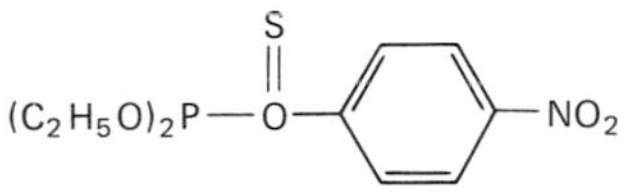

$C_{10}H_{14}NO_5PS$

Parathion

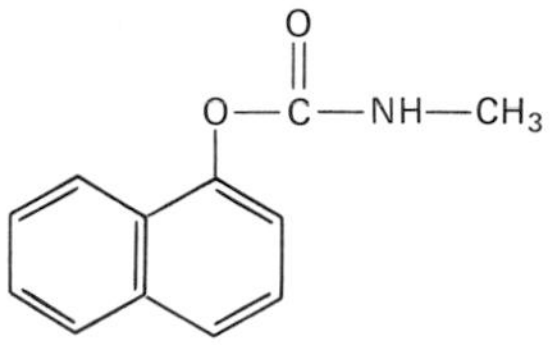

$C_{12}H_{11}NO_2$

Sevin

**Figure 9–1.**
*Structural formulae of three insecticides*

departments to cotton farmers. Without government subsidies, there just is not enough profit in the creation and production of a "boll weevilcide."

However, insecticides differ greatly in both *persistence* and toxicity to mammals. Some break down or volatilize quickly in most environments but others, such as DDT and lead arsenate, persist for years in the soil. A persistent insecticide is a two-edged sword: it helps the farmer by coating plants with long-lasting protection yet lasts so long that it can enter food chains and contaminate the biosphere. The ideal biocide should self-destruct as soon as it has done its job. *Mammalian toxicity* is another very important consideration because no one wants to hurt himself or endanger domestic animals. Despite this very natural prudence, many farmers use nerve poisons so potent that one drop of the concentrated solution on the bare skin can be lethal. Parathion and some other organophosphates, derived from nerve gases developed by Germans during World War II, fall into this category; however, even a "natural" organic such as nicotine sulfate is just as toxic. In creating new insecticides, it is necessary to find a "golden mean" between the persistent insecticides of low mammalian toxicity that harm other organisms (for example, DDT versus fish and birds) and the nonpersistent poisons that are so toxic they can kill the applicator.

How do insecticides work? For some, the *mode of action* is still obscure, but many seem to jam the transmission of nerve impulses. They reach the insect's nervous system by three routes: (1) those that penetrate the exoskeleton are called contact poisons; (2) those that go through the gut wall are stomach poisons, and (3) those that pass through the walls of the trachea (breathing tubes) are fumigants. Insects are not unfamiliar with poisons. As mentioned in Chapter 5, insects always have been engaged in a war with the plant world, for plants evolve everything from spines to psychedelic alkaloids in order to survive. Counterattacks by insects often have taken the form of detoxification mechanisms, enabling them to feed on poison-laden leaves. Some have simply bypassed the poison. Aphids feeding on tobacco leaves are quite sensitive to nicotine, but suck only sap that does not contain it. When we entered the fray, coating our crops with toxic compounds, many insect pests developed *resistant strains* that apparently are able to break down insecticides with detoxifying enzyme systems. This accelerated evolution has most often occurred when 99.9 percent of the pest population has been killed, leaving only the toughest to multiply. After a few generations, pest densities are as high as, or higher than, they were originally and the insecticide is no longer effective, even at greatly increased and uneconomic dosages. The usual ploy has been a simple one—try another spray. Unfortunately, the pest resistant to one chlorinated hydrocarbon can soon detoxify others. Therefore, an organophosphate is tried, and it works—until the pest population becomes resistant to organophosphates as well. So it has gone—and now there are some strains of mosquitos and certain agricultural pests that can cope with anything we throw at them—except a brick.[1]

Insecticides, even when used according to directions on the label or given by extension agents, can have other unfortunate effects. Many natural enemies of pests are killed. They actually may be more vulnerable to the insecticide, especially when they are walking on the poisoned surface of a leaf or stem trying to attack a pest boring within the plant. Ironically, certain leaf rollers and leaf miners achieve pest status only in areas where sprays have reduced their natural enemies. At the end of a spray campaign, a farmer may find that he has several new pests, in addition to the one he first set out to control. Other disruptions include bee kills with a consequent reduction of seed-set, detritivore decimation leading to a build-up of organic debris, and possibly even the elimination of certain weed-eating

**Figure 9–2.**
*Peach trees being sprayed with insecticide and fungicide* (U.S.D.A. photo)

insects, thus increasing weed densities. All of these beneficial insects—because they occur in many habitats outside farm areas—are not subject to the intensive selection needed to create strains resistant to insecticides. However, some researchers in California have tried to develop, in the laboratory, strains of useful insects that can survive in a poisoned environment (Figure 9–2).

All of these problems develop within the agricultural ecosystem but, sadly, insecticides can cause trouble elsewhere as well. Much of the insecticidal dust or spray misses the target area and drifts into surrounding woods or streams. With persistent compounds, there are also possibilities of later transport on wind-blown dust and organic particles or movement down into the water table. It is this sort of insecticidal contamination that worries both health authorities and ecologists. It is true that insecticide levels in human food are quite low, so low that they almost certainly cause no immediate damage to the consumer. However, there is the nagging worry that a lifetime diet of contaminated food does shorten life, possibly by increasing the incidence of certain cancers. Our liver is a good detoxifier and can render harmless many poisons consumed in small quantities, but stimulation of liver cancer may be the price exacted. With organisms other than man, the damage done by vagrant insecticides has been well documented. Reproductive failure traced to the insecticidal disruption of complex enzyme-hormone systems has occurred in fish, pelicans, falcons, eagles, and the osprey. DDT and some of its breakdown products can be *transported up food chains and concentrated* in the fat bodies of the top predators, especially fish-eating birds. If lethal concentrations are not reached, further contamination can be prevented and the birds saved from local extinction. On Long Island, osprey pairs are once again successfully rearing their young after years of thin-shelled, inviable eggs caused by DDT applications to marshlands during the 1960s. We have recognized the osprey's problems as a warning, just as early miners hastily left their mine shaft when their caged canary collapsed. In the United States, the use of DDT is restricted greatly. However, in many other countries, especially India, it is still used in large quantities because it is cheap, safe (to man), and effective against many agricultural and medical pests. Factories to produce DDT are being built in India and we are exporting 100 million pounds to developing nations each year. Some may come back to haunt us because DDT on dust can fall out on oceanic oil slicks, be dissolved, become incorporated in plankton, move up the food chain, and finally end up in the fish on our platter. Perhaps this is only fair when you realize that we have added DDT to the diet of penguins in Antarctica.[2]

## RODENTICIDES

Rodenticides have a chemical classification similar to that used for insecticides. Some are natural organics, such as red squill and strychnine, which are derived from plants; cyanide, although usually it is manufactured chemically, also could be placed here. However, as with insecticides, the new and popular poisons are synthetic organics, principally endrin, warfarin, and 1080 (sodium fluroacetate). Endrin, a chlorinated hydrocarbon with high mammalian toxicity, has been used in biscuits that are tossed into the cane fields of Hawaii to poison rats. Efforts to use it against rodents chewing on peach trees in Virginia led to a fish kill and the temporary separation of a reservoir from a municipal water supply. Compound 1080 is highly toxic, water soluble, and extremely stable. It is used against everything from prairie dogs to kangaroos. Because it is ordorless and flavorless, various baits can be rendered lethal without arousing suspicion. Warfarin is much safer, and repeated ingestion is necessary before death from slow internal hemorrhaging occurs.

As with insecticides, direct injury to humans has resulted most often from careless storage or use of rodenticides. At least thirteen people have been killed by 1080, but the real hazards have been to wildlife. Poisoned baits have helped bring the black-footed ferret and the California condor to the brink of extinction. Secondary poisoning through consumption of poisoned animals has affected many populations of scavengers and predators. It may turn out that we are doing a better job controlling the enemies of rodents than we are the rodents.[3]

Resistance to warfarin has developed in urban rats, first in Europe and now in the United States. Because rats are acknowledged to be reservoirs of pathogens and competitors for stored products, escalation to more potent poisons is almost inevitable. Building sanitized cities with no food or shelter for rodents would also solve the problem, but that is not likely to take place.

## HERBICIDES

Here we are dealing largely with a group of synthetic organic compounds that closely mimics auxins (plant hormones) and fools plants into growing themselves to death. Another group of herbicides are photosynthetic inhibitors. The former are generally most effective against broad-leafed plants and the latter against grasses, but both groups have wide spectrums and must be used with great care near crops or ornamentals. Until recently, the hazard to man and animals was considered minimal, although a few fish kills had been traced to herbicide drift or runoff and workers in herbicide factories sometimes developed a nasty skin condition (chloracne).

Now, however, there is ample evidence that we should treat herbicides with great respect or face the possibility of another thalidomide tragedy (in which hundreds of women who took thalidomide sleeping pills during their pregnancy gave birth to flipper-limbed babies). Such deformations to developing embryos are caused by chemicals collectively described as *teratogens,* and it seems that contaminants found in one herbicide, 2,4,5-T, are potent teratogens. No human birth defects in the United States or in Vietnam have been linked to 2,4,5-T, yet prudence dictates stringent restrictions on its use, perhaps putting it back on the shelf as we have done with DDT.

Both 2,4,5-T and 2,4,-D (the compound most commonly used against dandelions and other lawn weeds) are chemically related to a very widely used antiseptic, hexochlorophene. When it accidentally was added in high doses to baby power, this chemical caused a number of infant deaths in France. Laboratory studies in the United States have shown that it can also cause brain damage in baby monkeys. Although useful in preventing hospital nursery epidemics of staph (staphylococcus) infections, hexochlorophene has become a prescription item. Through guilt by chemical association, further restrictions, designed to protect mothers and children, may be placed on the use of all herbicides.[4]

So much for possible toxicological effects. What about *ecocide,* a category in which the now-terminated Vietnam defoliation operations can be placed? A number of observers have documented, often at great personal risk, some ecological consequences of *defoliation.*[5] In areas of rain forest, the removal of the upper canopies of trees subsequently permitted the growth of thick, junglelike vegetation characterized by bamboos and vines. Many of the secondary effects of the defoliaton have not yet been studied. Mangroves were completely killed in certain areas, but what effect this has had on fisheries or on the stability of deltas is not known. Nutrient cycling was presumably disrupted by defoliation, but it is not clear whether nutrients from decaying forest vegetation leached into aquifers or became part of a hard layer in soil. Either effect could cause long-lasting reduction in soil fertility. Finally, the persistence of defoliants such as picloram and the arsenic in cacodylic acid (used to destroy rice crops) has not been measured. Vietnam will have many problems in its postwar recovery, and ecologists should be able to help heal some of the scars of war. There is also a great need for critical ecological evaluation of herbicide use on fields, lawns, and roadsides in the United States.

## FERTILIZERS

This last category of agricultural chemicals is different from those considered earlier in that fertilizers are applied to agricultural ecosystems with the hope that they will stimulate life, not terminate it. Nonetheless, both toxicological and ecological problems have developed when fertilizers have leaked out from agricultural ecosystems into underground water supplies of nearby bodies of fresh water.

In the United States during the period between 1950 and 1964, there was a fourfold increase in annual applications of nitrogen fertilizer. Because farm acreage declined during the same period, the per acre application increased even more. From the farmer's viewpoint, this was a perfectly natural continuation of the "scientific agriculture" started by land-grant colleges and their associated networks of experiment stations and extension agents. However, the farmer may have been a bit puzzled when one government agency paid him not to grow crops (putting land in a "soil-bank") while another agency encouraged him to use fertilizers on his remaining acreage. To be sure, soil-bank funds invested in fertilizer purchase and application generally gave the farmer a handsome return, so he did not complain about apparently contradictory policies.

Spokesmen for chemical companies and the United States Department of Agriculture feel that, despite the high energy demands of fertilizer production, fertilizer applications will, and must, continue to increase. They argue that land in the United States is needed for many purposes other than food production and that other countries are so desperately short of food and land that the use of fertilizers, more intensively and extensively, is essential.[6] They may be right, but the hazards—of nitrate contamination, in particular—should be understood.

Nitrates in drinking water or in food can be dangerous to infants and to certain domestic animals. Denitrifying bacteria that normally transform nitrates to nitrites in the soil also can thrive in an intestinal tract if it is sufficiently alkaline. Milk-fed babies fall into this category, especially when they are suffering a digestive upset and the alkaline contents of the intestine deacidify the stomach. The *nitrite* produced under those conditions is a *poison* because it goes into the blood stream, combines with hemoglobin in the red blood cells, and, by interfering with oxygen transport, causes an often fatal "blue-baby"-type disease known as methemoglobinemia. During recent years, nitrate levels have been rising in food and drinking water in many areas. Cases of methemoglobinemia in California appear to be related to the change in irrigation practices after the completion of the Friant-Kern canal in 1950. The canal, which brings water from the north, raised the water table to the point where it reached and dissolved nitrates in a zone of deposition. Nitrate concentrations up to 90 parts per million (ppm), twice the recommended maximum, have occurred in some wells.[7] Cows and nursing mothers could transmit dangerous amounts of nitrate under these circumstances. A more direct result of fertilizer application is the increasingly high concentration of nitrates in baby foods, with the possibility that some of the nitrate may be converted to nitrite even before the baby consumes his food. Spinach is especially suspect, confirming a prejudice shared by children of several generations[8] (Figure 9–3).

The ecological effects of *fertilizer runoff* need to be mentioned but briefly here because they are similar to those that will be discussed in Chapter 20, "Sewage and Detergents." Lake Erie is burdened by drainage from 30,000 square miles of farmland; it is laden with nitrogen equivalent to that which would be found in sewage from twenty million people (twice the total population of the Lake Erie basin).[9] On a smaller scale, this phenomena has been observed in thousands of ponds and lakes where the fertilizer, instead of helping corn grow, fosters a stinking mass of algae. As any "organic" farmer will be glad to tell you—at length—it is possible to grow excellent crops without excessive reliance on chemical fertilizers. However, as long as a few sacks of N,P,K do the job, farmers will avoid the extra trouble and expense of hauling in a truckload of manure. There is a chance, however, that pesticide usage can be reduced, and that possibility is explored in the next chapter.

## SUMMARY

Although agricultural chemicals increase food production, they also can cause a number of ecological and toxicological problems. Broad-spectrum and persistent pesticides can kill many organisms other than the target

**Figure 9–3.**
*How nitrate fertilizer deposits ended up in California well water*

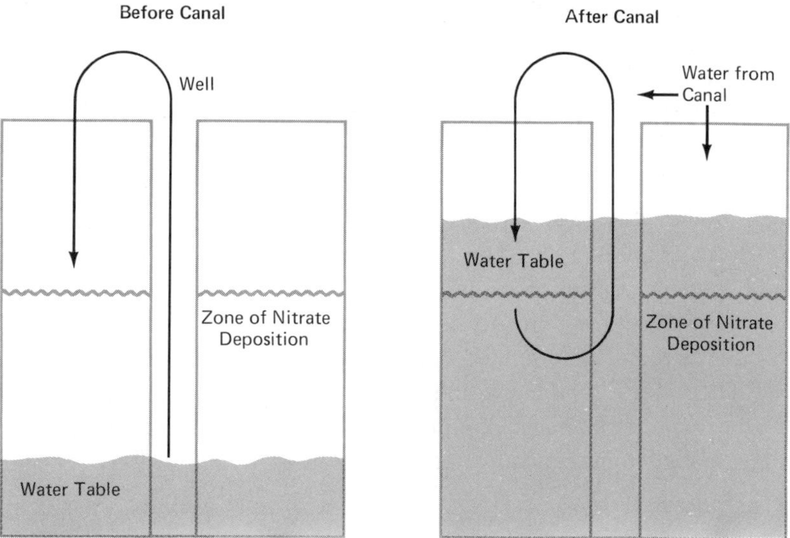

pests and may even have adverse effects on animals eating pesticide-contaminated food far away from the target area. Further complications ensue when pesticide-resistant individuals survive and multiply, forcing shifts to other chemical families of pesticides. Massive applications of herbicides or fertilizers can cause long-lasting changes in ecosystems and create health hazards, the latter usually through contamination of food or water. It is concluded that reliance on biocides may be reduced, but that the need for fertilizers will probably increase, despite the high energy inputs required for their production.

## Discussion Questions

1. In what ways do agricultural chemicals increase the production of food?
2. How can pesticides harm organisms other than those we classify as pests? How can pesticides harm us?
3. Discuss the accelerated evolution of pest strains resistant to pesticides and the problems caused by reducing beneficial insect populations.
4. Can fertilizers be applied so that they will contribute only to crop growth?

## Suggested Projects

1. Visit a store, read the labels on the agricultural chemicals being sold, and make a list of the types available, noting any suggested precautions for their use.
2. Ask a farmer or an agricultural extension agent for quantitative estimates of annual applications per acre for (a) insecticides, (b) herbicides, and (c) fertilizers.
3. If you have access to the chemicals needed to do simple analyses of water quality (for example, a Hach Kit), take samples from local ponds, lakes, reservoirs, and wells for estimates of nitrate concentration.

## Notes

1. As noted in Richard Garcia, "The Control of Malaria," *Environment*, **14**:2–9 (1972): "The probability is increasing that genetic resistance will render chemical insecticides useless before malarial transmission is completely interrupted" (p. 5).
2. The two most comprehensive indictments of persistent, broad-spectrum insecticides are by Rachel Carson, *Silent Spring* (Boston: Hough-

ton, 1962); and Robert L. Rudd, *Pesticides and the Living Landscape* (Madison: University of Wisconsin Press, 1964).

3. This possibility has been explored in Faith McNulty, *Must They Die?* (New York: Audubon-Ballantine, 1971); Jack Olsen, *Slaughter the Animals, Poison the Earth* (New York: Simon & Schuster, 1971); and Farley Mowat, *Never Cry Wolf* (New York: Laurel-Dell, 1965).
4. Thomas Whiteside, *The Withering Rain: America's Herbicidal Folly* (New York: Dutton, 1971) originally was published as notes and letters in *The New Yorker*; it is the most complete source of toxicological threats presented by herbicides and their relatives.
5. See these articles: G. H. Orians and E. W. Pfeiffer, "Ecological Effects of the War in Vietnam," *Science,* **168**:544–554 (1970); and A. H. Westing, "Ecological Effects of Military Defoliation on the Forests of South Vietnam," *BioScience,* **21**:893–898 (1971).
6. This viewpoint is embodied in C. J. Pratt, "Chemical Fertilizers," *Scientific American,* **212**:62–72 (1965); the article was reprinted in Paul R. Ehrlich, J. P. Holdren, and R. W. Holm, *Man and the Ecosphere,* readings from the *Scientific American,* (San Francisco: Freeman, 1971). See also T. C. Byerly, "Nitrogen Compounds Used in Crop Production," *Global Effects of Environmental Pollution,* ed. S. F. Singer (New York: Springer-Verlag, 1970), pp. 104–109.
7. "Poisoning the Wells," *Environment,* **11:**16–45, (Jan.–Feb. 1969), the article was reprinted in S. Novick and D. Cottrell, eds., *Our World in Peril: An Environment Review,* (Greenwich: Fawcett, 1971), pp. 321–335.
8. Barry Commoner, "Threats to the Integrity of the Nitrogen Cycle: Nitrogen Compounds in Soil, Water, Atmosphere, and Precipitation," in Singer, op. cit., pp. 70–95, deals with both toxic and eutrophic aspects.
9. Paul R. and Anne H. Ehrlich, *Population, Resources, Environment,* 2nd ed. (San Francisco: Freeman, 1972), p. 230.

# 10

# Integrated Control of Pests

## Key Concepts

- Pests
- Economic threshold
- Quarantine
- Protective management
- Control strategy
- Natural defenses
- Biological control
- Sterile release
- Pheromones
- Integrated control

Most of the organisms sharing Spaceship Earth with us are unnoticed passengers. A few attempt to share the provisions and we consider them pests. This is an anthropocentric classification with no biological foundation. In this, it differs from a pathogen, which can be objectively defined as a disease-causing organism. A *pest* is an organism that annoys us or damages something (food, furniture, and so on) we value. Included in this broad category is every sort of creature from tiny biting gnats to food-destroying birds, rodents, and insects.

## ORIGINS OF PEST STATUS

A very interesting and innovative book prepared by three Australians and a Canadian,[1] includes a good analysis of pest status. They recognize four ways in which this dubious distinction can be achieved. First, an organism can enter a previously uncolonized region. If it crosses a barrier (for example, an ocean or desert), it can leave its competitors and enemies behind and then go through a population explosion in its new habitat. A more subtle phenomenon underlies the second path to pestiness. A species can actually change genetically, adapting to a new host that is valued by man. Pests of oil palms in Malaysia may have undergone such genetic transformation as they spread from native palms in the surrounding forests. A third way in which pest status can be achieved involved no changes in the organism's genes, range, or numbers. Instead, human standards are altered, usually in the direction of fussiness. Buyers have been persuaded by Madison Avenue hucksters that fruits blemished with bumps or spots are somehow inferior to those covered with wax, dyes, and pesticide. This cosmetic aspect of pest control cannot be underrated because many control operations are justified in terms of increased marketability rather than reduced loss of production (Figure 10–1).

The final, and most important category, is related to increased abundance. An organism too sparse to worry about finds environmental conditions to its liking and its numbers increase to damaging or dangerous levels. The creation of pests by reduction of their natural enemies has already been discussed in the previous chapter. However, monoculture, the continuous growth of one crop for long periods or over large areas, also can foster pest status by greatly reducing the hazards of dispersal. Contrast the difficulties

**Figure 10–1.**
*Paths to pestiness*

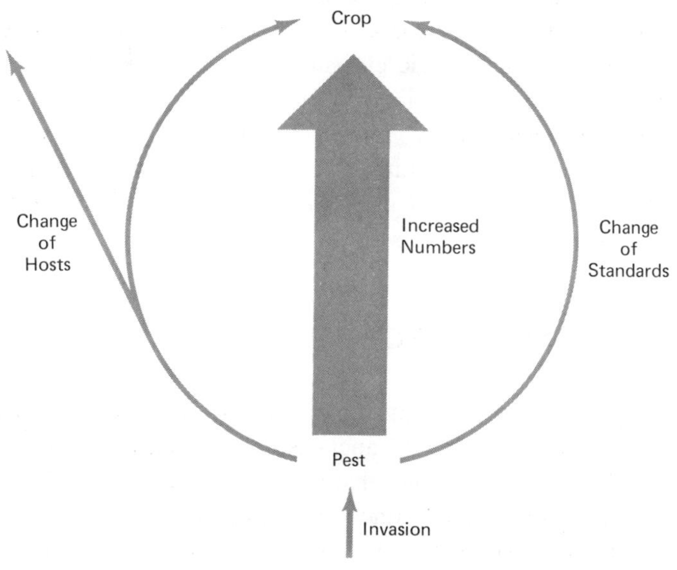

a palm eater has finding its favored host in a diverse tropical forest with the easy life it leads in a palm plantation. Uniformity also can be dangerous in other ways. The standardized, high-yielding varieties of grain that have created the green revolution may be susceptible to a superpest, or virulent pathogen. Trees planted at the same time may become susceptible simultaneously as they reach a critical stage in their development.

Usually, a cost-benefit analysis should be applied in the evaluation of pest situations. Only if pest numbers lead to value losses greater than control costs can the pest be said to have crossed the *economic threshold.* Of course, reduction in the control costs or increase in crop values can change the threshold. The analysis becomes very difficult in medical situations. If a single child dies during an outbreak of equine encephalitis, are the public health authorities justified in killing all horses and birds, which serve as a reservoir for the virus? No. Can they drain every marsh to prevent the production of vector mosquitos? No. However, they can immunize horses and urge parents to protect their children from mosquito bites.

*Quarantine* programs designed to prevent the invasion of pest species also are hard to analyze by cost-benefit ratios. Assumptions must be made about the potential harm that would be done if the pest were to break through the quarantine barrier. Although this is no more than glorified guesswork, you may see statements from government officials claiming that one million dollars spent on quarantine will prevent one billion dollars' worth of damage. Sceptics will ask: How many years of quarantine and how many years of damage?

## PRINCIPLES OF PROTECTIVE MANAGEMENT

Paul Geier, an Australian entomologist born in Switzerland, coined the phrase *"Vorbengender Wehrbetrieb gegen Insektenschaden"* to describe the strategy of preventing pest problems. Fortunately, the English equivalent is simply "protective management," and the underlying principles are quite straightforward. In fact, they are essentially the same principles that can be used for the intelligent management of all living resources, be they fish, wildlife, forest trees, rangeland grasses, or food crops. The main distinction is that with living resources we try to encourage favored species, whereas with pests we use any means, fair or foul, of discouragement.

"Know your enemy" is the first rule in dealing with pests. You should find out, with the help of specialists, the scientific name of a pest. Knowing where it fits in the Linnaean scheme of things will be your key to the literature, permitting you to learn what has been written about its life cycle, habits, and enemies. You should also, whenever possible, determine exactly how much harm the pest is doing or could do. Without this information, justification of funding for control operations can be based only on prejudice ("I don't like the fire ant because it's red").

Once the identity, weaknesses, and pest status of the organism have been determined, a *control strategy* can be developed. Because excessive abundance is the most common characteristic of a pest species, reduction in numbers is the usual goal, although prevention of increase is the ideal policy. Someday it may be possible to tinker with the genes of a pest species, changing its characteristics from noxious to benign, but that is still beyond the capabilities of genetic engineers. The best we can do with disease vectors is to dry up the reservoirs from which they transmit pathogens. A mosquito bite is no more than annoyance when the mosquito does not inject you with a virus, protozoan, or worm.

As Geier and his colleagues point out, the strategy of protective management aims to "create . . . conditions under which naturally-existing agencies and processes are so reinforced and/or supplemented . . . that endogenous stabilizing mechanisms" can hold pest numbers within tolerable limits.[2] Procedures used to achieve this can be evaluated in terms of

1. the required frequency and intensity of human intervention
2. the long-term reliability of protection.[3]

Ideally, human intervention should be minimal and protection should be permanent. We will see now how various techniques can be used in practical attempts to bring the ideal of protective management to the level of reality.

## ALTERNATIVES TO DDT

Chemical warfare between species has been going on for eons. Many plants and animals have evolved chemical weapons that protect them against consumption: alkaloids, irritants, repellants, pseudohormones, and many other toxic compounds. However, we have selected nontoxic, sweet-tasting varieties, propagating these as our food crops (see Chapter 9). Stripped of their *natural defenses,* these crops are quite palatable to pests and we find that artificial protection must be provided. It is, of course, possible to change the direction of selection and breed varieties that are resistant to pests or pathogens. However, we usually have relied on the last line of defense, coating our crops with toxic compounds. This, as was shown in the previous chapter, can kill friend and foe alike.

For many fiber and ornamental crops it may be better to use systemics, pesticides taken up through the roots, which make the plant toxic to any sucking or chewing pests, yet do not harm bees or other beneficial organisms. It also may be feasible to use antifeedants, which turn off the pest's appetite, or synthetic hormones, which prevent it from developing or breeding. These would be pest-specific and safe enough to be used on food crops.

Moving away from the mere protection of crops (or livestock), it is possible to use various biological, chemical, and physical weapons against pest populations to reduce or restrain them. The introduction, rearing, and release of predators or parasitoids that attack pests sometimes can prevent further damage without any additional expense or intervention after the initial project.[4]

In many locations, from the Fiji Islands to New England, the introduction of a natural enemy *(biological control)* has permanently solved a pest problem. More often, natural enemies serve to reduce the frequency, extent, and severity of pest outbreaks (Figure 10–2 a, b, and c).

Another group of potential biological weapons are the pathogens. Organisms infecting pests sometimes can be collected or reared in the laboratory and used as living insecticides. Examples include the milky spore bacillus for the Japanese beetle grubs, *Bacillus thuringiensis* for various caterpillars, and viruses for conifer-eating sawfly larvae. If pathogens are sprayed on a field or forest, an epidemic may be started in the pest population without any direct effects on beneficial organisms (or humans). Corpses of the dead pests can serve as foci for infection, preventing the rebound so often seen after chemical spraying. Of course, there is a chance that pests resistant to the pathogen may survive and multiply, but this should not happen unless the same strain of pathogen is used intensively against a sequence of pest generations.

In order to produce predators, parasitoids, or pathogens, we need large insectaries, or similar facilities, for rearing the pests and their enemies. Once these are built, usually under government auspices, they can serve as a source of material for pesticide screening or *sterile release*. The latter technique involves the use of high-energy radiation or potent chemosterilants to make males, and sometimes females, incapable of parenthood. Ideally, after sterilization, their behavior should be normal so that when

a

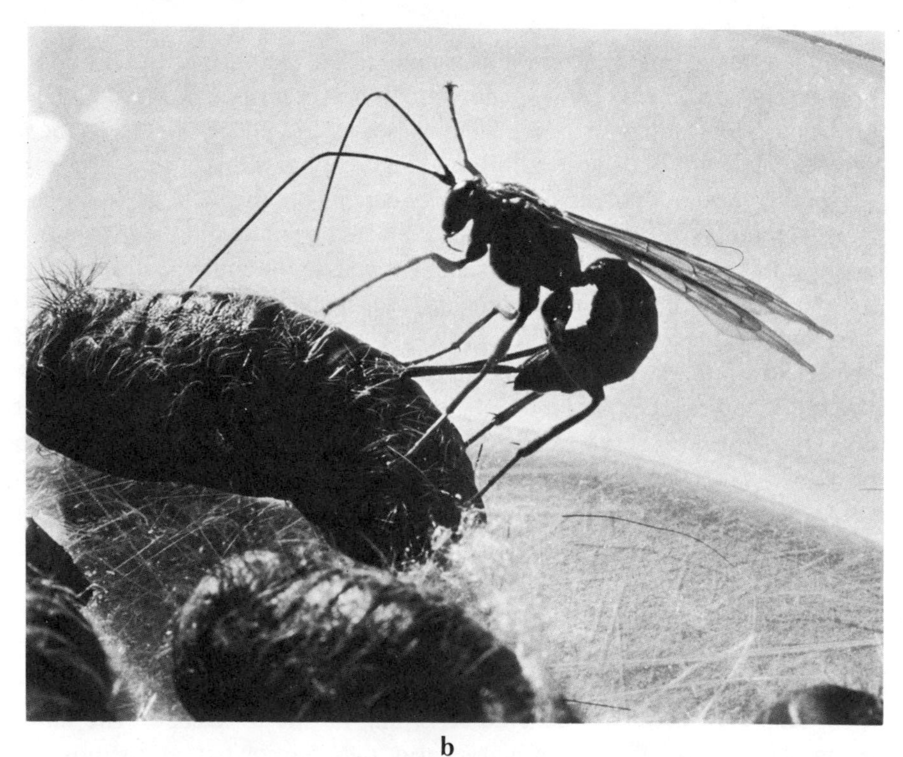

b

**Figure 10 –2.**

**a.** *Predator, a lady bug eating an aphid* **b.** *Parasitoid, a wasp depositing its eggs in the pupa of a gypsy moth* **c.** *Pathogen, a cabbage looper killed by a polyhedrosis virus* (U.S.D.A. photos)

C

**Figure 10–2.** *(Continued)*

they are released, they will mate with "wild" pests. This technique is most effective against sparse populations where the released "steriles" can overflood the wild population by ratios of 10 or 20 to 1. It has been used to eradicate the screwworm fly from the United States and fruit flies from several Pacific islands.

*Pheromones* (chemical communicators) can be used in conjunction with sterile-release or other control programs.[5] Perhaps the most spectacular programs involve the sex lures, which are emitted to attract the opposite sex and facilitate mating. When these potent perfumes are extracted or synthesized, they can be placed in traps to sample populations, thus monitoring changes in abundance or distribution. When overflooding with steriles is attempted, only color-marked individuals are released and their dispersal can be followed by recaptures in a grid of lure-baited traps.

Similar grids are used to keep track of the gypsy moth as it invades southern and western states, although some of the male gypsy moths captured may have hitchhiked from infested areas on campers or other vehicles during their pupal stage.[6]

There is a dangerous temptation to think that a technique or combination of techniques will permit us to wipe out pests. Eradication is rarely possible, and reduction below damaging levels is usually a far better goal—if only because the cost of killing every last member of a pest population seldom can be justified. The true spirit of *integrated control* is to use a wise combination of techniques, preventing the pest from doing damage, yet causing a minimal amount of environmental disruption. It may, however, be necessary to modify some field and forest ecosystems to keep pest populations within acceptable bounds. Such cultural practices as fallowing, rotation, or sanitation can disrupt the life cycle of a pest. It is also possible to time the planting of a crop so that its growth is out of synchrony with a climatically determined pest emergence or invasion. Perhaps the most important modification of all is the encouragement of diversity. It can be argued that any government policy that encourages the intensive cultivation of one plant species over large areas should be reevaluated, if we are to work toward peaceful coexistence as the ultimate alternative to DDT (Figure 10–3).

## THE COCONUT RHINOCEROS BEETLE

The UNDP–FAO–SPC coconut rhinoceros beetle project is an example of international research on the integrated control of an important agricultural pest. Funds from the United Nations Development Program (UNDP) were channeled through the Food and Agriculture Organization (FAO) to the South Pacific Commission (SPC), an organization devoted to cooperative efforts between governments in the South Pacific area for research and education. Why did a beetle merit all this organizational attention? Simply because it can kill coconut palms, the mainstay of the economy on many Pacific isles. The beetle, about 5 centimeters (2 inches) long, bores down the growing tip of a palm, slurping up the juices flowing into the burrow. Even if it does not kill the palm directly or make it more susceptible to lethal infections, the beetle attack cuts into the folded fronds and reduces the leaf surface available for the photosynthetic fixation of solar energy needed for maximum production of coconuts. In its grub stage,

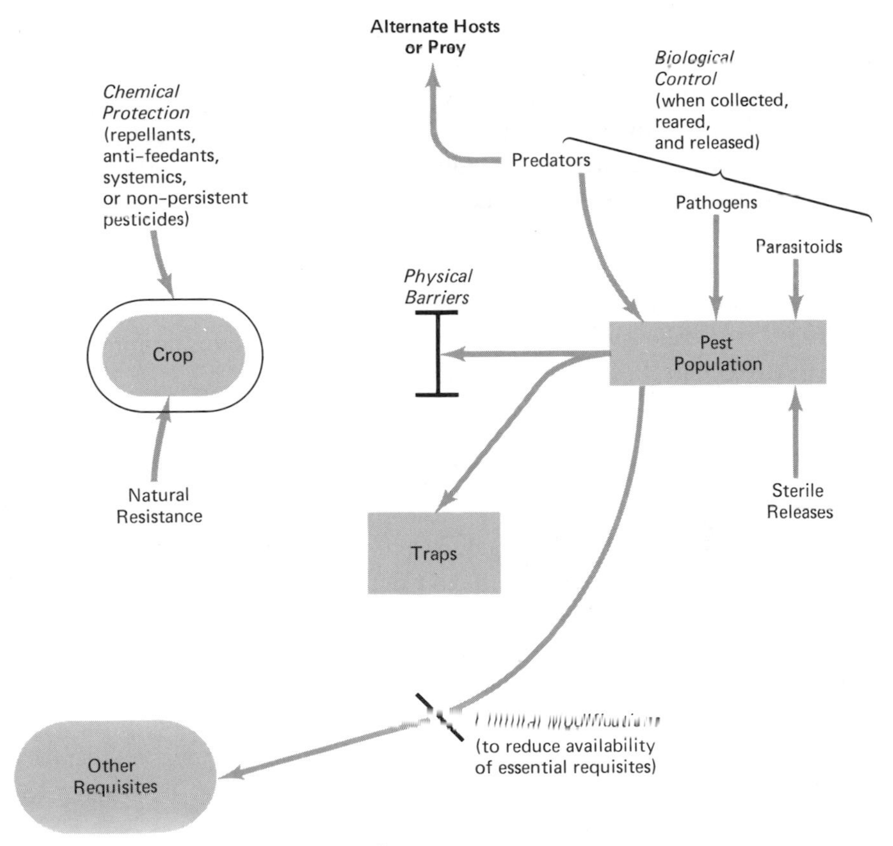


**Figure 10–3.**
*Strategies of integrated control*

however, the beetle is a harmless detritivore feeding on rotten logs or heaps of decaying material (breeding sites).[7]

For an integrated control campaign against the rhinoceros beetle, it is necessary to use the appropriate weapon for each situation. To protect especially valuable palms or to kill beetles flying off ships and attacking palms in port areas, crown treatment may be necessary. This requires intrepid climbers to place a mixture of sawdust and insecticide in the leaf bases of the palm crown every three or four months—new growth and tropical rains remove the protection. Natural enemies also can help, although not as effectively as in some other cases. Both a virus introduced from Malaya and a large parasitoid wasp introduced from Zanzibar kill some grubs that otherwise might reach the damaging adult stage. Traps, especially those made more attractive by artificial lures based on the scent of chrysanthemum, can catch adult beetles for estimates of population density, thus permitting the measurement of population increase after a hurricane creates numerous breeding sites or population decline when control measures have been effective. A final example of a tactic in the integrated campaign is directed against breeding sites. On Pacific islands invaded by the rhinoceros beetle, severe damage is most apt to be caused wherever breeding sties are abundant. Therefore, removal, poisoning, or destruction of these sites before they produce adult beetles continues to be an effective control of the coconut rhinoceros beetle.

## SUMMARY

When a pest has been identified, its damage properly assessed, and the weak points in its life cycle or behavior determined, an integrated program of techniques to control the pest can be developed. In a complex case, the integrated control might include a specific insecticide; a sex lure; the encouragement of natural enemies and barriers; and modifications of agricultural practices that had made possible increased damage by the pest. The objective of the campaign is damage reduction, not pest eradication, because the economic and ecological costs of eradication are usually too great.

### Discussion Questions

1. How can a pest situation be evaluated?
2. What are the principles of protective management and how do they compare with those governing management of forests, wildlife, or cultigens?
3. Can a home gardener use techniques of integrated control?

### Suggested Projects

1. Using the cost-benefit and integrated control concepts, estimate the costs of protecting a crop (a) with a maximum yield worth only fifty dollars per year, and (b) with a yield ten times more valuable.
2. Make a display showing some different kinds of beneficial insects—for example, praying mantis, ladybird (beetle), and caterpillar-killing wasp.

3. Develop an integrated control program to protect your home or school garden from pests and pathogens.

## Notes

1. L. R. Clark, P. W. Geier, R. D. Hughes, and R. F. Morris, *The Ecology of Insect Populations in Theory and Practice* (London: Methuen, 1967).
2. Ibid., p. 200.
3. Ibid., p. 201.
4. These are the three most useful books on biological control: the most technical is *Biological Control of Insect Pests and Weeds* Paul De-Bach, ed., (New York: Van Nostrand, 1964); less technical is Robert van den Bosch and P. S. Messenger, *Biological Control* (New York: Intext, 1973); Lester A. Swan, *Beneficial Insects* (New York: Harper, 1964) is a semipopular treatment of the topic.
5. See W. W. Kilgore and R. L. Doutt, eds., *Pest Control* (New York: Academic, 1967). This is an excellent, but quite technical, book in which there are sections on microbial pesticides, sterilization, pheromones, antifeedants, and integrated control.
6. See A. D. Hinckley, "The Gypsy Moth," *Environment* **14**:41–47 (March 1972), for a proposal for the integrated control of invading gypsy moth populations.
7. A. D. Hinckley, "Ecology of the Coconut Rhinoceros Beetle, *Oryctes rhinoceros (L.),*" *Biotropica,* **5**:111–116 (1973).

# 11
# Soil Conservation

## Key Concepts

- Dynamic interface
- Nutrient availability
- Flood deposition
- Erosion
- Solar-energy redistribution
- Turbidity
- Sedimentation
- Contour plowing
- Terracing
- Ground cover
- Shelter belt

On a BBC "comedy programme" there used to be a character who, in response to any question, claimed, "The answer lies in the soil." In a sense, he was right. Soil can be described as our most vital, most taken-for-granted, and most abused resource. There is good evidence that entire civilizations came to grief because they failed to recognize, and halt, gradual depletion of the soil, reduction in crop yields, and a decline in their economy. Soil is a fundamental component of all terrestrial ecosystems and, through erosion, has important effects on many aquatic ecosystems. In ecological studies, soil can be variously regarded as a renewable resource, as a habitat for organisms, as a depository for waste, and as a potential component in the degradation of air or water quality. In this chapter, soil formation, erosion, and conservation will be emphasized.

## SOIL FORMATION

Soils are at a *dynamic interface* between lithosphere and atmosphere, intermeshed with the terrestrial portion of the biosphere. Created by various interactions of climate, bedrock weathering, organic contribution, particle transport and deposition, as well as human activities, soils present a fascinating and complex array of combinations. Space here does not permit description of the regional types or the strata (horizons) found within each type.[1] In any situation, however, there is a gradient of characteristics from surface to bedrock, the intermediate unconsolidated debris being designated regolith, a fine word with a Stone Age ring to it. Generally, organic fragments decrease with depth. The patterns of air and water distribution within the soil are more complex, depending on frequency of precipitation, the level of water tables, and soil porosity (Figure 11–1).

Although lunar dusts demonstrate that "soil" can be formed in an abiotic environment by rock fragmentation from micrometeorite impacts and temperature fluctuations, organisms are important in the formation of most terrestrial soils. Ranging in size from microscopic bacteria to large burrowing mammals, soil organisms play many roles. Some, such as the fungal partner in the lichen symbiont, secrete organic acids which break down minerals, releasing nutrients in soluble form. Nutrients also are made available by fungi, bacteria, and other organisms of decay acting on the organic residues of plants and animals. Leaf litter, old logs, and corpses all are utilized by groups of specialized detritivores. Decomposition of such organic material is rarely complete and good soil usually has a component of organic fragments (humus) that, together with clay particles, forms a

**Figure 11–1.**
*Soil horizons*

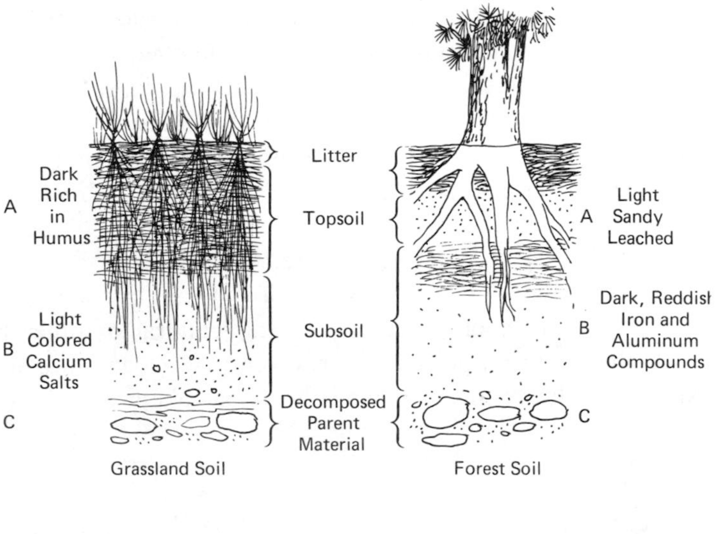

colloidal depository from which green plants can withdraw nutrients essential for their growth.

Another aspect of *nutrient availability* involving soil organisms is nitrogen fixation, the process whereby atmospheric nitrogen is converted into nitrogenous compounds. Heterotrophic bacteria and fungi, as well as autotrophic bacteria, living in the soil may be important, contributing 5 to 10 pounds per acre each year. Even more can be contributed by symbiotic bacteria living within the root nodules of leguminous plants, but these, strictly speaking, are not members of the soil community. One other group of microorganisms, the mycorrhizal fungi, are important in nutrient transfer within soil. Living on or within the minute roots of many trees, crops, and other plants, these fungi increase the uptake of nutrients, especially phosphorous, and accelerate the growth of their hosts. In turn, as in many other symbiotic relationships, they extract energy in the form of carbohydrates.[2]

The burrowing animals also play important roles, even if they do not subsist directly on the organic material on or in the soil. Transporting subsoil to the surface and letting air into the lower layers are contributions made by earthworms, some insect larvae, and burrowing insectivores (for example, moles) and rodents (for example, chipmunks, prairie dogs, and woodchucks). Many much less conspicuous animals spend their entire lives within the soil subsisting on organic material or preying on each other. Collectively known as cryptozoa, they can be extremely abundant and can be studied with various extraction techniques, yet they are often hard to identify and therefore remain in a neglected corner of ecology[3] (Figure 11–2).

Although the ecologist is fascinated by all this biological activity, he is forced to recognize the importance of physical and chemical processes in soil formation. Chemical reactions, proceeding at different rates on various rock and mineral substrates, include solution, hydrolysis, and oxidation. Physical factors also have a wide range of time scales, ranging from slow glacial abrasion to overnight *flood deposition* of alluvial soil material. The latter phenomenon is especially important because one third of the world's population is fed by flood-plain agriculture. Many of the same physical processes that contribute to the deposition of soil can, of course, remove soil from areas denuded of vegetation for agricultural or other human activities. A philosophical, but not too reverent, river bank farmer might put it like this: "The flood giveth and the flood taketh away"[4] (Figure 11–3).

a

b

**Figure 11–2.**
*Burrowing animals,* **a.** *earthworms* (U.S.D.A. photo) **b.** *prairie dogs* (U.S.D.A.-SCS photo)

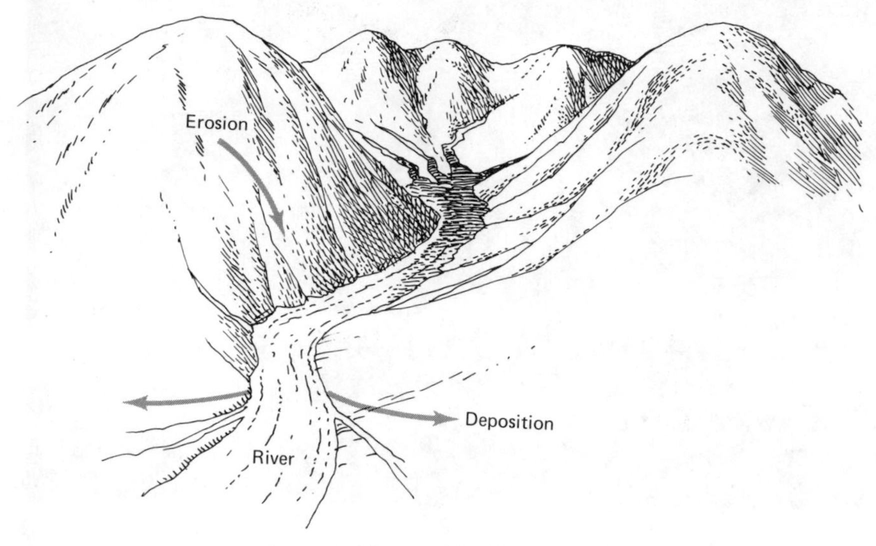


**Figure 11–3.**
*Flood plain*

## ACCELERATED EROSION

Many of the problems described in this book can be regarded as natural processes that have been accelerated by man's activities. However, such a benign evaluation may seem inappropriate when discussing the extinction of a wild species or the premature demise of a lake and it certainly seems wrong when we see a resource washing into reservoirs or into the depths of the oceans. Yet *erosion* is a natural consequence of *solar-energy redistribution*. Water transpiring from plants, perspiring from animals, and evaporating from our planet's surface must eventually come down again. When it pours down in large quantities on a steep slope, water can move huge boulders.[5] More typically, stream flow is able to move nothing larger than pebbles, and even the mighty Mississippi can carry only silt (suspended sediment); however, the Mississippi does push along large fragments on the river bottom (its bed load), and the quantities transported are impressive. The Mississippi dumps more than 2 million tons of sediment into its delta and the Gulf of Mexico each day.

Solar energy, in the form of convective air movements, is also involved in soil erosion by wind. By drying out soil, solar heat creates the predisposing conditions—fine dust unsecured by rootlets or bonds of surface tension—that can lead to a dust storm. Our planet contrasts with Mars where dust transported by high-speed (200 to 300 miles per hour) winds in the tenuous atmosphere obscures the surface for weeks at a time.[6] When the Martian surface is visible, some riverlike (*not* canal-like) features can be seen; however, it has been conjectured that, on Mars, erosion by liquids is much less frequent than wind transport. On earth, rivers move about ninty times more soil from land to sea than do winds.[7]

Even before the human species became a major geological force, erosion involved movement of $9.5 \times 10^9$ metric tons of material by rivers into the oceans each year. At this rate, the continents were being lowered 2.4 cm each one thousand years and would be reduced to sea level in the geologically short period of thirty-four million years if isostatic mechanisms did not cause compensating tilts and uplifts.[8] What we have done is accelerate the erosion part of the process approximately 2.5 times, so the annual movement is now $24 \times 10^9$ tons. The possible submersion of continents a mere 13.6 million years from now is the least of our worries because isostatic processes presumably also will accelerate and our sediments will be somewhat more promptly recycled into new mountain ranges.

We have achieved this remarkable ability to change the face of the earth, not by increasing the force of wind or water but by exposing and loosening the soil through agricultural and other activities. We have been doing this for a long time. Thousands of years of overgrazing, deforestation, and cultivation of the watersheds supplying the Tigris and Euphrates led to erosion that clogged irrigation canals with silt and moved the coast line 180 miles into the Persian Gulf.[9] The farmers of America, from pioneer days until the 1930s, did not fare much better. As long as the west remained open, it was easier to move on than to stay and repair a damaged landscape. In the words of an 1831 letter, "The scratching farmer's cares and anxieties are only relieved by his land washing away. As that goes down the river, he goes over the mountains."[10] It took the dual disasters of cotton lands washing out and the Dust Bowl blowing away to make Americans recognize the need for soil conservation on farmlands.

Ironically, the lessons are being learned all over again by the developers of suburbia. Huge tracts of land bulldozed bare for house sites are now the principal source of silt in many areas. Some unscrupulous developers compound the problem by trucking away the more fertile top soil for golf course construction leaving the homeowner to try to grow grass on barren subsoil. Another sharp practice is the use of uncompacted fill that, on steep slopes, settles unevenly, causing walls to crack, and is very hard to retain during periods of heavy rain. Let the home buyer beware! Fertile, stabilized soil may be almost as important as a dry basement or well-insulated walls (Figure 11–4).

What happens to runaway soil from a poorly managed farm or poorly supervised subdivision? Increased *turbidity* is one ominous-sounding effect, meaning simply that clear water becomes cloudy with fine, suspended particles. This, in turn, cuts down on the penetration of light and may reduce the photosynthetic activity of phytoplankton in a lake with the consequent lowering of oxygen available to aquatic organisms. Turbidity also adds to the frustration of fishermen trying to catch fish that can't see the bait! Another downstream effect is *sedimentation,* which can shorten the useful life span of dams (see Chapter 15) and may even increase the chances of a river spilling over its banks and into a downtown shopping district. Either way, the chief beneficiary is the Corps of Engineers, which can justify either building new dams or dredging out river bottoms.[11]

**Figure 11-4.**
*Suburban erosion* (U.S.D.A.-SCS photo)

## HOLDING THE SOIL

Soil conservation represents one of the older and more sophisticated forms of applied ecology. Any good text on conservation (such as Dasmann's *Environmental Conservation*) will include a section on engineering and biological methods of keeping soil where it will do more good than harm. Engineering methods include *contour plowing,* now widely practiced throughout hilly farmlands, gully damming with brush piles or straw bales, and *terracing,* most common in the ricelands of Southeast Asia. For subdivisions, a number of techniques can be used, including diversionary structures, subsurface drains, storm sewers, and sediment basins.[12] Because these techniques are expensive, a developer is reluctant to include them unless compelled to do so by a local ordinance enforced by a vigilant planning commission. If all builders in a region are so constrained, a builder complying with the antierosion laws will not be at a competitive disadvantage and will be able to pass any added construction costs on to the home buyer who will, hopefully, have the benefit of a less eroded environment (Figure 11–5).

Biological methods of soil holding include many forms of *ground cover,* ranging from crop residues to special plantings of leguminous vines or grass. Even if it is not practical to cover an entire area with vegetation, plantings in contoured strips or other vulnerable areas can help. Temporary mulches, such as straw spread over a slope, reduce the impact of rain and

**Figure 11–5.**
*Soil holding techniques*

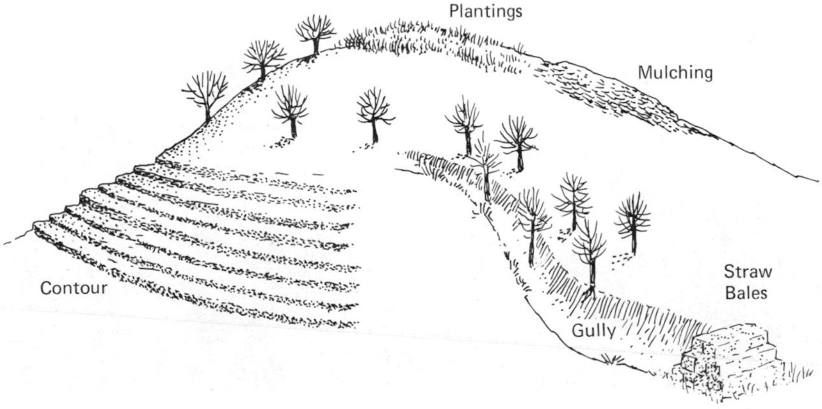

prevent erosion until seeds germinate and roots begin to stabilize the soil. Shrubs, vines, or trees can also be used, as a sequel to physical efforts, in healing the wounds of a gullied hillside. Although most of these biological methods are designed to counter erosion from water impact and runoff, there are methods used against wind erosion in both the United States and Soviet Union. By planting trees along the edge of farm fields, it is possible to create a *shelter belt* that reduces leeward wind velocity, creates a wildlife habitat, and increases crop yields. Ecological aspects of soil conservation, other than provision of cover crops or barriers to protect the soil from movement by wind or water, would include many of the wise management practices alluded to in earlier chapters. Forests should be protected from devastating fires and rangelands from overgrazing if watersheds are to be preserved as a source of water and not silt (Figure 11–6).

Although erosion—effects and prevention—has been emphasized, it should be mentioned that there are several other ways in which soil quality can be lowered. The lateritic soils of the humid tropics are baked to

**Figure 11–6.**
*Cover crop used to stabilize road cut* (U.S.D.A.-SCS)

bricklike hardness when their forest cover is removed.[13] Only tree crops, which shield the soil, can be safely substituted in place of the rain forest. In temperate regions, soils can be depleted of humus when no efforts are made to plow under manure, cover crops, or stubble. Ironically, this leads to applications of inorganic fertilizers in quantities far greater than would be needed just to replace nutrients hauled away in the harvested crops. Without the nutrient-holding power of humus, much of the fertilizer applied during winter washes out of the agricultural ecosystem before the growing season and ends up in ponds, lakes, or water tables (see Chapter 9). In arid regions, salinization is the most common ailment afflicting irrigated soils. Farmers must make sure that salts dissolved in the irrigation water remain in solution and do not precipitate on the soil surface or in the root zone. Thus, irrigation water must be supplied in amounts greater than would be needed just to maintain crop growth and evapotranspiration. The problem escalates when someone downstream trys to use the salt-laden water on his crops!

Making certain that land is used for purposes that are ecologically appropriate is one final aspect of soil conservation. However, this zoning approach will be considered in Chapter 25, "Resource Allocation" and Chapter 26, "Environmental Law."

## SUMMARY

Soil is a vital resource essential to the terrestrial portion of the biosphere; it is formed by a complex of biological, chemical, and physical processes. Soil erosion is a natural consequence of solar-energy redistribution in the forms of rain and wind, but we have loosened soil through agricultural and other activities, increasing erosion rates. The displaced soil has, in turn, clouded air and water as well as filled in reservoirs, channels, and harbors. Erosion can be slowed by various biological and physical techniques for soil stabilization, and other good management practices can maintain soil fertility.

### Discussion Questions

1. How is soil formed?
2. What are some effects of accelerated erosion?
3. In what ways, other than erosion, can soil quality and fertility be reduced?
4. Just how can we conserve soil?

## Suggested Projects

1. Find and photograph bad examples of erosion and good examples of antierosion techniques.
2. Set up a shallow wooden box with two equal-sized compartments. Fill both with top soil, seed one with grass, and sprinkle both regularly until the grass is well established. Then tilt the box at various angles (10 to 45°), or increase the water impact, and estimate the turbidity of water coming from each compartment.
3. Do a similar experiment with fertilizers, estimating the nutrient concentrations going in and coming out of the box.

## Notes

1. Harry O. Buckman and Nyle C. Brady, *The Nature and Properties of Soils,* 7th ed. (New York: Macmillan, 1969). This is a good standard text.
2. Ibid., pp. 122–123.
3. Theodore H. Savory, "Hidden Lives," *Scientific American,* **219**:108–114 (1968).
4. As strongly stated by William Vogt, *Road to Survival* (New York: Willaim Sloan, 1948), in one of the earliest and best books on overpopulation and its relation to the agricultural degradation of Mother Earth.
5. W. D. Ellison, "Erosion by Raindrop," *Scientific American,* **179**:40–45 (1948).
6. Bruce C. Murray, "Mars from Mariner 9," *Scientific American,* **228**:49–69 (1973).
7. Sheldon Judson, "Erosion of the Land, or What's Happening to Our Continents?" *American Scientist,* **56**:356–374 (1968).
8. Ibid.
9. Raymond F. Dasmann, *Environmental Conservation* 3rd ed. (New York: Wiley, 1972).
10. A. R. Hall, "Early Erosion Control Practices in Virginia," USDA Miscellaneous Publication no. 252 (Washington, D.C., 1938), p. 74. See also, Oliver S. Owen, *Natural Resource Conservation: An Ecological Approach* (New York: Macmillan, 1971).
11. My thinking on this subject has been strongly influenced by the ideas of Cullen Sherwood, now with the Geology Department at Madison College in Harrisonburg, Virginia. Cullen has worked closely with the

Virginia division of highways, helping them minimize the erosion associated with road building.
12. "Controlling Erosion on Construction Sites," USDA Soil Conservation Service, *Agricultural Information Bulletin,* **347** (Dec. 1970), 32 pp.
13. Mary McNeil, "Lateritic Soils," *Scientific American,* **211**:96–102 (1964).

# 12

# Sources of Energy

## Key Concepts

Pollution assessment
Misplaced resources
Solar origins
Fossil fuels
Radioactivity
Exposure to radiation
Energy consumption
Occupational hazards
Environmental degradation
Conservation of energy

This chapter is pivotal in two ways. First, the emphasis shifts from land to water. Secondly, the ecological role is not so much resource management as it is *pollution assessment*. The changes in focus should not be allowed to obscure underlying linkages between environmental problems. Pollutants can be described as *misplaced resources*. Furthermore, water interacts with land along shore lines and whenever atmospheric transport brings the hydrosphere in contact with the lithosphere over much of each continent (or, in simpler terms, wherever it rains or snows) (Figure 12–1).

Only two subheadings will be used to divide this chapter. Our energy environment will be described with a minimum of physical terminology. Then, human efforts to extract energy will be summarized with brief references to related pollution problems slated to be covered in later chapters. Consideration of alternative energy sources will be saved for Chapter 23, "Nonpolluting Technology." In keeping with the tone of the entire book, a conscious effort will be made to avoid using the word crisis.

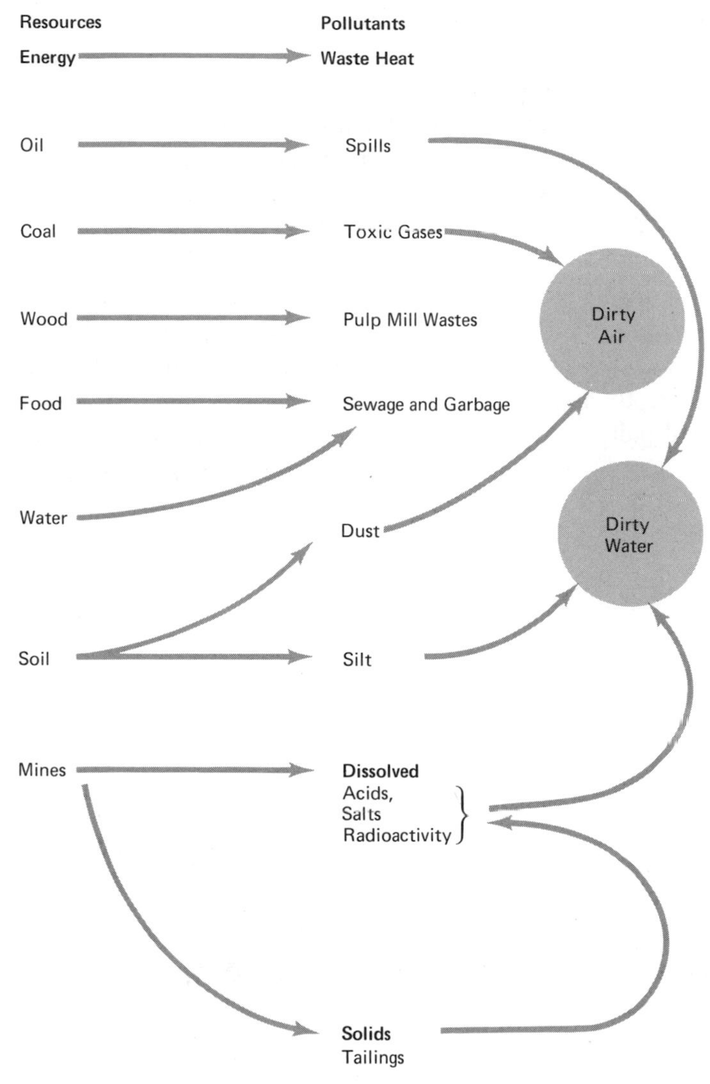


**Figure 12–1.**
*Pollutants as wasted resources*

## THE ENERGY ENVIRONMENT

The sun worshippers may have had something. Most of the usable energy in our environment is *solar in origin*. Green plants intercept sunlight, fixing it photosynthetically in carbohydrates, which can be used by the plants themselves or by animals feeding on the plants. Coal, oil, and gas are fossilized sunlight, a legacy of bogs, marshes, and swamps where, millions of years ago, deposition rates exceeded oxidation rates. Sealed and compressed under sedimentary deposits, *fossil fuels* are solar jinn we sometimes regret having uncorked. Solar energy also drives the hydroelectric turbines associated with giant dams, because evaporation and convection are both solar effects and contribute to the movement of moisture that eventually precipitates to form the hydrostatic head behind dams. To a nature worshipper, these huge edifices of concrete might be temples honoring the marriage of sun and water (Figure 12–2).

Although light, food, fire wood, fossil fuel, and falling water all represent solar energy, tides are mainly lunar in origin. The sun, 27,700,000 times more massive than the moon, is 390 times farther away, so the moon's gravitational pull is 2.2 times that of the sun.[1] Geothermal energy is also nonsolar. There is some question about its origin, one school contending

**Figure 12–2.**
*Solar energy pathways*

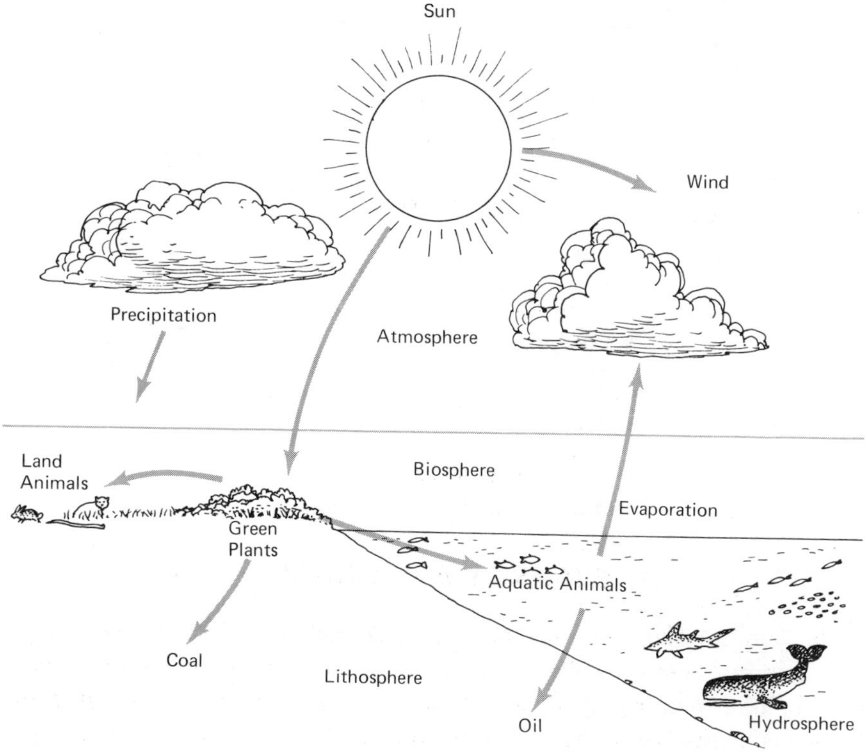

Sun
Wind
Precipitation
Atmosphere
Land Animals
Biosphere
Evaporation
Green Plants
Aquatic Animals
Coal
Lithosphere
Oil
Hydrosphere

that the earth's core has gradually warmed as radioactive isotopes split, the other arguing that the earth has retained its heat ever since its primal coalescence. An orthodox sun worshipper might claim that either form of earth heating should ultimately be credited to the sun, assuming that the earth did spin off from the sun. In any event, "the sun's contribution to the energy budget of the earth is five thousand times the energy input from all other sources combined."[2]

One form of energy that merits further discussion is *radioactivity,* which is locked up in unstable isotopes (forms of a chemical element) and released in the form of alpha, beta, and/or gamma radiation when the isotope "decays."[3] Alphas (with two neutrons and two protons, equivalent to the nucleus of a helium atom) are not very penetrating, betas (identical with electrons when negatively charged) are slightly more penetrating, and gammas (high energy X rays) are the most penetrating of all. Each radioisotope has a characteristic half life, this being the time it takes half the original mass to break into smaller atoms. Only a minute fraction of the mass is converted into energy waves, but that conversion follows the now famous law of $E = mc^2$, so the energy release is significant. Half lives cover a wide range, as shown in Table 12–1.

Rubidium 87 is one of the most common naturally occurring radioisotopes; it is found at a concentration of 75 ppm in the lithosphere, but rarer isotopes, as will be seen in later discussions, may play more important roles as sources of energy or hazards to health. Another component of our

**TABLE 12–1.**

Half Lives

| | |
|---|---|
| nitrogen 16 | 8 seconds |
| radon 222 | 3.8 days |
| phosphorus 32 | 14.3 days |
| iron 55 | 2.9 years |
| tritium ($H_3$) | 12.3 years |
| strontium 90 | 28 years |
| radium 226 | 1622 years |
| carbon 14 | 5760 years |
| potassium 40 | $1.28 \times 10^9$ years |
| uranium 238 | $4.5 \times 10^9$ years |
| rubidium 87 | $4.7 \times 10^{10}$ years |
| indium 115 | $6 \times 10^{14}$ years |

energy environment is formed by cosmic rays, high-speed atomic fragments that "zap" atoms in us or in our surroundings.

The approximate *exposures to radiation*[4] from natural and artificial sources (at sea level in the United States) are shown in Table 12–2.

Even if this exposure were received instantaneously, it would still be 1/2250 of the dose level that would be lethal to half an adult population. A few human groups are exposed to more than 1,000 millirem per year. Those living or traveling at high altitudes have less atmospheric shielding from cosmic rays. In fact, pilots are exposed to cosmic rays and to radiation from their instrument panels. Certain medical and research specialists working with X rays or radioisotopes also may be exposed intermittently. Finally, those living in regions in which the rocks are highly radioactive (Minas Gerais, Brazil; Kerala, India; Niue Island, South Pacific) also may have chronic exposures approaching the 1,000 millirem per year level. The possible effects of chronic exposure to low levels of radiation will be discussed in Chapter 16 (Figure 12–3).

## ENERGY AND POLLUTION

As shown in Table 12–3,[5] the energy supply in the United States in 1970 was largely derived from fossil fuel.

**TABLE 12–2.**

| | Millirem/yr |
|---|---|
| *Internal* | |
| potassium 40 | 20 |
| radium-thorium | 5 |
| tritium | 2 |
| carbon 14 | 1 |
| *External* | |
| cosmic rays | 50 |
| gamma emitting rocks, etc. | 50 |
| diagnostic X rays | 72 |
| other artificial sources (fallout, power plants, etc.) | 5 |
| | 205 |

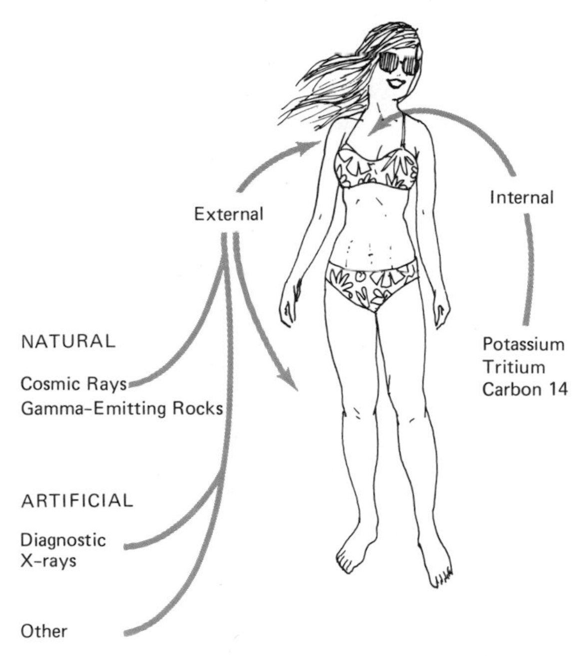


**Figure 12–3.**
*Radiation exposure*

Even the most optimistic spokesmen of the ERDA (Energy Research and Development Administration) or electrical utilities see only gradual shifts in this pattern, with no more than one half the nation's energy being available in electrical form by the year 2000 and only one half this electricity being produced by nuclear power plants.[7] Large power plants burning fossil fuels will continue to be built for various political and economic reasons.

If we had to derive all our energy needs from domestic production of one type of fossil fuel, demand would far exceed supply. Our annual *energy consumption* is equivalent to five years of coal production and three and one half years of oil production. Per capita consumption in the United States is 340 million BTU's (equal to 100 thousand kilowatt hours), about three times the consumption in Japan, France, or the Soviet Union. We have become quite dependent on our "energy slaves" and are not willing to set them free. This may prove tragic when we discover that our need to burn oil simultaneously distorts our foreign policy and deprives the petrochemical industry of building blocks that could be used to make anything from synthetic food to indestructible autos. The processes that fossilize solar energy may still be at work, but they are exceedingly slow and we are

TABLE 12–3. Use*

| Sources | Electricity Generation | Homes and Businesses | Industries | Transportation |
|---|---|---|---|---|
| Gas | 4,025 | 7,350 | 10,500 | 671 |
| Petroleum | 2,263 | 6,349 | 5,069 | 15,755 |
| Hard coal | 48 | 85 | 61 | |
| Soft coal | 776 | 314 | 5,499 | 9 |
| Hydropower | 2,647 | | | |
| Nuclear | 208 | | | |
| Totals (rounded) | 17,000 | 14,000 | 21,000 | 16,000 |

*Measured in trillion British thermal units (BTU).

going through a six hundred million year legacy in a matter of decades. Perhaps the sustained-yield principle is inappropriate in managing a fuel resource. Still, such rapid depletion of a virtually nonrenewable treasure seems prodigal!

We are paying for our energy in many ways—not just the portion of the GNP devoted to powering our technological society but, perhaps more importantly, in terms of *occupational hazard* and *environmental degradation.* Because the worker's on-the-job environment merges with the environment in general, these categories should be viewed as an additive rather than exclusive. The costs can be examined in the logical sequence of fuel or energy extraction, transportation, and final utilization. Coal mining involves hazards (black lung disease and bursting dams of mine wastes) as well as degradation (acid drainage and overburdening stripping). With oil and gas wells, the on-the-job dangers range from burns to frostbite, but the environmental contamination is more complex and insidious (see Chapter 18). Mining uranium can have many effects, from increased lung cancer among the miners to higher concentration of radioactive salts in water miles away (see Chapter 16). Even dams that do not burst extract their price in terms of construction injuries and drowned scenery (see Chapter 15) (Figure 12–4).

Moving fuel almost inevitably involves pipeline breaks and tanker spills. However, the transportation of electrical power is hardly free of controversy, as any utility executive trying to route a power line can tell you. The objections to power lines are that they waste land, endanger wildlife, and

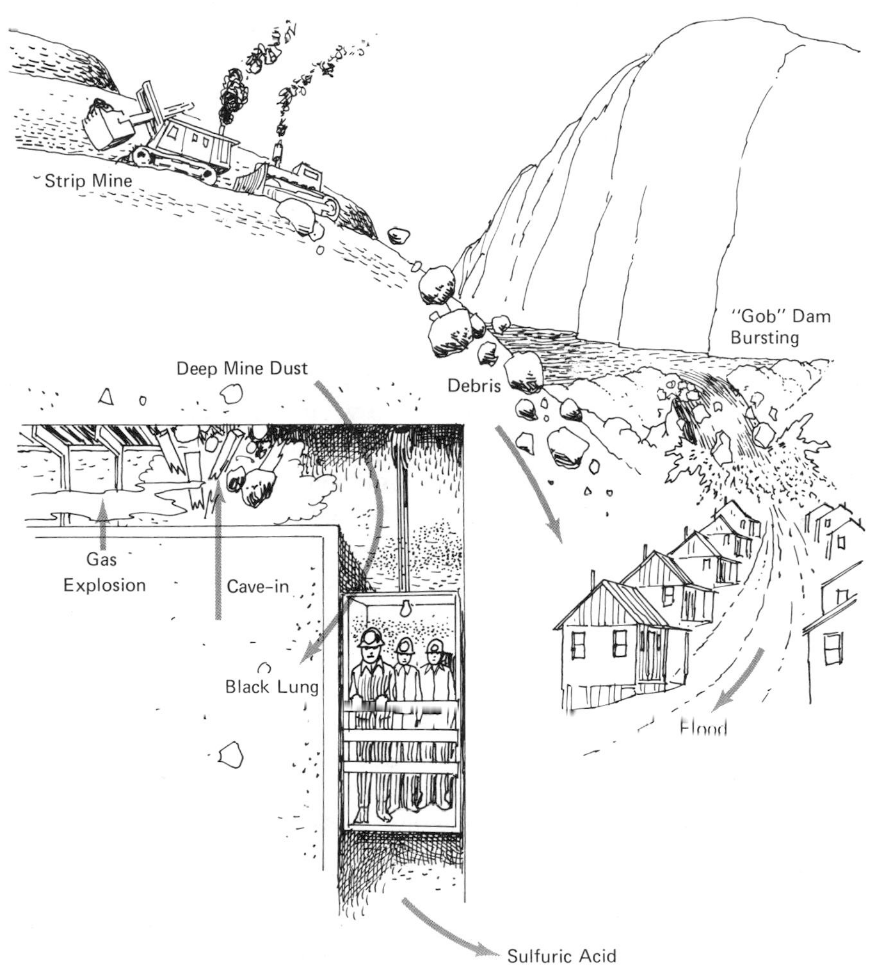


**Figure 12–4.**
*Coal mining hazards*

spoil views. There are also the problems of energy loss through heating and the wave lengths you pick up as noise on your car radio when you drive under a power line.

The conversions of heat into electricity and of energy into useful work also involve the release of waste heat, and in large quantities. The heat can modify the urban climate (see Chapter 19) or destroy entire aquatic ecosystems (see Chapter 17). Radioactive isotopes also are released from nuclear power plants, nuclear production facilities, and nuclear waste storage areas. Power plants that burn coal also release radioactive isotopes, as well as toxic heavy metals and acidifying $SO_2$. Finally, any device using coal, oil, or gas releases $CO_2$, $H_2O$, and various combinations of fuel fragments. The physical, toxicological, and ecological effects of this concentrated combustion is detailed in Chapter 21.

There is a certain inevitability about much of this. No process is completely safe or perfectly efficient. Any conversion or transfer of energy will entail some release, waste, or loss. The first law of thermodynamics shows that no energy is really lost; yet, according to the second law, the over-all trend is from high energy states and levels of organization to lower states.[8] Life, man, and technology are swimming up this mighty river of entropy, but nothing can be done to reverse its flow. In classical terms, we have taken the place of Prometheus and are paying for having stolen fire from heaven. We can hope only that Zeus is merciful or that we can somehow shift the burden and avoid the pain.

Despite the inevitability of hazards and waste, there is much we—especially those of us living in energy-consuming societies—can do to reduce our personal contribution to the problems. We can walk, rather than drive, to the corner store; support mass transit by vote and use; choose a house with good insulation and without central air conditioning; and boycott such luxuries as "instant-on" TV or automatic-defrost refrigerators.[9] Such sacrifices would not reduce the "American standard of living" in any meaningful way.

Government agencies, especially the Federal Energy Administration (FEA), also can institute urgently needed reforms in the production, distribution, utilization, and *conservation of energy*.[10] The nationwide 55 mph speed limit, if enforced, is a good example of what can be done to save fuel and lives. Increased supervision of energy use in transportation and industry also can yield many benefits, although it will be resented by executives leary of government control. As will be shown in Chapter 26, we now have the legal weapons needed to soften the environmental impact of any federally funded energy development, and we should continue to use them.

## SUMMARY

Energy is the key resource. Most pollution problems and many occupational hazards are related to our extraction, movement, and conversion of energy. Furthermore, we need energy to manage and extract other resources. A qualitative analysis of our energy environment shows that solar energy is available as food, wood, fossil fuels, falling water, and wind. Nonsolar forms include lunar tides, geothermal heat, and radioactivity. Because much of modern civilization depends on the continued availability of relatively cheap energy, it is vital that energy be used less wastefully.

## Discussion Questions

1. What is the "energy crisis"? Is it just a temporary, and somewhat artificial, shortage of oil? Or have our demands exceeded all available supplies?
2. Compare solar and nonsolar sources of energy, emphasizing differences in quantity and availability.
3. How many kinds of pollution are related to energy (a) extraction, (b) movement, and (c) conversion?

## Suggested Projects

1. Start a file or scrapbook of clippings on energy sources, use, and conservation.
2. Survey your own community and identify situations where waste energy is warming the environment or appearing as some other kind of pollution.
3. Make a list of energy-saving resolutions that you will be able to follow.

## Notes

1. Luman H. Long, ed., *The World Almanac and Book of Facts,* 1972 ed. (New York: Newspaper Enterprise Association, 1971), p. 248.
2. M. King Hubbert, "The Energy Resources of the Earth," *Scientific American,* **224**:61–70 (1971). One of the many excellent articles on energy written by Hubbert, this one appeared in an issue of the *Scientific American* devoted to energy and power.
3. Jacob Kastner, "The Natural Radiation Environment," Understanding the Atom, United States AEC, (now ERDA) Division of Technical Information, (Oak Ridge, Tenn., 1968) This booklet, like the others in the series, has useful information presented in a popular style.
4. Based on data from ibid., see Melvin A. Benarde, *Our Precarious Habitat* (New York: Norton, 1970); and Robert Gillette, "Radiation Standards: The Last Word, or at Least a Definitive One," *Science,* **178:**966–967, 1012 (1972).

5. Based on *New York Times,* 6 July 1971.
6. *New York Times,* 8 July 1971.
7. Paul R. and Anne H. Ehrlich, *Population, Resources, Environment,* 2nd ed. (San Francisco: Freeman, 1972, p. 68.)
8. Ibid., pp. 62–63. See also, Freeman J. Dyson, "Energy in the Universe," *Scientific American,* **224**:51–59 Sept. (1971).
9. Many electric utilities have tried to prevent "brownouts" by sending their customers booklets: for example, "Some Helpful Hints on How to Conserve Energy" (Northeast Utilities, 1973).
10. Reduction of "industrial energy consumption by 10 to 15 percent" could save "the equivalent of 1,100,000" barrels of oil each day. See "Pondering the Tasks Ahead," in "Energy," *Time,* 65–66 (May 27, 1974).

# Summary of Part II

Terrestrial ecosystems include the fields, range lands, forests, and wild places that we use as sources of food, fiber, and wood and that we also prize because of their value as recreation destinations or wildlife habitats. To manage these ecosystems wisely or to preserve them from degradation, we must understand the evolution of terrestrial organisms, the patterns of succession in terrestrial communities, and the movement of energy and nutrients through or within the ecosystems. When we seek to foster certain species (cultigens, conifers, or game), we must recognize the price we are paying in effects on other species. Similarly, the use of biocides to reduce pests or weeds must be evaluated carefully and chemical control techniques must be integrated with other, less damaging, techniques. Finally, the conservation of soil and energy resources can be regarded as fundamental to the successful management of terrestrial ecosystems.

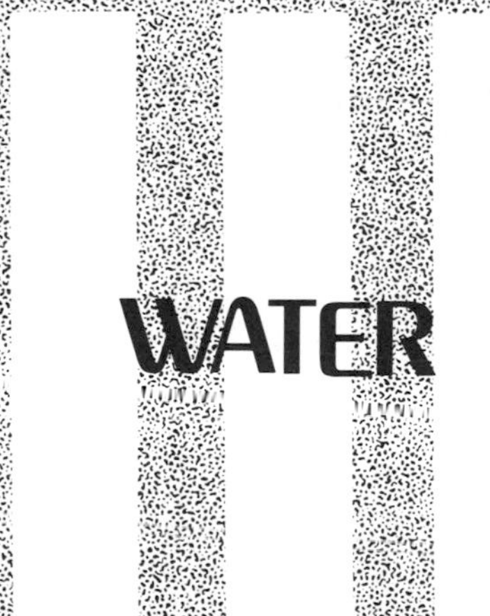

# WATER

# 13

# Aquatic Ecosystems

## Key Concepts

- Physical gradients
- Phytoplankton
- Herbivore food chain
- Limits to growth
- Taxonomic uniqueness
- Aquatic succession
- Eutrophication
- Accelerated eutrophication
- Stopping succession
- Coastal interactions
- A renewable resource
- Repository for waste

As indicated in Chapter 5, the distinction between aquatic and terrestrial ecosystems is not sharp. All life depends on water, and the underlying principles of evolution, adaptation, or survival can be demonstrated with examples from any environment. Yet, it is profitable to consider aquatic ecosystems separately, especially in discussions of water pollution. It is also illuminating to contrast environments of air and water, remembering at all times that generalizations about either medium must be modified to reflect unique circumstances.

Classifying aquatic ecosystems is not as tidy as grouping terrestrial ecosystems into climatically determined, and vegetationally characterized, biomes. The best we can do is speak of fresh-water, brackish-water, and salt-water ecosystems, with ponds, lakes, streams, rivers, estuaries, shallow seas, near-surface ocean layers, and ocean depths forming important subgroups. Land-water interfaces include bogs, swamps, marshes, tide pools, mangrove "forests," reefs, dunes, and rock-bound coasts. As in the case of terrestrial biomes, *gradients of temperature* from the equator to the poles determine many aspects of community composition and levels of productivity. Furthermore, aquatic ecosystems with open water of any great depth also have a *gradient of light* penetration from surface to depths. This impressed Marston Bates because he recognized that forest and ocean communities both are stratified along the vertical gradient of dimming light, with active photosynthesis concentrated in the forest canopy and near the ocean surface and various heterotrophic organisms subsisting on "packaged sunlight" in the lower strata[1] (Figure 13–1, a, b, c, d, e, and f).

The world ocean can be regarded as one huge ecosystem, covering 70 percent of the earth and containing 98 percent of the water. Because the nutrients needed by *phytoplankton* (microscopic, floating algae) reach the sunlit surface in large quantities only in certain areas of up-welling currents, biological productivity in the open ocean is generally quite low. Therefore, it is not surprising that green plants in the ocean and those on land contribute equally to the oxygen pool of the atmosphere, despite the larger area of the ocean. If someone with great patience were to calculate the total surface area of leaves on terrestrial plants and estimate the number of cells actively photosynthesizing on land and in the sea, the parity of oxygen contribution would be even more understandable.

The generally low productivity of the ocean has other important implications. We cannot blithely assume that the human population's growing needs for animal protein will be met easily by increased oceanic fishing. As shown in Chapter 4, overexploitation to the point of extinction has already been the great whale's sad fate, one that could befall the tunas and other deep-water species. Potential for increased harvests from the sea is greater near coasts, especially where rivers meet the sea in estuaries. The problems associated with such developments will be discussed in the aquaculture portion of the next chapter.

## UNIQUE ASPECTS OF AQUATIC ECOSYSTEMS

Although there are basic similarities underlying aquatic and terrestrial ecosystems, there are some differences well worth keeping in mind.[2] Terrestrial autotrophs are long-lived. This is true not only of forest trees but also of lichen patches and grass clones whose longevity can be measured in decades. In many aquatic ecosystems, however, the primary producers are phytoplankton with life spans of days or hours. This simple fact has many implications, enabling us to explain differences in biomass distribution, productivity, and response to stress. On land, plants generally live longer than animals, and plant biomass outweighs animal biomass by a considerable margin, relationships that are reversed in the open ocean.[3] Although detritivores and herbivores are active in all ecosystems, the flow of energy in open-water communities is predominantly along the *herbivore food chain* (phytoplankton → grazing zooplankton → small fish → large fish), whereas fixed energy in terrestrial ecosystems is more apt to be utilized by organisms of decay (organic debris → detritivores → secondary consumers).

Other unique characteristics of aquatic ecosystems are fairly straightforward consequences of water's physical-chemical characteristics. The increase of terrestrial green plants is limited by the availability of sunlight, nutrients, and water; terrestrial animals multiply up to the limits set by the availability of food, water, or shelter. For phytoplankton, the *limits to growth* are set by light or the depletion of an essential dissolved nutrient. For fish, crustacea, and many other aquatic animals, dissolved oxygen concentrations can be critical. In estuaries, a gradient of salt concentration from the river, with less than 1 part per thousand (ppt) to the sea, with circa 35 ppt, determines the locations of plants and animals with varying degrees of tolerance to salt. In all ecosystems, terrestrial, fresh water, estuarine, and oceanic, many organisms also are limited in their distribution and abundance by other organisms (including us) that eat them.

The final elements of aquatic *uniqueness* are essentially *taxonomic*. Many large groups of algae and invertebrates never evolved terrestrial forms; some did not even invade fresh water. Insects, on the other hand, are, with few exceptions, confined to terrestrial and fresh-water habitats, perhaps being excluded by crustacea occupying many potential insect niches in salt water. To be sure, some vertebrates enjoy the advantages of both worlds. Amphibians, with herbivorous larvae in fresh water and carnivorous adults on land, are one example. Diving birds and pinniped mammals (seals, sea lions, and walruses) forage in the sea but maintain breeding colonies on land. Cetaceans (whales and porpoises), and sirenians (dugongs and manatees) have gone all the way back, reverting to completely aquatic lives. There is an intriguing possibility that modern man's ancestors had a long period of coastal living while the continental interiors of Africa and Eurasia were even less hospitable than they are at present.[4] Following the sea otter example, they could have evolved into a species, amphibious or possibly even oceanic, with ecological relationships far different from those that we now seek to understand and manipulate.

a

b

**Figure 13–1.**

*Aquatic ecosystems* **a.** *Waterfall,* **b.** *Stream,* **c.** *Pond,* **d.** *Swamp,* **e.** *Estuary,* **f.** *Surf* (**f** Courtesy U. S. Department of the Interior, National Park Service photo. Photographer: Dick Frear)

c

d

**Figure 13 –1.** *(Continued)*

e

f

**Figure 13 –1.** *(Continued)*

## SUCCESSION IN AQUATIC ECOSYSTEMS

All impoundments of fresh water, natural or man-made, can be filled in with detritus and silt to the point where they are aquatic no more. This process may take millions of years in a Great Lake created by glacial retreat, or it may be completed within decades in a beaver pond. The successional stages for the pond would be open water with phytoplankton and other floating vegetation and then a gradual accumulation of bottom muck, which leads to the establishment of lily pads, cattails, and other rooted vegetation. When the plants fill the water from shore to shore, the pond has become a marsh. However, the succession continues with further accumulations of silt and organic material and more invasions of plants, culminating in a valley-bottom meadow. This is the end of the *aquatic succession* and the beginning of a terrestrial sequence that could lead to a maple-forest climax (Figure 13–2).

Because bodies of water that are rich in nutrients can be termed *eutrophic*, aquatic succession, at least in its early stages, can be called eutrophication. This is not necessarily a bad thing because a lake with low concentrations of nutrients (for example, oligotrophic) is unproductive, with few plankters, insect larvae, or fish. Some nutrient input can sustain enough fish to keep the anglers happy without destroying the enjoyment of those who like to see where the bottom is when they dive off a raft. Unfortunately, however, we *accelerate eutrophication* partly through siltation (Chapter 11), partly through fertilizer-contaminated runoff (Chapter 9), and through the nutrient-rich effluent flowing out from municipal sewerage systems (Chapter 20). It is, perhaps, misleading to claim that accelerated or cultural eutrophication leads to the death of lakes and ponds, because these aquatic ecosystems are being overladen by life. Nutrients foster the growth of algae which, if they are in the blue-green taxon, can further increase nutrient availability by fixing atmospheric nitrogen. When the algal blooms or masses exhaust dissolved nutrients, or overshade themselves, they die, triggering sequences of problem phenomena. Bacteria, fungi, and other heterotrophic organisms subsist on the dead algae, simultaneously depleting dissolved oxygen and releasing cell-bound nutrients (nitrates, phosphates, $CO_2$, and carbonates). The lowered oxygen concentration can cause fish kills. Obnoxious odors and flavors can be, quite naturally, produced by the dead algae, fish, and other organisms. Yet, all this decay is merely setting the stage for another bloom, starting the cycle (vicious, of course) all over again. It has been suggested by Barry Commoner[5] that no

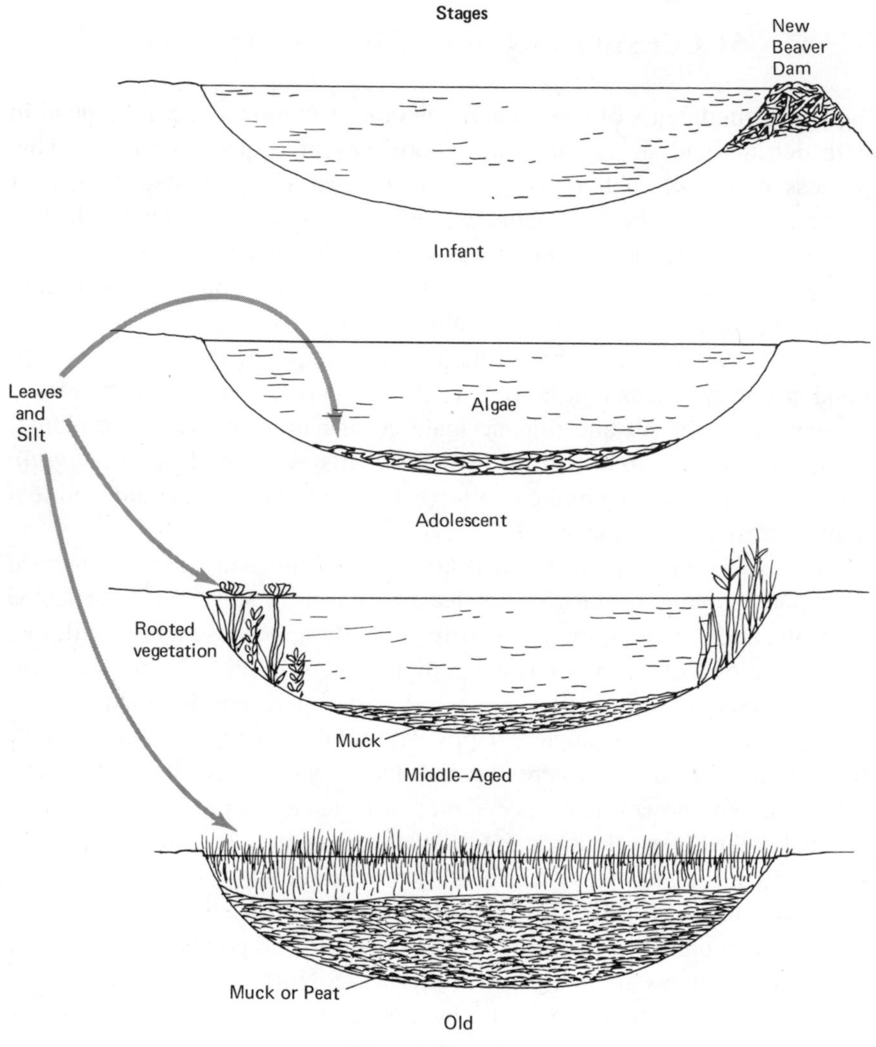


**Figure 13–2.**
*Pond succession*

further inputs of nutrients are needed to keep the cycle going. The bottoms of many lakes, including the "much abused but far from dead" Erie, are covered by a thick layer of muck, rich with nutrients that are sealed off from the water above by a skin of insoluble iron oxides. Unfortunately, that skin becomes soluble, breaks, and releases nutrients when oxygen concentrations in the water are low. If this is true, certain forms of eutrophication may be virtually irreversible and some lakes are going to proceed toward the meadow stage no matter what we do now. In other situations, diversion of nutrients or purification of inflowing water will certainly help improve the health of lakes and ponds.

Management of such aquatic ecosystems involves many operations that are similar to those characteristic of our standard agriculture strategies. In both situations, we regard certain species as invasive weeds and try to stop them with chemicals (herbicides and algicides) or mechanical techniques while we encourage other species, cultigens in agricultural ecosystems and semidomesticated game fish in ponds or lakes. In either case, the instability of an early successional stage should be recognized. The degree to which misplaced nutrients encourage weeds in farm fields, as they foster algae in ponds, is not clear. The basic quandary of *stopping succession* without causing ecological repercussions remains quite similar on land and in water.

## VIEWS OF AQUATIC ECOSYSTEMS

In the following chapters, the water world will be viewed in three distinct ways. First, water will be treated as it *interacts with land forms* and human activities along coasts; these relationships, once understood, are being used in a more sophisticated management of bays, wetlands, beaches, and dunes. Secondly, water will be considered as a *renewable resource,* with some attempts made to show how the distribution of water, in time and space, can constrain human activities. The final approach, to be explored from several aspects in Chapters 16, 17, 18, and 20, concerns our use of water as a *repository for waste*. Throughout these discussions water pollution will be regarded as symptomizing the larger problem of misused resources, and suggestions for the cure or prevention of our wasting disease will be made.

## SUMMARY

Although aquatic and terrestrial ecosystems operate under the same basic principles, aquatic ecosystems have certain unique characteristics. Water is the supporting medium for groups of organisms—phytoplankton, fish, and many invertebrates not represented in the terrestrial biota. In ponds and lakes, aquatic succession proceeds through predictable stages, eventually terminating with filled-in wetlands. Ecological perspectives can clarify land-water interactions, water conservation measures, and problems of water pollution.

## Discussion Questions

1. What limits the growth of phytoplankton and all animals dependent on the phytoplankton?
2. In what ways does succession in a pond resemble succession in an old field?
3. To what extent is water an international resource?

## Suggested Projects

1. Return to the pond you visited as a project for Chapter 2 and record any changes observed.
2. Start and maintain an aquarium, not just as a show place for pretty tropical fish, but as a microcosm of a contained and managed aquatic ecosystem. Record all inputs (hours of illumination and additions of fish, snails, plants, and food), growth rates of organisms (plankton and fish), and removals (dead or alive).

## Notes

1. Marston Bates, *The Forest and the Sea* (New York: Vintage, Random, 1960), pp. 15–27.
2. Many of these distinctions should be credited to William E. Odum, my colleague in the Department of Environmental Sciences, University of Virginia, Charlottesville.
3. H. W. Harvey, "On the Production of Living Matter in the Sea off Plymouth," *Journal of Marine Biology Association, U.K.N.S.*, **29**:97–137 (1950).
4. A. C. Hardy, "Was Man More Aquatic in the Past?" *The New Scientist,* **7**:642–645 (1960).
5. Barry Commoner, "Soil and Fresh Water: Damaged Global Fabric," *Environment,* **12**:4–11 (1970), covers some aspects of accelerated, cyclic eutrophication.

# 14

# Coastal Utilization

## Key Concepts

- Coastal concentrations
- Multiple use
- Dune stabilization
- Aquaculture
- Nutrient trapping
- Filter feeders
- Pollutant trapping
- Excessive harvesting
- Underwater parks
- National seashores

Looking at a map that shows population densities of the human species, you can see that we have a strong tendency to *coastal concentrations*.[1] This is most noticeable in the Southern Hemisphere, and least so in the great Eurasian land mass where population densities are also high along rivers. If states with Great Lake shorelines are included, thirty of the United States can be described as coastal, and they contain 83 percent of our total population. There is no need to invoke any atavistic yearning for the amphibious life to explain these concentrations because they seem to be rooted in the historical development of trading posts into cities. To an ecologist, however, the presence of so many people near vulnerable sand dunes and wetlands is a very important fact of life.

In Chapter 6, some of the problems caused by the use of forests for mutually incompatible purposes were described. *Multiple use* may encounter even more difficulties when applied to coasts. We soon will have to sort out our priorities and decide whether we will continue to use coastal wetlands for dumping urban and industrial waste or we would prefer to use this unique resource for a wise combination of recreation, food production, and wildlife preservation. In this chapter, emphasis will be on the ecological restraints that must be recognized before our management of coastal ecosystems can be deemed wise.

## RECREATION

Ranging in intensity from the August Sunday crowds on Coney Island to the brave bird watchers making a Christmas count at Cape May, the use of shorelines for rest and renewal seems a most natural thing to do. Yet, man is not content to visit, he wants to stay. This has led to a proliferation of cottages, motels, boardwalks, and roads along sandy shores. In a way, this is just as unwise as building in a flood plain, astride an earth-quaking fault, or on a volcano's flank. Beaches and dunes have but one real owner, the ocean. It may tolerate our occupancy for some years but some dark, winter night, it will storm ashore and affirm its claim. At all times, wind and waves are moving some sand, often in directions we find displeasing. We try to *stabilize dunes* with heavily-fertilized plantings of grass. We attempt to retain beaches where we want them by building barriers perpendicular to the shore. Both forms of interception almost inevitably deprive someone else of sand, with the result that millions of cubic yards must be pumped or hauled to replace the natural flow. Stabilization and fill projects are expensive, so much so that even the wealthiest citizens of coastal resorts prefer to pass the cost on to the general public and get the U.S. Corps of Engineers to undertake the tasks[2] (Figure 14–1).

When we "reside by the sea side," other problems develop. Nearby marshes are sprayed to control mosquitos and green-headed flies. Sewage and trash are dumped wherever it seems convenient to do so. Furthermore, fresh-water reserves beneath the sands are depleted with consequent salt-water intrusion and frantic projects to maintain a drinkable supply. Even mere footsteps can be troublesome. Dune grasses cannot tolerate trampling and the demise of the dune grasses is often followed by wind erosion. Compounding these problems are those caused by recreational boats and buggies, contributing noise, oil and other jarring notes to the coastal serenity. The innate attractiveness of our coasts, as our forests, puts them in jeopardy of being loved to death.

## AQUACULTURE

Food production in aquatic ecosystems is a large and fascinating subject with important ecological implications and applications to fresh-water fish

**Figure 14–1.**
*Dune* (U.S. Department of the Interior, National Park Service photo. Photographer: Cecil W. Stoughton)

ponds, oceanic sustained-yield fisheries, and the cultivation of organisms in bays or estuaries. Here, only the latter topic will be covered, even that not getting the in depth treatment that might be demanded by a confirmed clam lover. First, one question must be answered: Why are shallow waters along coasts so productive? At least three processes are involved. *Nutrients* from rivers, aquifers, and other land sources wash into coastal waters where they are temporarily *trapped* by an efficient combination of physical barriers (including incoming tides), chemical bonding (in bottom oozes), and biological processes (uptake by algae, eel grass, and so on). A second, closely related input comes in the form of organic debris from partially awash coastal vegetation (mangroves in the tropics and marsh grasses in the temperate regions). Many *filter feeders* (clams, oysters, and the like) and small fish (including the fry of numerous oceanic species) subsist on photosynthetic energy encapsulated in tasty (to them) morsels of detritus. This brings us to the third process, photosynthesis itself, when can reach very high levels of efficiency in shallow waters where $CO_2$ and essential nutrients are not limiting growth (Figure 14–2).

With several interlinked processes contributing to the productivity of coastal waters, it is not surprising that imbalances occur. On the West Coast, sewage outfall caused a population explosion of sea urchins that then proceeded to chew up the holdfasts of giant kelp. Expensive applications of quicklime kill the urchins and permit kelp regrowth, but the urchins soon return.[3] In the bays between Fire Island and Long Island, waste from

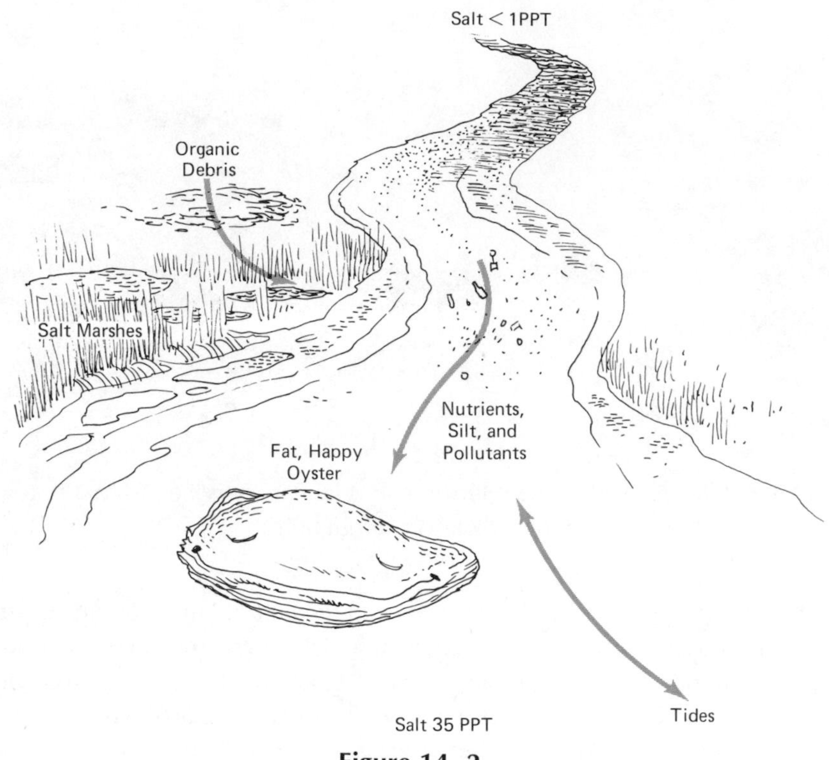


**Figure 14-2.**
*Estuarine diagram*

septic tank seepage, duck farms, and other sources has favored certain species of plankton at the expense of others. Clams are quite content with the now abundant algae, but the oysters find them indigestible. Consequently, the famous blue point oyster, despite heroic efforts to restock the beds, is close to extinction.[4]

Ironically, the same processes that make estuaries and bays productive also can make them *poisonous!* Mechanisms that trap detritus or nutrients also can *capture* viruses, bacteria, radioactive isotopes, and toxic compounds.[5] When this happens, a clam is a very dangerous delicacy indeed. Obviously, any hope of harvesting more food from coastal waters depends largely on our ability to maintain eutrophication without contamination. It can be done, as the Japanese have shown in some of their best-managed oyster farms, but it will not be easy.[6]

## PRESERVATION

As you can see, utilization of the coastal zone is beset by many difficulties. In fact, there is genuine concern that little will be left to utilize unless strong efforts toward the conservation of wetlands, bays, beaches, and their associated biota are started now. Pollution is a major threat to shore birds. The spectacular kills caused by oil spills will be discussed in Chapter 18, but here we will deal with some of the more insidious forms of chronic poisoning. Although DDT is no longer applied to marshes by mosquito-control crews, quantities of DDT and its breakdown products remain in the mud and are slowly released into the food web. Fortunately, concentrations reaching fish eaters, such as osprey, are lower than they were in the 1960s and these birds now have a good chance of rearing their offspring successfully. One technique that further increases the odds in their favor involves the construction of nesting platforms in clean areas (for example, Smith Island in the middle of Chesapeake Bay, Fisherman Island at the southern tip of the Delmarva Peninsula, and Gardiners Island, east of Long Island).[7] The vulnerability of birds forced to fish in polluted waters has been shown by a study of deformed chicks of the common tern. Polychlorinated biphenyls (PCB), industrial compounds with affinities to chlorinated hydrocarbon insecticides and the 2,4,5T herbicide, have been implicated as the food contaminants causing these deformations in tern colonies along the East Coast of the United States.[8] (Figure 14–3, a and b).

Coastal organisms also can be threatened by *excessive harvesting*. Lobsters on the East Coast and certain huge clams on the West Coast must be harvested on a sustained-yield basis or else they may be reduced to rarity. Even inedible organisms can be overcollected. Tide pools and coral reefs are especially attractive to large groups of eager science students out to bag a wide variety of marine invertebrates in one day. With hammers, nets, and poisons, they can harvest such a high proportion of the organisms that many years must pass before immigration and successful colonization replace the toll.[9] A happy trend is the establishment of *underwater parks* (John Pennekamp, off Key Largo, Florida; Hanauma Bay, Oahu, Hawaii; and several areas off California). In these sanctuaries, snorkeling and fish watching are encouraged, but collecting and spear fishing are forbidden (Figure 14–4).

Preservation also has been advanced by the establishment of *national seashores,* "operated intelligently and devotedly by the National Park

a

b

**Figure 14 –3.**

**a.** *Osprey* **b.** *Tern* (Bureau of Sport Fisheries and Wildlife photos)

**Figure 14–4.**
*Underwater coral* (U.S. Department of the Interior, National Park Service photograph by M. W. Williams)

Service."[10] Cape Cod, Fire Island, Assateague, Cape Hatteras, and Cape Lookout all form links in a chain along the Atlantic Coast. Also included in the national seashore system are Padre Island, south of Corpus Christi, Texas; Point Teyes, north of San Francisco, California; and a number of islands in the Gulf of Mexico. These, beautiful and ecologically valuable though they may be, represent only a small fraction of our coast line. Many other equally attractive segments are threatened still by overdevelopment. Marshes are filled in to dispose of solid waste and/or make sites for factories, homes, and parks: Boating enthusiasts demand dredging and spoil bank projects to create new marinas and channels. Even dams far inland have their effect, intercepting silt and nutrients that otherwise would have helped keep estuaries productive. Many of the true costs of all these development projects are never factored into the equations used to justify them. The loss of a fish nursery, a wildlife habitat, or a biological filtering system recycling organic waste should certainly be weighed against any immediate economic or recreational benefits. There is even the possibility that dredging can have deleterious effects less obvious than the smothering of oyster beds. A recent outbreak of toxic red algae along the New England coast may have been triggered by nutrients released in dredging operations near Cape Ann, Massachusetts.[11] Sometimes the sacrifice of coastal wetlands is rationalized on the grounds that they are degraded already. This is as illogical as cutting down forests simply because they no longer contain cougars and chestnuts! In many ways, our coastal marshes are more threatened than our inland forests. They occupy less area, they are closer to urban concentrations, and they seem less beautiful or valuable in their natural state. Ecologists must work with private groups, such as the Nature Conservancy, and with government agencies to insure that large portions of our coasts will be preserved. This may turn out to be the wisest form of utilization.[12]

## SUMMARY

Coasts, like forests, are of value for recreation, production, and conservation. However, large cities near coasts foster overdevelopment and concentrate waste, both of which degrade coastal ecosystems. Ecologically sound management practices that can reduce technological impacts and help preserve the ecosystems include restrictions on sea-side building, protection of productive estuaries, and establishment of parks or sanctuaries along the shore or underwater. These practices are essential because many species of fish and wildlife require coastal habitats during at least part of their life cycles.

### Discussion Questions

1. Compare the recreational uses of forests and coasts.
2. What is the potential value of coastal aquaculture?
3. How can the preservation of marshes benefit fish and wildlife species?

### Suggested Projects

1. Identify your state's (or country's) most vulnerable coast lines.
2. If possible, participate in a well-planned field trip to a coast, recording some of the problems observed.
3. Find out how much protein is now obtained from coastal aquaculture and estimate the annual yield per unit area.
4. Write your government representative in support of coastal conservation (for example, land acquisition and sanctuary designation).

## Notes

1. N. J. W. Thrower, *Man's Domain, A Thematic Atlas of the World,* (New York: McGraw-Hill, 1970), p. 11.
2. See W. Marx, "In Pursuit of Beaches", *The Frail Ocean* (New York: Sierra Club-Ballantine, 1967); as well as Ian L. McHarg, "Sea and Survival," *Design with Nature* (Garden City, N.Y.: Am. Museum of Natural History—Doubleday, 1971).
3. J. E. Brown, "Wheeler North: Environmental Scientist," Houston, Tex.: *The Humble Way* (now *Exxon, USA*), 4th Quarter, **11**:2–7, (1972).
4. Richard H. Wagner, *Environment and Man* (New York: Norton, 1971) pp. 157–161.
5. William E. Odum, "Insidious Alteration of the Estuarine Environment," *Transactions of the American Fish Society,* **99**:836–847 (1970).
6. C. P. Idyll, "Farming the Sea: Fact and Fancy," *FAO Review,* **5**:43–46 (1972).
7. D. R. Zimmerman, "Man and Osprey, Strategies for Survival," *National Parks,* **47**:16–19 (1973).
8. H. Hays and R. W. Risebrough, "The Early Warning of the Terns," *Natural History,* **80**:38–47 (1971).
9. Marx, op. cit., pp. 105–108.
10. J. N. Leonard, *Atlantic Beaches* (New York: Time-Life, 1972), p. 19.
11. J. Darnton, "Red Tide in New England Costs Thousands of Jobs," *New York Times,* 24 September 1972.
12. Very good arguments for the preservation of coastal ecosystems (especially salt marshes) are presented in John and Mildred Teal, *Life and Death of the Salt Marsh* (Boston: Atlantic Monthly Press, Little, Brown, 1969); Steve Hitchcock, "Can We Save our Salt Marshes?" *National Geographic,* **141**:728–765 (1972); and Ernest F. Hollings, "Will We Save Our Coasts?" *Sierra Club Bulletin,* **59**:5–7, 38 (1974).

# 15

# Water Conservation

## Key Concepts

A nonrenewable resource
A living resource
Uses of water
Hydrologic cycle
A limiting factor
Drought
Flooding
Trade offs
Draining wetlands
Dam building
Desalinization
Rain making

It is easy to see that water is a resource essential to man and all other organisms. Yet, the resource status of water is not always clear. Water in deep aquifers can be mined far more rapidly than it is replaced by seepage from the surface. In this situation, now all too typical of the southwestern United States, water is like a fossil fuel, a nonliving, essentially *nonrenewable resource*. However, in many other situations water can be treated as if it were a *living resource* and can be managed on a sustained-yield basis. This rationale underlies most dam and reservoir projects designed to intercept enough runoff to insure a steady supply of water for drinking, irrigation, and other purposes.

The many *uses of water* further confound its resource status. Not only does it support all life, it also serves vital roles in cooling, as a raw material for industry, and as a transport medium for the movement of everything from ships to sewage. For those on a vacation by the seashore or lake side, the recreational uses—swimming, boating, fishing, or just wave watching—seem most important. Once again multiple use almost inevitably leads to conflicts that will be detailed in the last part of this chapter.

**TABLE 15–1.**

| | Volume (thousands of) | |
|---|---|---|
| | Cubic Miles | Cubic Kilometers |
| Atmosphere | 3.1 | 13 |
| Ocean | 317,000 | 1,320,000 |
| Ice | 7,000 | 29,000 |
| Fresh-water lakes | 30 | 125 |
| Fresh-water rivers | 0.3 | 1.25 |

**TABLE 15–2.**

| | Volume | |
|---|---|---|
| | Cubic Miles | Cubic Kilometers |
| *Annual input to oceans* | | |
| Precipitation | 78 | 320 |
| Runoff from rivers and icecaps | 9 | 38 |
| Ground water outflow | 0.4 | 1.6 |
| | 87.4 | 359.6 |
| *Annual output from oceans* | | |
| Evaporation | 85 | 350 |

## WATER INVENTORY

First, we should try to assess the availability and quantity of water as we have done with other resources.[1] A world view shows how only a minute fraction can be classified as fresh water. (See Table 15–1.)

A dynamic analysis shows a slight imbalance in the *hydrologic cycle,* indicating that sea level is slowly rising. (See Table 15–2.) The net gain of 2,400 cubic miles is almost lost in an ocean of 317,000,000 cubic miles, but it will represent a 1 percent increase in 1,300 years (Figure 15–1). For completeness, the annual budget for land area is shown in Table 15–3. A daily budget for the forty-eight contiguous United States does not tell the whole story of our water-use patterns. Of 1,200 billion gallons flowing toward the sea each day:

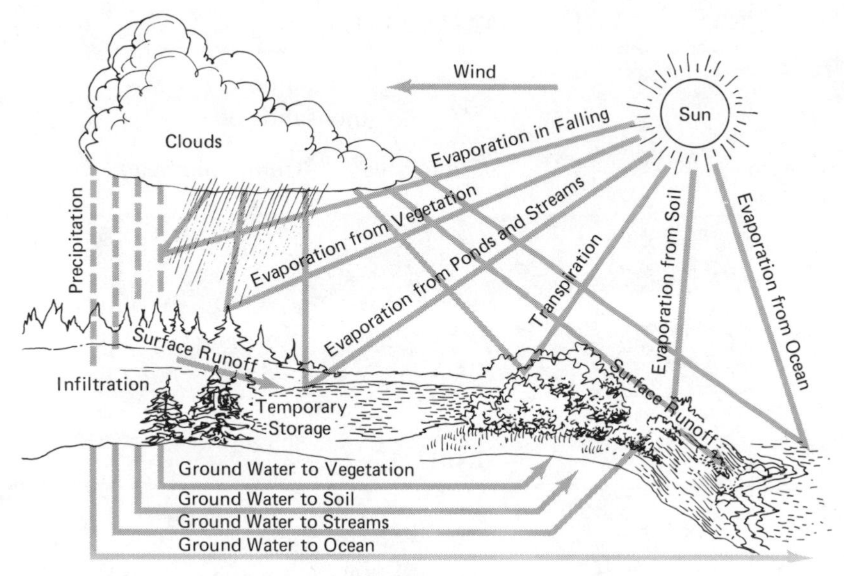


**Figure 15–1.**
*Hydrologic cycle*

370 go through hydroelectric turbines with little change in quality.
310 are withdrawn and then are returned in a used condition (contaminated or heated).
5 are consumed by industry and 73 by agriculture.[2]

The withdrawn and returned category includes 27 billion gallons of drinking quality, only 100 million gallons of which are actually drunk; the rest is used

**TABLE 15–3.**

| | Volume (thousands of) | |
|---|---|---|
| | Cubic Miles | Cubic Kilometers |
| *Annual input* | | |
| Precipitation | 24 | 100 |
| *Annual output* | | |
| Evaporation | 17 | 70 |
| Runoff and outflow | 9.4 | 39.6 |

for everything from lawn watering and cooking to washing and flushing. Those of us on public supplies used about 115 gallons per capita per day (gpcd) for domestic and public use and 51 gpcd for commercial and industrial uses.[3] Like most aggregate figures, these national estimates are misleading. They indicate an over-all surplus when, in actuality, some regions have too little water and others have too much.

## WATER AS A LIMITING FACTOR

Both extremes of water supply can *limit* human activities, including those connected with industry, agriculture, and urban development. The arid portions of the American West look temptingly unoccupied to "grand planners" with visions of new cities in the sun. They should pause and ask why all that space has remained empty for such a long time. Droughts can be chronic in zones to the lee of mountain ranges that lift, and wring dry, the prevailing winds. Shifts in the patterns of higher, faster winds (the jet streams) can bring periods of desiccation to any region. The Dust Bowl received enough rain for good yields of wheat during the periods 1914 to 1931 and 1940 to 1951 (helping "our side" win two world wars), but the rain cannot be described as reliable. The Soil Conservation Service has warned that "at least 14 million acres in the Great Plains currently under cultivation should be returned to grass."[4]

*Drought* afflicted the Delaware River basin from 1961 to 1965, affecting the lives of twenty-two million people living in New York, New Jersey, and Delaware. Designed with the conviction that no regional drought would last longer than two years, New York State's system of reservoirs had a capacity of 572 billion gallons. By August 1965, they held only 212 billion gallons and, if rains had not come, they would have been empty by January 1966. This emergency led to drastic measures. New York City stopped releasing water from its reservoirs into the Delaware with the result that salt water, "advancing at a rate of one-half mile a day, corroded expensive industrial equipment,. . . and became a threat to Philadelphia."[5] "Water wars" between cities are not confined to the West! (See Figure 15–2.)

The opposite of drought, *flooding,* is also caused by vagaries of wind and precipitation. In a list of the fifty floods that did the most damage in the United States, fifteen were described as "hurricane, tidal, and river floods," three were related to melted snow, two were aggravated by dam failure, and the rest were simply "rainfall-river floods."[6] The dollar losses have increased in recent years as more and more homes, businesses, and

**Figure 15–2.**
*Drought* (Courtesy Library of Congress)

industries have been built in flood plains. Fortunately, improved warning and evacuation techniques have reduced the human toll so that we are less apt to have disasters comparable to those at Johnstown, Pennsylvania (2,100 died when a dam burst in 1889); Galveston, Texas (more than 6,000 were killed by a hurricane tidal flood in 1900); and Lake Okeechobee, Florida (2,400 lives were lost in 1928 when a hurricane breached dikes around the south end of the lake). Generally, the hazards of floods, even when they recur several times in a decade, do not limit regional development. Wise builders can always ‘‘take to the high ground’’ and avoid the danger. This option contrasts with those open to a developer in a region characterized by prolonged or chronic aridity where water shortage cannot be so easily sidestepped (Figure 15–3).

**Figure 15–3.**
*Flood* (bottom photo courtesy U.S. Army Corps of Engineers. Photographer: James N. Sanders)

## WATER MANAGEMENT

The policies and techniques of water management form a vast subject, too complex to be analyzed in depth within the confines of this chapter, yet so important that it must be considered. Typically, ecologists become concerned with water management whenever utilization involves a change in an entire ecosystem (drainage of a marsh, impoundment of a stream, or irrigation of a field). However, they, together with authorities responsible for the welfare of fish, wildlife, and humans, also take an interest in any use that causes a significant change in water quality. The latter set of problems will be dealt with in the following chapters. Here, *trade offs* at the ecosystem level will be the theme.

*Draining* a marsh to control mosquitos or to permit agricultural development might seem completely innocuous. It is true that some wetlands can be converted from breeding grounds for disease vectors into richly productive fields. As suggested in the previous chapter, however, the value of marshes as a wildlife habitat should be recognized, especially in areas such as those to the north of Everglades National Park in Florida where any form of development could intercept or contaminate water flowing into a delicately balanced ecosystem. Another benefit of fresh-water marshes is that they often serve to recharge aquifers that provide well water for distant cities. If hydrostatic pressure is not maintained in these areas, the wells go dry or become contaminated by salt-water intrusion.

*Dam building,* by providing a steady supply of water and preventing floods, would seem even more beneficial than a drainage project. Once again, we should know exactly what we lose before we rhapsodize over the benefits. It is true that the "vegetative sponge" of a watershed can intercept and hold only so much rainfall. Yet, a flood-control program that builds dams while it permits the watershed to be denuded of vegetation is doomed because the dams will soon be filled with silt. Dam building should complement, not replace, watershed conservation. Furthermore, the prevention of floods would be much less important if flood-plain utilization could be restricted to agriculture, recreation, and transportation (Figure 15–4).

Dams also are justified as sources of electric power, irrigation, and drinking water. Each of these "reasons" should be examined closely whenever a dam site is chosen.[7] Would it be cheaper to use nuclear energy as a power source? Is irrigation really needed when the same crops would cost less to grow in a rainy region? How much reserve is really needed in a

**Figure 15-4.**
*Dam* (U.S. Army Corps of Engineers photo)

drinking-water supply; enough to cope with a drought of such severity that it is apt to occur only once in a century; enough to provide for unbuilt cities? In answering many of these questions, the water manager faces the danger of a "self-fulfilling prophecy." If electricity and water are cheap enough, industrial and urban development eventually will reach limits set by supply, and the cycle will start again with further demands. A multipurpose dam has its virtues, but all those purposes could be achieved by a mix of alternatives, perhaps giving better control and direction to regional development. The central question, "How much growth is desirable?" is especially important in evaluating schemes for moving water from one region to another. When you think about the growing pains already experienced by California, you wonder if it really would be wise to bring Canadian water all the way down to California's central valley, as proposed in the 220 billion dollar North American Water and Power Alliance Plan.[8]

"Recreation" is the final justification for dam building, and it has been voiced more loudly in recent years. Many communities feel that they are entitled to a lake, and it is true that lakes enhance the value and beauty of the "new towns" of Reston, Virginia, and Columbia, Maryland. However, the creation of an artificial lake often destroys a stream, fresh-water marshes, rich farmlands, and diverse low-land forests. Those responsible must be sure that recreational opportunities are really increased. Bird watchers and trout fishermen have rights equal to those of bass catchers and water skiers!

If you think there are ecological, economic, and ethical problems associated with drainage or dam projects, wait until *desalinization* and *rainmaking* projects get going! The vast quantities of water with 34 ppt salt near coastal concentrations of people and machines have seemed a temptingly boundless source of fresh water and valuable minerals to many engineers. Cheap energy, nuclear or thermonuclear, may bring desalinization and "mining sea water" into large-scale operation. At present, however, desalinization relies on fossil fuels, produces much waste heat and brine, and is useful only as a source of drinking water in remote locations such as Key West, Florida. Any enlargement of desalinization will be subject to economic constraints that, in turn, should include environmental costs.

Rainmaking will be even more difficult to develop without legal and ecological complications. Clouds will be seeded (with silver iodide) to produce rain for a power company trying to fill its reservoir. Unless everything goes just right, the company may find itself facing the wrath of lettuce farmers whose crops were destroyed by hail or ranchers whose livestock drowned in a flash flood. Farmers with parched crops may enter the fray, accusing the company of "stealing rain God had intended for them." It may be easier to continue our present strategy of capturing and piping precipitation after it falls, rather than trying to redirect clouds (Figure 15–5).

One final and very important aspect of water conservation is the possible modification of the use patterns that now often are wasteful. Farmers, engineers, and householders all can find ways to reduce water consumption or recycle "used" water. We should recognize that a reliable supply of clean water is a very precious resource, the preservation of which may require a combination of ingenuity and control.

## SUMMARY

Water is a resource of many facets and uses. We rely on the small fraction flowing from mountains to seas in aquifers or rivers for drinking, cooling, irrigation, flushing, transportation, and hydroelectric power gener-

**Figure 15–5.**
*Cloud seeding* (Bureau of Reclamation, Dept. of the Interior photo)

ation. With such reliance, it is natural that human activities, especially the development of cities, can be limited by the availability of water. Increasing constraints on the habitation of flood plains may be based also on recognition of natural limits. Management of water supplies often leads to loss of some resources and development of others, a trade off that must be evaluated carefully in each case of drainage, dam building, or tapping new sources.

## Discussion Questions

1. How much water do you use and how much is used to provide things you need?
2. Contrast the constraints on urban development imposed by droughts with those imposed by floods. To what extent should we try to circumvent these constraints?
3. Do you think rain making is a good idea?

## Suggested Projects

1. Find out where your community obtains its supplies of drinking-quality water.
2. Make a map of areas near your community that would be inundated if the river (or lake, estuary, or the like) rose 50 feet above its average level. (This can be done simply by shading in the zone on a topographic map.)
3. Measure the amount of water wasted each day from leaky taps in your home or school.

## Notes

1. These water-supply and budget statistics are abstracted from Table 2–3 in D. K. Todd, ed., *The Water Encyclopedia* (Port Washington, New York: Water Information Center, 1970), which also has many other kinds of water data.
2. C. R. Murray, *The World Almanac, 1973 ed.* ed. by G. E. Delury (New York: Newspaper Enterprise Association, 1972), p. 477.
3. H. H. Landsberg, *Natural Resources for United States Growth* (Baltimore: Resources for the Future, Johns Hopkins, 1964), pp. 121–148, has a good assessment of water supply and demand in the United States.
4. Raymond F. Dasmann, *Environmental Conservation* 3rd ed. (New York: Wiley, 1972), p. 143.
5. O. S. Owen, *Natural Resource Conservation: An Ecological Approach* ( New York: Macmillan, 1971), p. 126. See also "The Northeast Water Supply Crisis of the 1960s," U.S. Department of the Interior Geological Survey (Washington, D.C.: U.S. Govt. Printing Office, 1973).
6. Todd, *op. cit.,* p. 169.
7. A. E. Morgan, *Dams and Other Disasters A Century of the Army Corps of Engineers in Civil Works* (Boston: Porter Sargent, 1971). The book is not very well written, but it is interesting nonetheless.
8. See the map in Owen, *op. cit.,* pp. 166–167.

# 16

# Radioactive Pollution

## Key Concepts

- Radioactive isotopes
- Internal sources
- External sources
- Nuclear holocaust
- Atmospheric testing
- Uranium mines
- Tracers
- Underground disposal
- Reconcentration
- Threshold dose
- Chromosome damage
- Zero emission

As was shown in the description of our energy environment (in Chapter 12), we are exposed to radioactivity of several kinds from various sources. There are naturally occurring *radioactive isotopes* in the air we breathe, the food we eat, and the liquids we drink *(internal sources)*. We also receive radiation from *external sources,* both natural (cosmic rays and gamma-emitting isotopes in rocks, soil, or bricks) and man-made (X rays used for medical or dental diagnostics).[1] Added to these exposures are the various forms of radioactive pollution, defined simply as the contamination of our environment by radioactive waste materials. Although these problems are discussed in the section on aquatic ecosystems, they also form part of air pollution. However, many of the most interesting and ecologically important aspects of radioactive pollution can be illustrated with aquatic examples.

## MAN-MADE SOURCES OF RADIOACTIVITY

The horrors of Hiroshima and Nagasaki have not been repeated since that tragic week in August 1945, but the possibility of a *nuclear holocaust* continues to haunt the human species. Rational members of any group, party, or nation recognize that this would be the ultimate form of pollution, the only kind that could quickly destroy most of mankind and civilization. Yet, the same discoveries and technology that endanger all of us can be applied to many good purposes, so we must be careful not to confuse the hazards of nuclear warfare with the environmental problems caused by the development of nuclear power or by use of radioisotopes in medicine and agriculture. These problems are real and must be dealt with, but they are much less terrifying than a rain of thermonuclear rockets.

Preparations for the war we pray will never come do contribute to radioactive pollution. *Atmospheric testing* by the United States, the United Kingdom, and the Soviet Union until the signing of the limited nuclear test-ban treaty in July 1963, and by France from 1960 on and by China from 1964 on, has contaminated the atmosphere with long-lived isotopes. Even underground tests have shown a distressing tendency to vent, sending up a radioactive plume that may drift across international borders causing, at least, a technical violation of the test-ban treaty. Fortunately, the monitoring of fallout in milk and water shows that most forms of atmospheric radioactivity have been declining from peaks achieved during the early 1960s[2] (Figure 16–1).

Other human activities, however, still contribute to the radioactive contamination of our environment. Radioactive salts may be leached from *uranium mines* and from the piles of waste rock produced by such mines, ending up in stream or well water. At research establishments and medical institutions, radioactive chemicals *(tracers)* used to trace biochemical pathways sometimes are washed down a drain, although the authorities frown on such practices and suggest that wastes be held until a number of half lives have elapsed. Holding tanks and ponds also are required at nuclear reactors, giving short-lived radioisotopes ample time to break down into relatively harmless atoms. However, some radioactivity, in gaseous and liquid forms, is released from reactors, with efforts being made to insure atmospheric or aquatic dilution to a point where it will not be hazardous.[3] Other sources of leakage are fuel reprocessing plants, where spent fuel rods are treated to extract reusable isotopes, and waste disposal areas where

**Figure 16–1.**
*Mushroom cloud of atmospheric bomb test* (US Air Force photo)

unreusable isotopes are stored. In recent years, steel drums filled with concrete and low-level radioactivity have been dumped at eleven sites off the East Coast of the United States, six off the West Coast, and one in the Gulf of Mexico.[4] The current policy is to keep even the low-level alpha and beta emitters away from water. ERDA is looking for a dry, *underground disposal* site and had hoped that it would be able to use the salt mines of Kansas, but container breakdown, heat flow, and movement of radioisotopes through the salt are problems not yet solved.[5] For some time to come, boiling high-level wastes will continue to be held in steel and concrete tanks at Hanford, Washington; Arco, Idaho; and Savannah River, Georgia. Leakage from these "hell-holes" into air or water must be prevented[6] (Figures 16–2 and 16–3).

Other possible sources of radioactivity include "Plowshare" programs, in which leftover nuclear devices are used to create instant harbors or stimulate the release of natural gas from underground rock formations.[7]

**Figure 16–2.**
*Nuclear reactor* (AEC photo)

The problems of radioactivity containment have been one of the main reasons these well-intentioned projects have met with little success (Figure 16–4).

## RECONCENTRATION OF RADIOACTIVITY

By releasing radioactivity into our environment, we are increasing radiation exposure, but the increase is slight and accounts for no more than 2 of the 205 millirems the average American receives each year. The situation is complicated by the special problems of higher exposures near the points of release and at the tops of food chains, both categories showing that dilution cannot always reduce radioactivity below possibly hazardous levels. The Japanese fishermen and Marshallese islanders caught in the fallout of a 1954 bomb test received high external exposures, a thousand times the average external dose an American gets each year. Apparently the islanders, living on Rongelap, 100 miles east of Bikini, also ingested iodine 131 (whose half life is eight days) because nineteen of the eighty-two exposed have had operations for thyroid nodules caused by concentration of the radioactive

**Figure 16–3.**
*Underground transporter designed for use in salt mine depository of radioactive waste* (AEC photo)

isotope in the portion of the thyroid producing the hormone thyroxine ($C_5H_{11}I_{14}NO_4$). Although three had cancerous symptoms, none have died of thyroid cancer. However, one other, Lekoj Anjain, died of myelogenous leukemia in 1972.[8] Children who drank milk from cows that foraged on grass contaminated by fallout from the Nevada test site also have developed thyroid nodules.[9]

In aquatic ecosystems, physical, physiological, and ecological processes all may combine to bring about reconcentration. There is the famous case of White Oak Lake, which was used for waste disposal from the Oak Ridge National Laboratory in Tennessee. Phosphorous 32, cesium 137, and other radioisotopes were concentrated in algae and then further concentrated in the tissues of fish and ducks.[10] When the "hot" ducks, contaminated at Oak Ridge, were shot and eaten by hunters in Canada and Texas, the pond was drained, although it has since been refilled with uncontaminated water. Another example, also used by Sheldon Novick in *The Careless Atom,* is based on studies of radioactivity in the Columbia River, near the plutonium

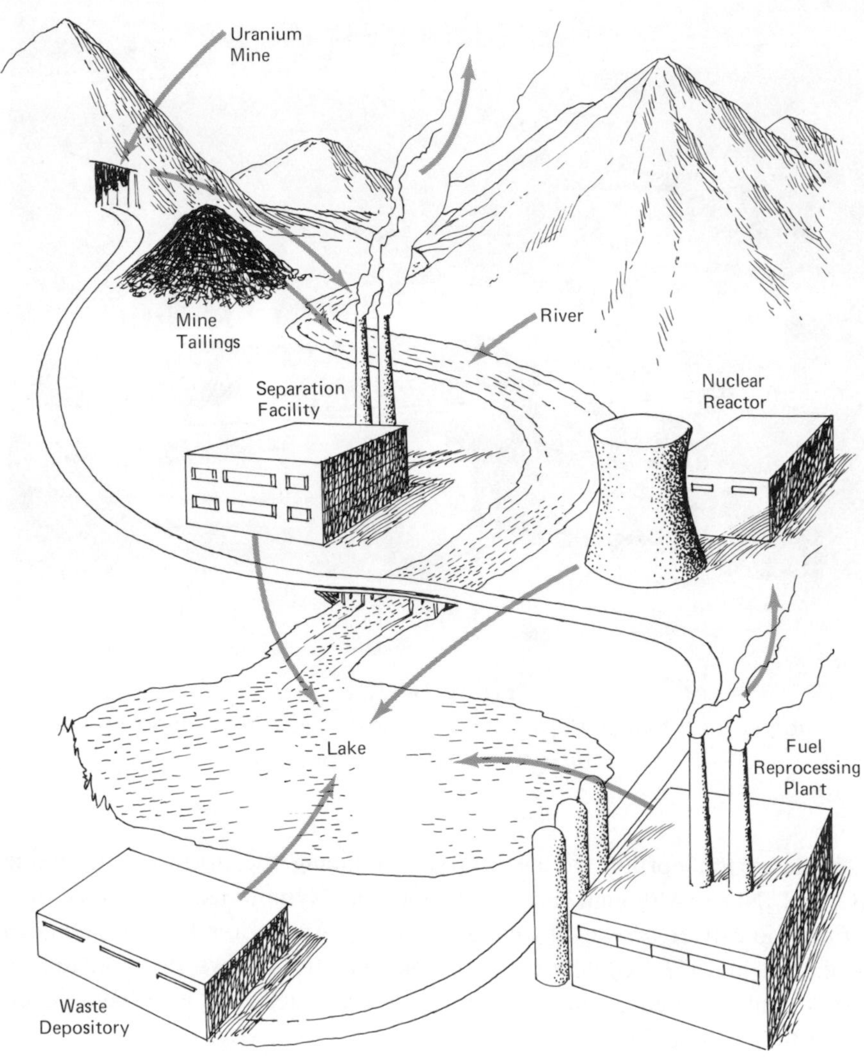


**Figure 16–4.**
*Radiation leaking from nuclear industry*

factories at Hanford, Washington. Radioactive phosphorous was concentrated two thousandfold by plankton. Caddis fly larvae, presumably filtering out the plankton, achieved levels 350,000 times those measured in the water. Swallows, feeding on adult caddis flies, and many other less radioactive insects, had a "concentration factor of 75,000." Comparable observations have been made in estuaries. Zinc 65 (half life, 245 days), from the sheathing of reactor fuel rods near Bradwell in the United Kingdom, was concentrated 240,000 times as it moved up the water → plankton → oyster food chain; and iron 55 (half life, 2.9 years) was concentrated ten million-fold by barnacles on the California Coast.[11] Although we do not eat barnacles, we do eat oysters and other filter feeders, so health authorities sometimes find it necessary to ban shellfish harvesting near nuclear facilities.

Much of what has been learned about the movement and *reconcentration* of radioactive isotopes in ecosystems has increased our understanding of potential hazards from other chemicals.[12] In many ways, heavy metals (mercury, cadmium, and lead) and persistent organic compounds (DDT, PCB, and the like) behave like long-lived radioisotopes. They can be trapped in lakes or estuaries; they can be stored in certain tissues (for example, lead in bone, DDT in fat); and some, especially the organic compounds, are concentrated as they move up food chains. These nonradioactive chemical contaminants may be the ones we really should be worrying about!

## EFFECTS OF CHRONIC IRRADIATION

The debate over radiation effects has been entirely anthropocentric—and rightly so. Unlike the pollution problems to be discussed in the next two chapters, radioactivity has not been considered a hazard to fish and wildlife. We want to know if radiation is contributing to cancer, premature aging, or fetal deformation in the human species. In answering these questions, there has been great disagreement among the experts, often over the existence of a *threshold dose* below which natural mechanisms function to repair any damage done by ionizing radiation. All the authorities agree that high-level, acute exposures, such as those received by the Marshallese caught in a cloud of fallout, are hazardous. However, they are not sure if chronic, low-level exposure is as dangerous.

Some statistical problems further confuse the issue. Even if radioactive contamination causes an increase in the incidence of a form of cancer (such as leukemia), that same disease also may be triggered by a cat virus, various chemicals, or synergistic combinations of several carcinogens. It becomes very difficult to correlate a slight increase, possibly coming twenty years after an unrecorded exposure, with an environmental factor.

To be on the safe side, we should assume that every little bit hurts, that *damage to chromosomes* in somatic or gametic cells is cumulative, and that increased exposure to radiation should be regarded as undesirable, both occupationally and environmentally. Rather than have permissible rates of release, perhaps the ideal for everything from color TV sets to nuclear power plants should be *zero emission.* There will be great costs and many technological difficulties in achieving this ideal under all circumstances. We will have to decide just how much we are willing to pay for a slight, possibly unmeasurable, reduction in the incidences of certain forms of cancer and birth defects (see Chapter 22). As Karl Morgan, director of the Health Physics Division at the Oak Ridge Laboratory, has said often in speeches and public testimony, it would seem prudent to keep exposures low, but we should not become so concerned about emissions from nuclear power plants that we fail to recognize and reduce the hazards of medical and dental X rays.[13]

## SUMMARY

Radioactive pollution, added to natural and diagnostic exposures, comes from bomb-testing, uranium mines, nuclear reactors, nuclear fuel reprocessing plants, and nuclear waste depositories. Although the addition is small, it is worrisome because some of the radioactive isotopes released have long half lives, are concentrated as they move up food chains, and may end up in our tissues. The effects of long exposures to low levels of radiation are hard to assess because many other factors also can increase the incidence of cancer, birth defects, or other diseases caused by chromosome damage. Reduction of radiation exposure can be accomplished by more cautious use of diagnostic X rays and by a zero-emission standard for all man-made sources of radiation.

### Discussion Questions

1. Do you think man has done more good or harm with radioactivity since its discovery?
2. Which man-made sources of radioactivity are likely to become more important in coming decades?
3. Why is it so difficult to find out exactly how much damage is being done to our chromosomes by natural and artificial irradiation?

## Suggested Projects

**1.** The next time you have a medical or dental X ray, ask what precautions are being taken to keep your exposure, and the exposure of the X ray technicians, to a minimum.

**2.** If possible, visit a nuclear research or power generating facility and find out what means are used to monitor radiation leakages and to prevent large-scale accidental releases.

## Notes

1. A comprehensive summary of "background" radiation is provided in D. T. Oakley, *Natural Radiation Exposure in the United States* (Washington, D.C.: U.S. Environmental Protection Agency, 1972).
2. *Environmental Quality* (Washington, D.C.: Council on Environmental Quality, 1971), p. 222.
3. J. F. Hogerton, *Atomic Power Safety* (Oak Ridge, Tenn.: Division of Technical Information, AEC, 1967), pp. 17–18.
4. P. Nobile and J. Deedy, eds., "Maps from Ocean Dumping: A National Policy," *The Complete Ecology Fact Book* (Garden City, N.Y.: Anchor, Doubleday, 1972), pp. 230–231.
5. "The Kansas Geologists and the AEC," *Science News,* **99:**161 (March 6, 1971).
6. See S. Novick, "Earthquake at Giza," *Environment,* (Jan.–Feb. 1970) **12:**2–13; reprinted in S. Novick and D. Cottrell, eds., *Our World in Peril* (Greenwich, Conn.: Fawcett, 1971).
7. P. Metzger "Project Gasbuggy and Catch–85" *New York Times Magazine,* (Feb. 22, 1970) pp. 26–27, 79–84.
8. M. Malone, "It Was 'Snow' that Brought Death," *Pacific Islands Monthly,* **44:**7 (1973).
9. Barry Commoner, *Science and Survival* (New York: Viking, 1967), pp. 7–9.
10. S. Novick, *The Careless Atom* (New York: Delta, Dell, 1969), p. 100.
11. B. Aberg and F. P. Hungate, *Radioecological Concentration Processes* (Elmsford, N.Y.: Pergamon, 1967).
12. G. M. Woodwell, "Radioactivity and Fallout: The Model Pollution," *BioScience* **19:**884–887 (1969); also Woodwell, "Toxic Substances and Ecological Cycles," *Scientific American,* **216:**24–31 (1967); the latter article was reprinted in Paul R. Ehrlich, J. P. Holdren, and R. W.

Holm, eds., *Man and the Ecosphere* (San Francisco: Freeman, 1971), pp. 128–135.

13. K. Z. Morgan, "Adequacy of Present Standards of Radiation Exposure." Preprint of testimony before the subcommittee on Air and Water Pollution of the Senate Committee of Public Works, 4 August, 1970, at Washington, D.C.

# 17

# Thermal Pollution

## Key Concepts

Waste heat
Physical pollution
Noise
Background
Lethal limit
Thermal plume
Defaunation
Cooling towers
Man-made islands
Potential use

Thermal pollution is an area in which euphemisms often have been substituted for an honest phrase. Some engineers, impressed no doubt by the power of positive thinking, prefer to describe the release of hot water from power plants as "thermal enrichment." Some scientists, trying to attain a neutral stance, describe the same situation as "calefaction."[1] By any name or phrase, they are simply describing the dumping of *waste heat* into aquatic ecosystems. This form of pollution is quite distinct from those involving chemical contamination of local ecosystems or the world's biosphere. Thermal pollution occurs whenever and wherever hot water discharge raises the natural background temperatures. The only comparable form of *physical pollution* is *noise,* which is, like heat, a by-product of energy conversion and adds to a natural, ambient *background*.

Either noise or heat can reach levels stressful to organisms. With noise, however, we humans are the ones who usually have cause for complaint, whereas thermal pollution is much more apt to affect uncomplaining fish. This is the main reason it often is so difficult to arouse public concern over thermal pollution. Despite the expression "poor fish," very few people can empathize with finny creatures. Unless there is clear danger to a species of economic or recreational importance, little response from citizens or government can be expected. This is where aquatic (or, at least, amphibious) ecologists can help—by showing just what losses in species diversity or primary and secondary productivity can be expected when water is warmed above levels natural for each location and season.

## EFFECTS OF THERMAL POLLUTION

Fish and other aquatic organisms can be killed by hot water in a number of ways. During the summer in temperate regions and any time of the year in the tropics, hot effluents can raise ambient temperatures above the *lethal limit* tolerated by one or more species. This may lead to the elimination of all species except a few tough snails and blue-green algae in the zone heated by the discharge. For fish, death can also come through various indirect effects. Swimming more rapidly in the warmer water, they may not be able to get enough oxygen, especially when less can be dissolved and demands caused by their increased activity exceed the concentrations available; or they may be more susceptible to fungal infections; or they may starve to death when their favored food insects are forced to emerge in the dead of winter.

Ironically, fish mortality also can occur when there is a sudden drop in temperature. This sometimes happens when a power plant shuts down for repairs or refueling during winter months and fish that had been overwintering in the *thermal plume* (instead of migrating south), literally find themselves "out in the cold." Other common problems at power plants are fish mortality at the water intake or within the cooling system itself. Fish too small to swim away from the intake suction may be battered to death against protective grills at the entrance. Fry and plankton may be sucked right through the cooling coils and parboiled. When the same lake or bay water is used over and over again for cooling, this latter phenomenon can lead to *defaunation* of the entire aquatic ecosystem because the power plant functions like a huge filter feeder (Figure 17–1).

## TWO POWER PLANTS

In order to emphasize the wide range of situations that must be dealt with in thermal pollution and the related problem of cooling-water intake, it is necessary to examine the case histories of two power plants. One is at

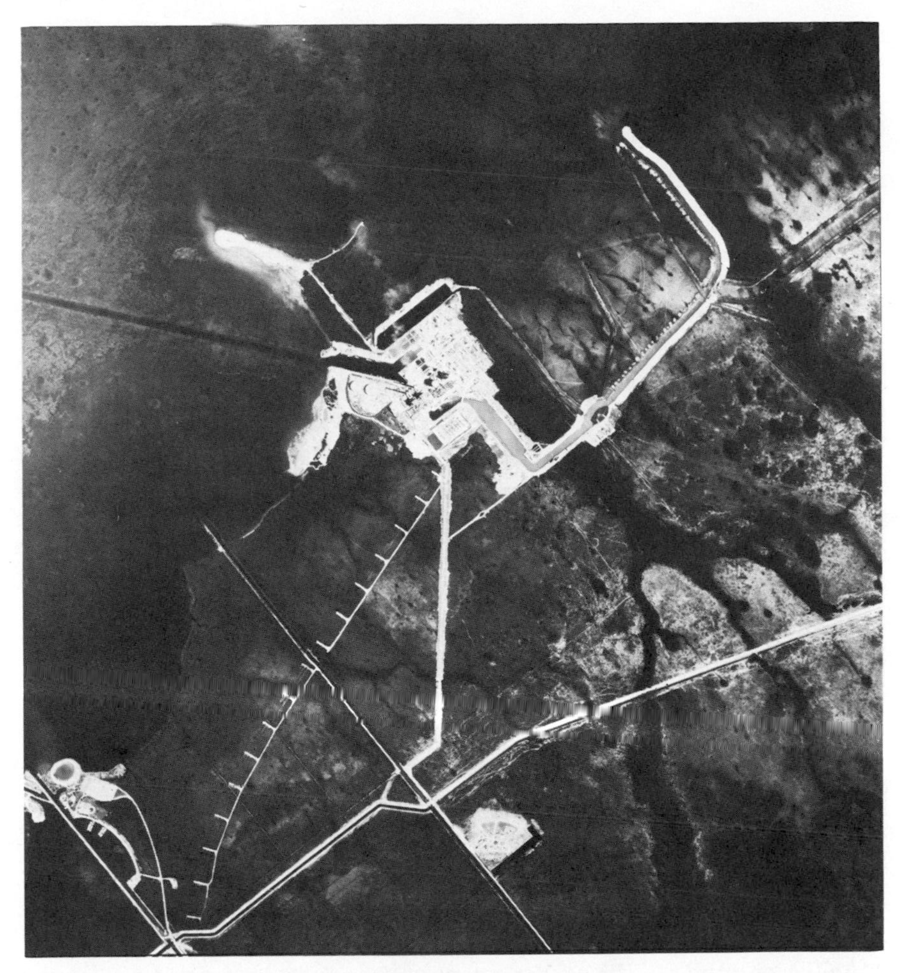

**Figure 17–1.**
*Thermal plume at Turkey Point* (NASA photo)

Turkey Point on the east coast of Florida, south of Miami. The other is at Haddam Neck on the Connecticut River, southeast of Hartford. The Turkey Point site was picked because it was near the Ja-Mi (Jacksonville-Miami) megopolis, yet not so close that pollution would be a problem conspicuous enough to frighten away tourists. In fact, the Florida Power and Light Company did its best to maintain good "public relations." Much of the site was designated as a wildlife refuge and certain areas were opened to recreation, including Boy Scout camping. The power plant itself now has four units. The first two, powered by gas or oil, became operational in 1967 and 1968. The second two, both nuclear, started generating electricity in 1973, somewhat behind schedule. A number of problems, most of them related to cooling, contributed to the delay. It turns out that the surveyors of the original site missed several very important environmental constraints. For one thing, a current moving south to north along the shore pushed warm water dumped into Biscayne Bay back toward the cooling intake. Moving the outlet farther south solved that problem, but it still created a zone of devastation in the bay. You might think that organisms living in shallow tropical waters could tolerate warm water. However, because they live very close to their lethal limit under natural conditions, a 5° C. (9° F.) rise kills them. Even when only the fossil fuel plants were operating, using 1,490 cubic feet per second (cfs), all eel grass, clams, and many crustacea and fish were eliminated near the outfall. Ecologists recognized that the problem could get much worse when the nuclear units started up because that would triple the cooling-water impact and warm-water output. Visions of Biscayne Bay inhabited by only tough snails and noxious blue-green algae worried such diverse groups as the Miami Chamber of Commerce and the government officials charged with the protection of national seashores.[2]

Florida Power and Light had very few options open. The air conditioners of Miami Beach and the gadgets of Disney World needed the electricity; but the Corps of Engineers would not let them dump any more warm water in the bays. Cooling towers would need fresh water, a scarce commodity in south Florida. They could not use salt water because the resultant drift of salt spray would kill 160 square miles of Everglades. Use of the cool ocean depths was considered for dumping and pumping, but that meant a willingness to spend 106 million dollars building two pipes 15 feet in diameter and 15 miles long and then using 25 percent of the power output to circulate the water. Finally, it was decided that the lesser of the evils was to create a 7,000-acre canal network in which the warm water from the power plants could be held until it is cool enough to be pumped back into the secondary coils—in effect, tacking a huge radiator onto the plant. This, by no means, solves all the problems of Turkey Point because the canal system needs periodic topping up and flushing out, processes that may have some deleterious effects on the bay's biota, even if temperature limits are strictly adhered to. The cooling complex also may have other effects, such as modification of the local climate (huge clouds already form over the fossil fuel units) or replacement of fresh water in aquifers by salt water (Figure 17–2 a and b).

To counterbalance the troubled history of Turkey Point, let us examine

DESTRUCTION OF BOTTOM BIOTA BY THERMAL POLLUTION

CONCEPT: USE OF AERIAL PHOTOGRAPHY AND THERMAL IR IMAGERY TO TRACE EXTENT OF THERMAL POLLUTION

TEST SITE
TURKEY POINT POWER PLANT
BISCAYNE BAY, FLORIDA

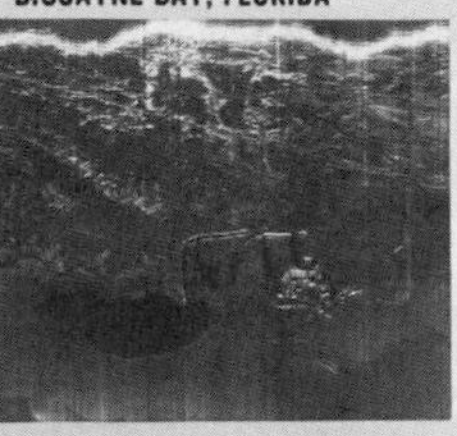

COLOR PHOTO

AIRCRAFT: NASA MSC 926
ALTITUDE: 20000 FT.
CAMERA: WILD RC-8
FILM: ANSCO D-200
INVESTIGATOR: DR. M. KELLY, NYU

THERMAL IR SCAN

(1) DARK AREA IS 7° C WARMER THAN AMBIENT WATER
(2) INSTRUMENT - RECONOFAX IV

SURFACE TRUTH ANALYSIS

M - VISIBLE INNER AREA OF BOTTOM DAMAGE
K - OUTER ZONE OF BOTTOM DAMAGE
I - COASTAL GRASS ZONE
J - MIXED BOTTOM COVER ZONE

**a**

**b**

**Figure 17–2.**

*Turkey Point* **a.** *Hot water effluent* (NASA photo) **b.** *Cooling canals* (Courtesy Florida Power & Light, AEC photo)

the relatively trouble-free record of Haddam Neck.[3] Starting up in 1967 after extensive site studies, this plant has remained under ecological surveillance. The intake diverts 828 cubic feet per second (cfs) of the average 16,000 cfs Connecticut River flow. There have been some problems with young or sickly fish being sucked against or through the intake grill. Young shad, for example, may pass through the entire system, emerging unscathed (although it would be interesting to study their subsequent survival). Various combinations of floating booms and immersed electric probes have been tested in efforts to keep fish away from the intake. Perhaps they should imitate the Surry plant near Williamsburg, Virginia and use underwater loud speakers blaring rock music! (Figure 17–3.)

There have been some other effects on fish populations at Haddam Neck. Striped bass overwinter in the thermal plume, putting themselves in some jeopardy should the plant suddenly close down in midwinter. Catfish moving into the discharge canal also seem to do so at some risk, perhaps through a combination of poorer nourishment and increased fungal infec-

**Figure 17–3.**
*Haddam Neck Nuclear Power Plant*

tion. Generally, however, there have been few problems—no major fish kills or zones of devastation. There is, however, one remaining concern relating to periods of low flow: What happens when 828 cfs are taken out of a river trickling by at fewer than 1,000 cfs? This could be disastrous to the river fauna, especially if more nuclear power plants are built above and below Haddam Neck.

This brings us to the basic constraint of cooling-water availability. Each day, 1.2 trillion gallons of water flow from the continental United States into the sea. In 1970, 10 percent (120 billion gallons) of this runoff was used for cooling. By 1980, the proportion may rise to 17 percent, and by 2000, if all planned nuclear power plants are in operation, 50 percent of the runoff will be used at least once for cooling before it reaches the oceans. A long drought, even if it only affected one region, could lead to shutdowns of key plants, with massive blackouts at the very times everyone needed electric heating or air conditioning. It is unlikely that deliberate weather modification will have advanced to the point where we can increase precipitation, especially over a large area, so we will have to learn to live within the constraint imposed.

## COOLING TECHNIQUES

When picking a site for a nuclear power plant, engineers now give heavy weight to the cooling potential of the immediate environment, in addition to such traditional requisites as a firm substrate, access to railroads, and reasonable proximity to consumers of electricity (close enough so that little energy is lost in the high-tension lines and yet not so close that the consumers become nervous about "nuclear mishaps"). Rivers and estuaries have been attractive because the natural flow disperses the warm effluent, but these same circumstances contribute to the chances of fish kills. Therefore, more sites suitable for the construction of cooling ponds or towers are being chosen. Even more impressive than the power plants, the *cooling towers* may be 400 feet high and add $100 million to the 220 million dollar cost of the plant. They do their job through various combinations of convection and evaporation. Another possibility, also expensive, is the construction of power plants on *man-made islands* off the coast where there is an unfailing supply of deep, cool water.[4] This has been suggested for Los Angeles and New Jersey, but the threats of waves and storms may make this alternative less promising than those that rely on self-contained systems, dumping waste heat into the atmosphere (Figure 17–4).

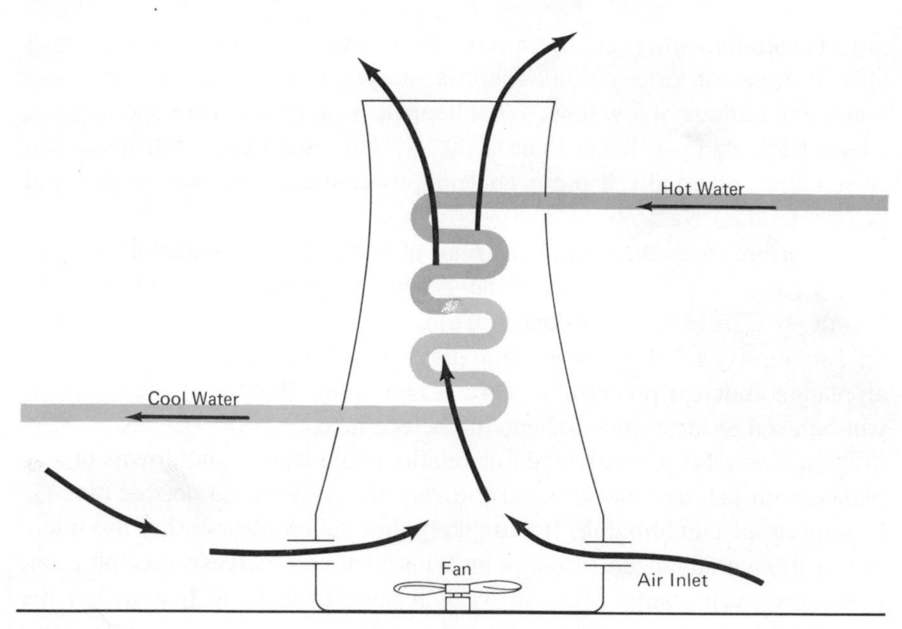


**Figure 17–4.**
*Cooling tower*

Perhaps the most common questions arising in discussions of thermal pollution concern the *potential use* of the waste heat. Why dump it? Two major difficulties have frustrated most efforts in this direction: (1) power plants produce warm water year round, but few things need heating during the summer; and (2) the water is not really hot enough to be useful during the other seasons. At present, there is little economic justification for pumping effluent from a power plant to a home, greenhouse, or fish pond. Growth rates of plants or fish are limited by factors in addition to ambient temperature, and the addition of carbon dioxide to a greenhouse or food scraps to a fish pond may give better returns in increased productivity. Still, the experiments continue in the hope that warm water may help extend the growing season for corn or increase the spawning of clams.

The only place where water from a nuclear power plant has been successfully used for home heating is in a suburb of Stockholm. There engineers deliberately designed a plant that produced less electricity and hotter water. An added benefit is that streets are kept frost free by the heat from pipes that link the plant to the community. However, such a system requires closer proximity to a reactor than government agencies and most Americans are willing to accept. It is ironic that the nuclear power plant, supposedly a source of cheap electricity, produces wastes, heat, and radioactivity, which are hard to handle let alone put to good use. Here is a real challenge for engineers, ecologists, and any other specialists who want to accept it. They have a choice: either tap the atom's energy so efficiently that little waste is produced or, if waste production is unavoidable, turn the waste into a useful resource. A Nobel Prize (or its equivalent) awaits those who meet this challenge.

## SUMMARY

Heat, like noise, is physical pollution and a by-product of energy conversion. However, noise is bothersome to humans in cities, whereas waste heat is most likely to harm fish and other aquatic organisms near power plants. Aquatic organisms can be killed directly when water temperatures exceed their specific limits, they can starve when their food supply is disrupted, and they can become more susceptible to infection. A power plant also may damage aquatic organisms by sucking them through its cooling system or by a sudden cessation of its warm outflow in midwinter. Waste heat from power plants can be transferred to the atmosphere through cooling towers or to the ocean from off-shore power plants, but these alternatives to the present use of lakes, rivers, and estuaries are expensive.

### Discussion Questions

1. If precautions to protect aquatic ecosystems near power plants are fully implemented, who will pay?
2. What do you think about the proposal to build nuclear power plants on man-made islands off the coast?
3. Can you think of ways in which waste heat can be put to good use?

### Suggested Projects

1. If you are able to visit a nuclear power plant on a "radioactive pollution" field trip, also note the cooling system being used and ask if there have been any fish kills.
2. Do some simple experiments with guppies, goldfish, or other easily maintained species: (a) use an immersion heater to gradually increase the water temperature and observe changes in behavior; and (b) transfer some fish from 75° F. to 95° F. or to 55° F. water and measure the average survival times.

## Notes

1. D. Merriman, ''The Calefaction of a River,'' *Scientific American,* **222**:42–52 (1970); see also J. R. Clark, ''Thermal Pollution and Aquatic Life,'' *Scientific American,* **220**:18–27 (1969).
2. Much of this information comes from my colleague J. C. Zieman and from a beautifully illustrated article by B. Atkinson, ''Biscayne Bay,'' *Audubon,* **72**:36–47 (1970).
3. Merriman, *loc cit.;* and Peter H. Judd, ''A River and a Nuclear Power Plant,'' (Northeast Utilities Service Company, 1970), 30 pp.
4. G. Smith, ''Contract Signed on Offshore Nuclear Plants,'' *New York Times,* 19 September 1972.

# 18

# Oil Pollution

## Key Concepts

Continuous process
Prediction
Oceanic pollution
Chronic leaks
Spills
Off-shore wells
Supertankers
Lighter fractions
"Mousse" masses
Blowout
Oil skimmers
Detergents

As with other forms of pollution, it is possible to view oil pollution as a *continuous process,* starting at sources, following the pollutant as it disperses, and then measuring its impact on organisms. Quantification helps clarify the pollution process: for example, 10,000 tons of oil spills from the tanker, it spreads southeast at 3 knots (18,000 feet per hour), and kills 50 percent of an auk colony during the following week. However, *prediction,* the hallmark of science at its best, remains difficult. It is next to impossible to say where the next oil spill will occur, where it will go, and what it will do. All that is certain is that our increasing use and movement of oil increases the chances of spillage.

In this chapter, oil is used as an example of *oceanic pollution,* as opposed to the various forms of fresh-water contamination discussed elsewhere in the book. Many other pollutants enter the ocean. Some—for example, plastic fragments used for packing—may have little effect on man or fish; others, especially mercury in its methylated form, can be picked up by marine animals and transmitted to man in toxic concentrations.[1] Limits of space do not permit a full discussion of these problems, but they should be recognized as reflecting the common view that the oceans can swallow the wastes of civilization without a burp.[2]

## SOURCES OF OIL

Although the most spectacular releases of oil into oceans occur when a tanker breaks open or an off-shore oil well has a blowout, there are many *chronic leaks* from our oil-based technology. Garages, with their routine oil changes for automobiles and other motor vehicles, may be more important than all of the off-shore sources put together if the estimates in Table 18-1 are correct. Sometimes motor oil and industrial lubricants are cleaned and reused, but often they are poured down the drain, going through sewers into rivers, estuaries, and the sea. Even *spills* (defined as "the sudden release of oil in large quantities") are more common along shores than on the high seas, four out of five being the result of refinery leaks, dock-side sloppiness, or similar accidents.

There is no denying, however, that tankers and *off-shore wells* have a good chance of moving up in the oil-source rankings. The world fleet of tankers now numbers more than four thousand and some *(supertankers)* have a 500,000-ton capacity. A spill from one of these leviathans would match the current annual average for all tanker accidents. Oil wells in the continental shelf are also increasing (from 500 in 1961 to 1,800 in 1971—actually 5,000 wells drilled from 1,800 platforms). There is great economic

**TABLE 18–1. Sources of Oil Entering the Oceans***

| | 100,000 metric tons/yr |
|---|---|
| *Land sources* | |
| Motor vehicles | 18 |
| Factories | 13 |
| Refineries and other facilities | 5 |
| *Off-shore sources* | |
| Tankers | 5 |
| Other ships | 5 |
| Wells | 1 |

*Adapted from Tony Loftas, "The Oceans Have Become the Sinks of the World," *Ceres*, **5**:35–39 (1972).

and political pressure to permit drilling along the eastern seaboard, even in the Long Island Sound. Oil that close to market areas is tempting indeed, but the potential customers are as worried about fish and beaches as they are about heating oil and gasoline. The most recent candidate for oil-spill notoriety is, of course, the yet-to-be-completed Alaska pipeline. If it does break at a point where it crosses a river, several hundred thousand barrels of crude oil could be released and washed down to the sea before automatic check valves stop the flow. Even without a break, the increased tanker traffic from the pipeline terminus at Valdez, Alaska to the West Coast and other destinations portends spills that make many environmentalists feel the Trans-Canadian route would be safer and more logical, bringing the oil where it is most needed—to the urbanized Midwest and Northeast[3] (Figure 18–1).

In summary, oil—crude or used—can come from many sources—on land or off-shore—pouring slowly or rapidly into the seas. Oil companies hasten to point out that natural seeps have existed for millions of years, but they must admit that we have, as in so many other environmental matters, greatly accelerated a natural process.

## EFFECTS OF OIL SPILLS

"Oil and water don't mix." Like many old sayings this is only true in part. When first spilled, oil floats on water, but it does not remain trapped at the interface between atmosphere and ocean. *Lighter fractions,* those we use for gasoline, volatilize into the atmosphere. Wave action churns the denser, tarry fractions into lumps that resemble an unappetizing version of the dessert known as chocolate mousse. Depending on the specific gravity of these *"mousse" masses,* they either float for long periods or gradually sink to the ocean floor.

How can marine organisms be affected by such a spill? Some effects are immediate and obvious. Up to 90 percent of sunlight is intercepted by an oil slick, greatly reducing the photosynthetic activity and growth rate of phytoplankton in the shaded area. The natural water repellancy of diving birds is destroyed and they may drown or be chilled to death. More subtle and chronic effects also have been observed. As an oil-soaked bird (Figure 18–2) attempts to clean itself, it ingests some of the sulfur-laden oil, changing the acidity of its gut and making it susceptible to a lethal fungal infection. Or tarry fragments may be filtered out by clams and oysters, rendering them inedible for months thereafter. Perhaps the most worrisome

a

**Figure 18–1.**
**a.** *Supertanker, Esso Malaysia* (Courtesy EXXON Company, U.S.A.) **b.** *Alaska Pipe Line,* [EPA-Documerica (Dennis Cowals)]

possibility is that oil slicks may serve as a trap for air-borne pollutants that are oil-soluble, especially DDT and the PCB group. If this is happening on a large scale, it would help explain why so much chemical fallout is appearing in marine food chains. For example, plankton may be incorporating microscopic globules of oil with PCB (see Chapter 14). The plankton are consumed by small fish, which next contaminate carnivorous fish, and finally

b

Figure 18–1. *(Continued)*

contribute to the death, deformation, and poor reproductive success of marine birds.[4]

You will note that there has been no mention of oil-spill effects on human health. So far, the evidence is inconclusive on this point. We do not eat sea food that obviously has been tainted by oil, but we may not be able to avoid some of the more insidious forms of food-chain contamination. It has been suggested that some of the compounds in oil are potential carcinogens and that any contact, internal or external, should be prevented. How far such caution should be taken must be determined by further studies in the lab and along the shore. One thing is certain: no resort area is happy when its beaches are befouled by oil drifting ashore. This, as will be seen in the two following case histories, has been the most common concern of coast dwellers and visitors threatened by spills.

## TWO INFAMOUS OIL SPILLS

In 1967, the tanker Torrey Canyon ran aground 15 miles west of Land's End, the southwestern point of England. Altogether 118,000 tons of oil

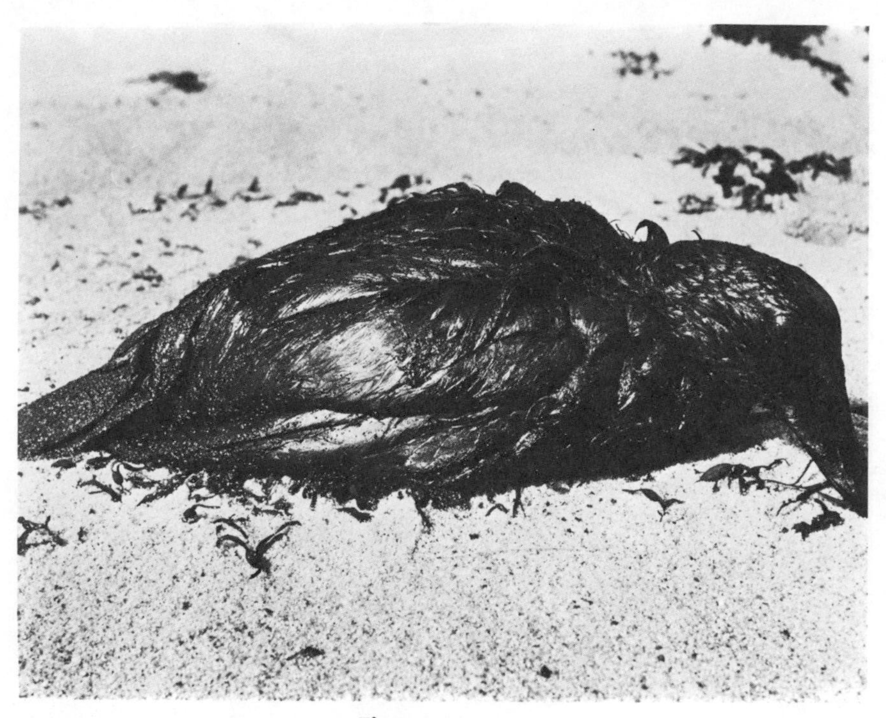

**Figure 18–2.**
*Oily duck* (Bureau of Sport Fisheries and Wildlife. Photo by Wallace Bailey)

spilled, soon fouling both British and French beaches, despite bombing runs by the RAF to try to ignite it before it spread. Other aerial assaults involved spraying 2.5 million gallons of detergent (a 1.5 million dollar operation) on the spill in an effort to sink it. Between the oil and the detergent, there were some very real hazards for marine organisms in the vicinity of the wreck. At least twenty-five thousand sea birds were killed. Certain fish eggs were killed or deformed. Even some free-swimming protozoans died in the melee, and it is safe to assume that the bottom fauna also suffered in zones where toxic mixtures of detergents and oil fractions settled.[5] Where the mousse mess washed ashore, intertidal animals (barnacles, limpets, and mussels) also were devastated, although attached algae (seaweeds) survived quite well. In fact, removal of the grazing snails often led to luxuriant growth of the algae.

Moving to another ocean and another source of oil, we can see some of the characteristics common to off-coast oil spills. In January 1969, an oil well off Santa Barbara had a *blowout* (Figure 18–3). Human error per-

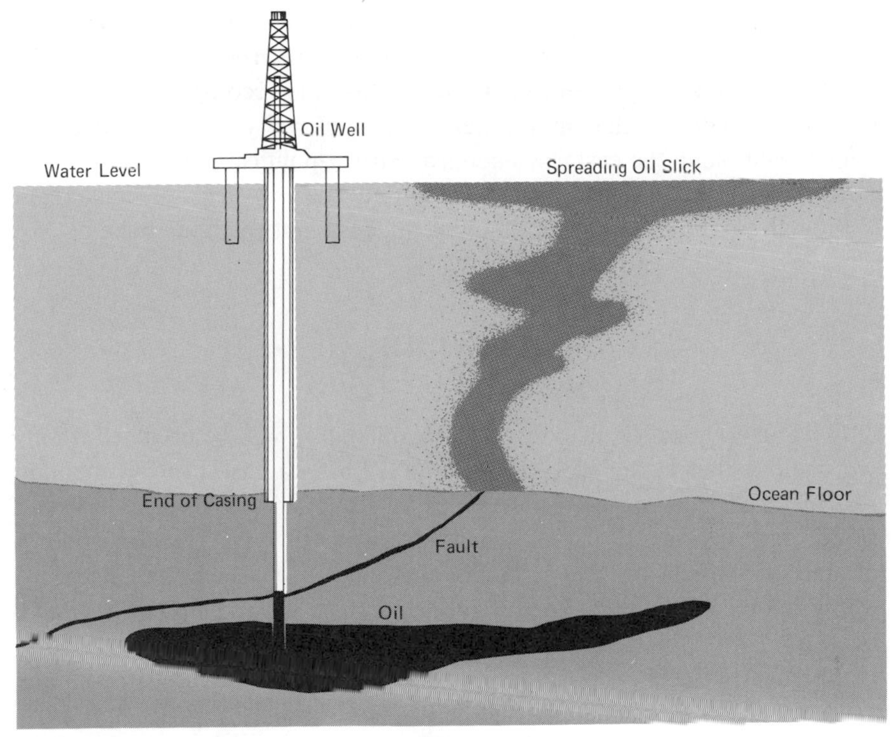


**Figure 18–3.**
*Blow-out*

mitted a pressure build-up and four different safety systems failed to contain the oil. Attempts to sink the oil with dispersants (detergentlike chemicals) or scoop it up with *oil skimmers* also were unsuccessful. Until mid-March, the leak continued at a rate of about 45,000 gallons per day. From then until mid-July it averaged 1,000 gallons per day, continuing to decline thereafter. Outrage is a very mild word for the reaction of Santa Barbarans who had long objected to the government policy of granting drilling leases off *their* shore. However, the immediate and long-range damage done by this oil as it washed onto California's coast is still the subject of debate. Birds of many species were killed or driven from their nesting areas, but marine mammals (grey whales, porpoises, elephant seals, and sea lions) apparently suffered little harm. Nor was there any evidence of massive fish kills. On the other hand, mussels, surf grasses, and certain species of algae were decimated and may be recovering still their former status as components of the coastal biota.[6] If it is true that the most toxic fractions of the oil volatilized into the atmosphere before the slick reached the coast, then the damage could have been greater if the blowout had been closer or the easterly winds stronger. However, the relative toxicity of oil fractions remains a subject requiring much more study by chemists, toxicologists, and ecologists.[7] We need means for predicting the environmental costs of wells drilled in the continental shelf along the eastern seaboard. Strong political pressure for such "convenient" oil wells is being brought to bear on decision makers in Washington. They will have to know if the costs outweigh the benefits.

## CLEAN-UP

Obviously, much of the concern over oil spills could be obviated if only we could gather in the slick. In the Santa Barbara case history, mention was made of oil skimmers. These specially equipped vessels can work well in harbors or other situations where the water is calm. Floating booms around oil-shipping or refining facilities also are useful in containing spills. Many materials to soak up oil have been tested. Wood chips or hay have been used with some success but a foamed plastic (for example, polyurethane) might be even more effective, although with all these absorbents, the problem of disposal remains (Figure 18–4).

When there is a danger of fire, dispersing and sinking the spill with *detergents* that make the oil wettable may be necessary, even though this means wasting oil and endangering bottom organisms. Materials that are not themselves toxic would seem preferable. In dealing with the Torrey Canyon slick, the British used toxic detergents, but the French used chalk dust. The oil industry now has a compound, Corexit 8666, that they claim can be used to sink oil safely. This can be applied anywhere in the world within hours of the spill, the cost of materials and application being borne by an emergency fund established by the major oil companies. There is a fascinating possibility that someday the oil slicks will be sprayed with bacteria rather than chemicals. Certain bacteria can actually live in oil, breaking it down into $CO_2$ and $H_2O$. These oil eaters may occur in natural seeps or oily harbors. Getting a bacterial strain that would multiply quickly enough to prevent oil damage seems to be the main problem with this unique form of biological control.

One other clean-up problem demands attention here. How do you get oil off a bird? Because they are the most obvious, and most pitiful victims of spills, birds have received the attention of many rescue operations. Proce-

**Figure 18–4.**
*Offshore oil skimmer* (Lockheed Missiles and Space Co., and U.S. Coast Guard)

dures have improved through experience and the survival rate can be satisfyingly high. Various cleansing agents have been used. Polycomplex A-11 (as a 1–2% solution in water) does a fine job removing crude oil from feathers, but it also removes the natural oils that provide essential water repellancy. The clean birds may have to be held in captivity from six weeks to six months before they can be safely released.[8] Perhaps a better material is Larodan 127, which, like a car wax, cleans and, at the same time, provides a protective coating.

Obviously, the prevention of oil spills is, in many ways, easier than the clean-up. Yet, it is unrealistic to assume that prevention can be accomplished by creating a world free from wells, tankers, pipelines, and refineries. They will be with us until the last well runs dry. What we should work toward is a combination of technological safeguards and legal restraints designed to keep spills to a minimum.

## SUMMARY

Oil is just one of many pollutants we accidentally or deliberately dump into the ocean. Because our reliance on oil as the favorite fuel of modern technology has increased greatly in recent years, the incidence of oil leakage or spillage presumably will increase. Although this may not create any great hazards to human health, marine organisms, especially diving birds, can be seriously affected. There is also the possibility that oil slicks may facilitate the entry of oil-soluble pollutants into marine food chains. Oil can be conserved and kept out of aquatic ecosystems by more secure oil transport and quicker retrieval systems.

### Discussion Questions

**1.** How does an oil embargo by producing nations affect the incidence of oil spills?
**2.** Have you ever seen an oily beach? If so, describe your reaction.
**3.** How would you clean an oily duck?

### Suggested Projects

**1.** Try some experiments with aquatic organisms in the following combinations (a) lubricating oil and fresh water, (b) lubricating oil and salt water, (c) detergent in oil and in fresh water, and (d) detergent in oil and salt water. Observe effects on behavior and survival.
**2.** Contact Phillip B. Stanton for specific instructions on cleaning oily birds. (See note 8 on p. 215.)

### Notes

1. One of the best discussions of possible mercury hazards is in Peter and Katherine Montague, "Mercury: How Much Are We Eating?" *Saturday Review,* (Feb. 6, 1971), pp. 50–55.
2. For an evocative, although sometimes inaccurate, defense of King Neptune, see Wesley Marx, *The Frail Ocean* (New York: Ballantine, 1969).
3. See Tom Brown, *Oil on Ice* (San Francisco: Sierra Club, 1971); Ron Moxness, "The Long Pipe," *Environment,* **12**:12–23, 36 (1970); and Charles Cicchetti, "The Wrong Route," *Environment,* **15**:4–13 (1973).

4. H. Hays and R. W. Risebrough, "The Early Warning of the Terns," *Natural History,* **80**:38–47 (1971).
5. J. Fisher and S. Charlton, "A Tragedy of Errors," *Audubon,* **69**:72–85 (1968).
6. C. Steinhart and J. Steinhart, *Blowout* (North Scituate, Mass.: Duxbury, and Belmont, Calif.: Wadsworth, 1971) p. 37.
7. "Oil's Aftermath," *Time,* (March 1, 1971), p. 37.
8. Further information can be obtained from a biology instructor at Framingham (Massachusetts) State College who has, since 1968, concentrated on the treatment of oil-soaked birds: Philip B. Stanton, Wildlife Rehabilitation Center, Grove Street, Upton, Massachusetts 01568.

## Summary of Part III

Vast though the water world may be, the impact of man and technology on aquatic ecosystems is becoming increasingly apparent. We are intercepting larger and larger portions of the finite fresh-water runoff, using it in hydroelectric facilities; then loading it with silt, salts, fertilizers from irrigated soils; and wastes from homes and industries. In addition, our need for energy has placed stress on aquatic organisms as a result of thermal plumes and oil spills. Radioactivity concentrating in aquatic organisms is another problem related to energy demands because nuclear power plants and related facilities can be sources of radioactive isotopes, dumped or leaked into the aquatic environment.

Many of the interactions between human activities and natural ecosystems are most obvious in the coastal zone, especially where we have residential or recreational concentrations. The development of a high protein aquaculture in estuaries and the preservation of habitats vital to fish and wildlife are hampered by contamination, land filling, and other consequences of overcrowding. Human population growth also has increased the frequency of problems related to water extremes. Expansion into arid regions (for example, sub-Saharan Africa) has set the stage for famine during a prolonged drought, while residential and industrial expansion into flood plains (for example, the Mississippi Valley) has created greater vulnerability to spring floods.

Ecologists studying fresh-water, estuarine, and marine ecosystems are compiling mounting evidence that human activities are the factors limiting the growth of aquatic populations. Perhaps our need for fresh and clean water will, in turn, limit both population growth and urban concentration, thus protecting aquatic ecosystems from further stresses.

# IV

# 19

# Urban Ecosystems

## Key Concepts

Urban ecosystem
Input-output analysis
Interdependence
Metropolitan agglomeration
Mid-city
Accumulation
Population density
Impact of a city
Waste management
Rural support
Collective watershed

Some ecologists and many urban experts argue that there is no such thing as an *urban ecosystem*.[1] They point out that natural ecosystems evolve as combinations of living organisms uniquely determined by climatic, edaphic (soil), and other physical-chemical factors. In natural ecosystems, many processes contribute to the transfer of energy and the continuation of biogeochemical cycling. Organisms that achieve excessive density in a natural ecosystem do so at the peril of exhausting finite requisites or increasing their vulnerability to other organisms. If, perchance, space, food, or some other requisites are underutilized, opportunistic organisms will exploit them over a short ecological time span or a long evolutionary period. In short, "Nature abhors a vacuum" but it's not too keen about crowding either.

Contrast a natural ecosystem (diverse organisms governed by a painfully evolved system of checks and balances) with an urban ecosystem (machines, roads, buildings, lawns, and parks dominated by one organism—man). If a slum is destroyed by fire, there is no reason to expect an invasion of log cabins—representing a temporary reversion to the city's earliest successional stage. Instead, any development is determined by a combination of politics and economics. There are pressures to use the space, but these are generated by the need to earn income and pay interest or taxes not by the availability of nutrients and sunlight. Furthermore, the patterns of competition within the city are quite different from those in the forest. Businesses may displace other businesses, one ethnic group may supplant another, but there are no examples of a different species shoving man out of his urban niche, and this will continue to be highly improbable (unless rats get very well organized).

## INPUT AND OUTPUT

After all these caveats, why have a chapter about urban ecosystems? Simply because the ecosystem concept provides a good framework for *input-output analysis*. If all the water, energy, and other resources brought into a city are measured, this gives some indication of the city's dependence on other ecosystems. Output measurements of combustion products, sewage, and solids provide some basis for estimating the degree to which the city environment has become overloaded with waste. For certain geographic or economic subunits within a city, input-output analysis also can be used to identify relationships and determine responsibility. The diagram in Figure 19–1 shows how this might be done.

It is also possible to examine input-output rates for a school or a home.[2] These studies, which do not have to be detailed or expensive, can serve to stress a recurring theme of ecology: *interdependence*. Very few units in a modern society, with the possible exception of the remaining family farms, approach self-sufficiency. We need others to provide essential goods and services, but often we fail to recognize this simple fact until the power goes out or the garbage men go on strike.

Returning to the urban level, an example with some representative statistics might be useful. Consider a city together with the suburbs surrounding it as a unit, a *metropolitan agglomeration* in the census takers' jargon. In the United States, a typical urban area might cover 230 square miles and be inhabited by 1,200,000 people. This is difficult to visualize. However, if you have ever visited one of the following cities:

| | |
|---|---|
| Atlanta | Indianapolis |
| Buffalo | Miami |
| Cincinnati | New Orleans |
| Dallas | San Diego |
| Denver | Seattle |

**Figure 19–1.**
*Urban ecosystem model*

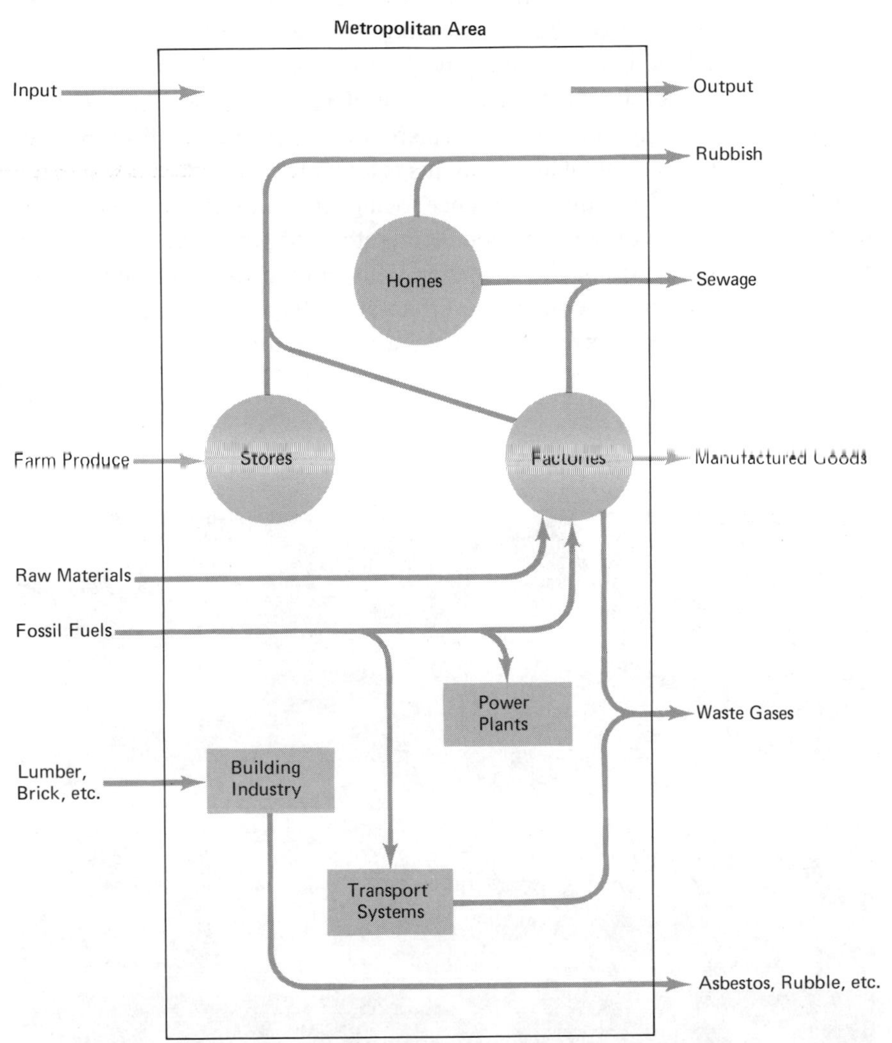


(simplified by omission of water, electricity, and merchandise distribution)

you have been in the midst of such an "agglomeration" (Figure 19–2). For convenience, let us call an urban area in this general size category *Mid-City* and proceed to make some estimates of the resources consumed and materials (especially waste) produced each day.[3] Focusing on one day makes the numbers easier to grasp and they remain impressive without being overwhelming. As you will see in Chapter 21, certain conditions can lead to the *accumulation* of air pollutants in a period of three or more days. This addition of daily emissions creates most air-pollution alerts. Another form of intensification can be recognized best when Mid-City is compared to Manhattan Island in New York City. Because the *population density* on that haven of skyscrapers is forty times that of Mid-City, the concentration of sewage or trash (in tons per acre) is also forty times greater. Fortunately, the per capita production of air pollutants is lower for New Yorkers than for residents of Mid-City, this difference being attributable to reliance on subways and to strict regulations on incinerator and power plant emissions in New York City. Although population density (and the concentration of certain pollutants) may be higher in urban areas larger than Mid-City, the converse is not necessarily true. Even towns of ten thousand to thirty

**Figure 19–2.**
*Typical city* (HUD photo)

**TABLE 19–1. A Day in Mid-City***

| Consumption (Input, tons per day) | | Production (Output, tons per day) | |
|---|---|---|---|
| water | 800,000 | feces | 300 |
| drinking water | 2,700 | sewage | 600,000 |
| coal and oil (½ used for production of 22 million kwh electricity) | 6,000 | | |
| gasoline | 2,400 | carbon monoxide | 600 |
| food | 1,700 | nitrogen oxides | 160 |
| paper | 840 | sulfur dioxide | 230 |
| plastic | 100 | hydrocarbons | 250 |
| steel | 2,500 | particulates | 100 |
| aluminum | 80 | total air pollutants | 1,340 |
| | | solid waste | 2,400 |

Concentration (8 people per acre)

| | |
|---|---|
| sewage | 4 tons |
| air pollutants | 20 pounds |
| solid waste (including 6 cans and 3 bottles) | 32 pounds |

*Many of these estimates are simply annual United States figures divided by 60,000.

thousand may have population densities similar to the 8 per acre characteristic of Mid-City. However, small towns surrounded by open areas often can dump pollutants quite easily (too easily perhaps), whereas the citizens of Mid-City must build and maintain elaborate systems for the collection, transportation, treatment, and disposal of waste (see Chapters 20 and 23 and Figure 19–3).

What else can be concluded from the numbers shown in Table 19–1? Mid-City is taking in, and contaminating, huge quantities of water. Very little of this is used for drinking, but the other uses (as shown in Chapter 15) are also essential—although not always handled as efficiently as they might be. The weights of other inputs are much less than that of water, yet they are clearly related to the production of air pollutants and solid waste. It would be interesting to know just how efficiently fuels are converted to

**Figure 19–3.**
*City scenes* (HUD photos)

**Figure 19–3.** *(Continued)*

useful work, and raw materials into finished products, in Mid-City. These processes may be only 30 to 40 percent efficient, leaving much room for improvement. Ultimately, of course, the potential energy within fuel must be released into the environment to warm water (Chapter 17) or air (Chapter 21); however, before release, we must get as much use from it as we possibly can (Figure 19–4).

## RELATIONSHIPS WITH OTHER ECOSYSTEMS

The *impact of a city* on its environs takes many forms. Some are obvious: for example, bulldozing rolling terrain to create a parking lot for a shopping center. Others are more subtle: dumping wastes that exceed the biodegrading capability of the ecosystems. This category is of particular

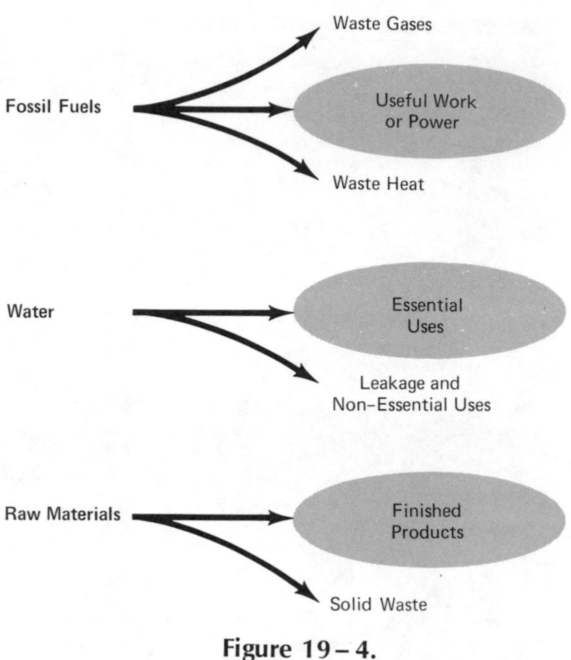


**Figure 19–4.**
*Urban inefficiencies*

interest to ecologists because they have become involved increasingly in problems of *waste management*. Some materials, especially glass, aluminum, and plastic, do not break down rapidly when exposed to normal ranges of temperature and moisture. Unfortunately, heavy metals (lead and mercury) and certain synthetic organic chemicals (such as PCB) are also quite stable and may remain hazardous to man and beast long after they are dumped. There are still other materials that can be broken down by organisms of decay if these organisms are present and sufficiently abundant. For example, tissue paper dropped in a forest will be processed by detritivores that normally work on leaves, but similar paper dumped into a pond may rot quite slowly if few organisms accustomed to eating cellulose are present. That aquatic ecosystems often are overloaded near cities is hardly surprising when one remembers the huge volume of sewage with its high concentration of nutrients.

The other major set of relationships between an urban ecosystem and other ecosystems might well be described as *rural support*. This includes the farms supplying cotton, grain, vegetables, and fruits; the ranches producing cattle; and the forests yielding pulp and lumber. If all of these areas are not overexploited, but are managed on the basis of sustained yield, there should be no degradation attributable to the needs of those dwelling in Mid-City. However, there will be inevitable modification of the natural ecosystems and continued dependence on those created by our favoring certain productive species (for example, conifers, corn, alfalfa, and domestic animals). The largest component of the rural-support system is the *collective watershed,* those portions of the landscape that provide not only the water moved from reservoirs or aquifers into the city but also the water needed to maintain productive pastures, crops, and forests. In arid parts of the United States, this may amount to an aggregate three hundred times greater than the area of Mid-City itself. You can build a city in a desert, but such a city remains completely dependent on produce from wetter areas (Figure 19–5).

The urban-ecosystem concept may be useful to those who are planning the growth or placement of cities.[4] Cities, when considered at the same abstraction level (see Chapter 2) as forests and lakes, can be seen to have definite physical, chemical, and biological needs, as well as impacts or

**Figure 19–5.**
*Collective watershed supporting a city*

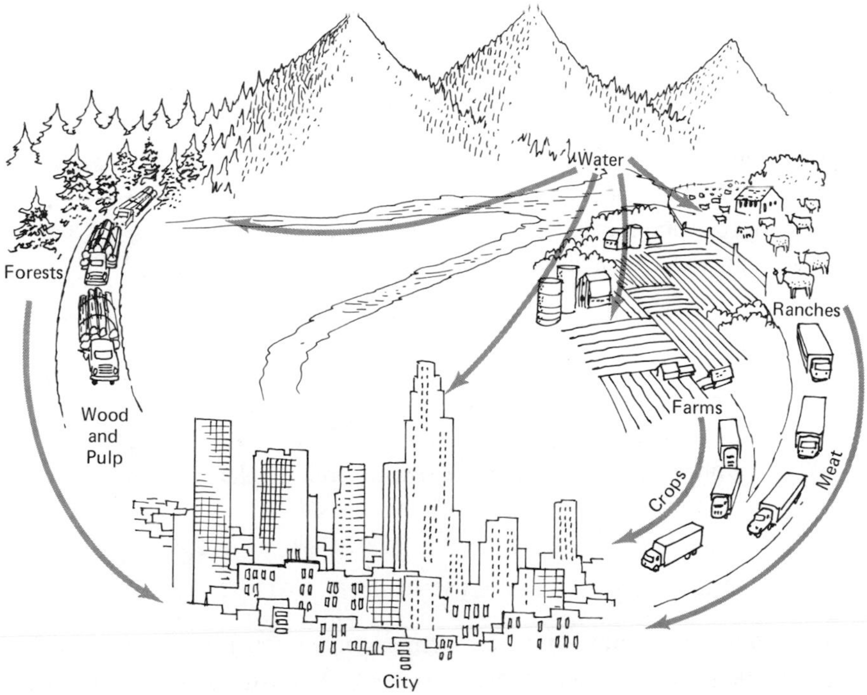

effects. Wise planning includes constraints on urban growth whenever and wherever environmental costs seem too high. Happily, political support for such decisions is becoming stronger and stronger as citizens turn from the philosophy of the Chamber of Commerce to that espoused by a local chapter of Zero Population Growth (ZPG). Furthermore, there are many ways in which cities can be made more self-reliant; for example, chemicals and other resources can be recycled very much as the forest ecosystem taps the nutrients released by a decaying log. It may even be possible for an urban area to reduce its dependence on fossil fuels and make more use of solar energy, not through photosynthesis but through roof-top units well suited to ranch houses in sprawling suburbs (see the discussion of energy alternatives in Chapter 23). A combination of constraints on growth and encouragement of self-sufficiency may bring cities closer to the urban-ecosystem concept.

## SUMMARY

The ecosystem concept can, with some stretching, be applied to urban areas. It is especially useful in assessing the dependence of cities on inputs from distant rural support areas and the impact of urban waste outputs on natural ecosystems nearby. Daily consumption and pollution figures for a middle-sized American city (Mid-City) show the relative quantities involved. Water is the largest input and sewage the largest output, but fossil fuel-air pollutant quantities are also impressive. It is important to remember that urban ecosystems differ greatly from natural ecosystems both in energy sources and the degree of chemical recycling, but there are possibilities that cities can be made more "natural" in both respects.

### Discussion Questions

1. If you live in an urban area, can you see ways in which your city (a) resembles a natural ecosystem or (b) differs from a natural ecosystem?
2. Where would you (if you had the responsibility) place a new city?
3. How can cities be made more self-contained?

### Suggested Projects

1. For your home community (or some smaller unit) estimate the daily inputs of food, fuel, and water and outputs of waste. (Local government

agencies and environmental groups *may* be able to help you get this information.)

**2.** Find out the size and population density of your home community and any numerical changes that have occurred in recent decades.

## Notes

1. This argument has been presented strongly by some of my former colleagues at the University of Virginia.
2. Mark Terry, *Teaching for Survival* (New York: Ballantine, 1971), shows the pedagogic value of simple input-output analysis at levels relevant to the experience of students.
3. These estimates are similar to those made independently by Abel Wolman, "The Metabolism of Cities," *Scientific American,* **213**:179–89 (1965), for a hypothetical city in the United States whose population is one million.
4. In 1973, the Institute of Ecology sponsored a workshop on urban ecosystems, bringing together specialists from many disciplines, and producing a summary report, Forrest W. Stearns and Tom Montag (eds.) *The Urban Ecosystem: A Holistic Approach* (Stroudsburg, Pennsylvania: Dowden, Hutchinson and Ross, 1974).

# 20

# Sewage and Detergents

## Key Concepts

- Pure water
- Water-borne disease
- Organic compounds
- Inorganic load
- Primary, secondary, and tertiary treatments
- Trickling filter
- Activated sludge
- Anaerobic digester
- Chlorination of final effluent
- Dissolved oxygen (DO)
- Biological oxygen demand (BOD)
- Detergents
- Biodegradable material

The most paradoxical fact about sewage is that it contains 99.9 percent *pure water* with the other 0.1 percent of contaminants causing a lot of trouble. The danger that pathogenic organisms in sewage will end up in drinking water still governs most decisions about the treatment and disposal of sewage, and there is no denying the reality of such dangers. In some parts of the world, *water-borne disease* accounts for a high proportion of the deaths and disabilities that afflict both indigene and tourist. Cholera, dysentery, typhoid, and hepatitis are but a few of the many diseases that can be acquired by inadvertently drinking water contaminated by untreated human waste.

Is it then permissible to release into a convenient waterway sewage that has been disinfected thoroughly? No. That 0.1 percent contains troublesome material other than pathogens. There are also suspended and dissolved *organic (carbon) compounds*. These include not only the derivatives of feces and toilet paper, but also, in many communities, "disposall" grindings and gutter washings.[1] Furthermore, waste water is burdened with an *inorganic load.* As with the organic compounds, some of this is in solution (dissolved nutrients, salts, and so on) and the rest is suspended particulate material (silt and fine sand) that is washed into the sewers through cracks and gutter drains then is carried along to the outfall or sewage treatment plant.

## SEWAGE TREATMENT

You will notice that the options are outfall or the sewage treatment plant. In the United States, the sewage from thirteen million people, most of them living in coastal cities, such as New York, is dumped untreated.[2] Another thirty-three million are served by systems that have only *primary treatment:* that is, some of the suspended inorganic and organic material is removed. They could add *secondary treatment* (the breaking down or trapping of even more of the organic material), and thus catch up with the eighty million Americans served by municipal systems that at least attempt primary and secondary treatment of sewage. A surprisingly large number, at least seventy million, must still rely on cesspools, septic tanks, or other back-yard facilities, often because sewer hookups are not available.[3] Very few communities have *tertiary treatment,* facilities capable of removing dissolved nutrients before the effluent is released.

A sewer tour may not sound like much fun, but it is one way to understand how the system is supposed to work. Most cities have combined networks that carry waste water from homes, stores, and certain industries as well as the water running off streets after a storm. Wherever possible, sewers are kept ventilated because oxygen must be available for the microorganisms that break down waste into $CO_2$, $H_2O$, and dissolved nutrients. If the oxygen is not available, other organisms of decay, which do not need it, take over the breakdown job. The end products of their efforts include methane (explosive "sewer gas"), $H_2S$ (hydrogen sulfide which smells like rotten eggs), and $H_2SO_4$ (sulfuric acid, which corrodes the walls of the sewers). In situations where ventilation is not possible, it may be necessary to use more expensive corrosion-resistant, gas-tight pipes (Figure 20–1).

Treatment of sewage mainly depends on physical and biological processes, although chemical treatments are becoming increasingly important. The first material removed at a sewage treatment plant (hereafter called STP) is the suspended sand that is trapped in a grit chamber. Screens also

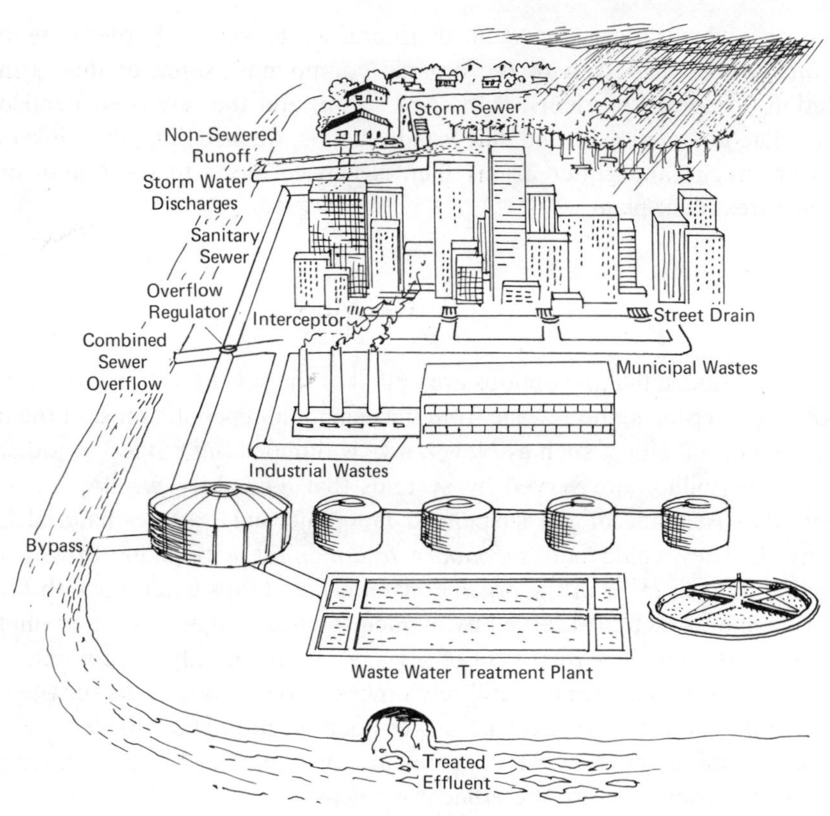


**Figure 20–1.**
*Sewerage system*

are used to intercept large floating objects. If they are not removed, such coarse materials can damage the pumps that keep the waste water moving through the plant. After a period in a settling tank where fatty scum is skimmed off the top and settled sludge is pumped out the bottom, the sewage is aerated. Since their introduction during the 1890s, large rotating booms have sprinkled sewage on a filter made of rock layers *(trickling filters)*. Now, however, oxygen can be provided more directly by pumping air into the bottom of a tank. This so-called *activated-sludge* method requires less space and can be used to increase the efficiency of a plant. If, after initial screening and settling, the waste water is pumped through a cycle of settling and aeration, it is said to have received secondary treatment and up to 95 percent of the suspended material should have been removed. Tertiary treatment is not more of the same but involves precipitation, or other extractive techniques, to remove dissolved nutrients.[4]

a

b

**Figure 20–2.**
*Sewage treatment plants* **a.** *setting tank* [E.P.A-Documerica (Belinda Rain)]
**b.** *trickling filter* (E.P.A.)

As in the sewer environment, different microorganisms work at the STP. Those that need oxygen function most effectively in the upper portions of the trickling filter or in the oxygenated zones of sludge. An entire ecosystem may be present because the steady supply of food and water supports a community of bacteria, fungi, algae, snails, worms, and flies. Those bacteria and yeasts that do not need oxygen are seeded in large tanks known as *anaerobic digesters*. The scum and sludge from other parts of the plant are pumped into the digesters, temperatures are maintained near 95° F., and methane is produced in sufficient quantities to be a source of heat for drying the final residue. After aeration and digestion, much of the organic material originally present in the sewage has been reduced to $CO_2$ or methane ($CH_4$) but some is left. This must be dried and, like the sand from the grit chamber, hauled away. Odorless and germ free, the dried sludge is useful as a soil conditioner, although it is low in nutrients and really cannot be described as a fertilizer.

What are the main accomplishments of primary and secondary treatment? The organic material present in raw sewage is largely removed, and most pathogens are killed. Just to make sure, the effluent leaving a STP is *chlorinated,* a parting shot at any pathogen still present. (Of course, chlorination is also used as part of the treatment in a municipal water supply to kill bacteria from any source.) These accomplishments are important, but they depend on the continuous, normal operation of the STP. Many things can go wrong. A sudden dose of toxic oils or other chemicals may kill organisms in the trickling filter, or cold weather may greatly reduce their efficiency. Or, the organisms in the anaerobic digester may die out, requiring quick readjustment and restocking. Overloading is the most common problem and comes in two forms: organic excess and storm runoff. Many plants simply were not designed to cope with the amounts of sewage they are now expected to treat. City authorities may find themselves caught in a very nasty situation with no money for upgrading the STP and a court order from the Environmental Protection Agency (EPA) or the state water-control board stating that the facilities must be improved. Coping with sudden surges of storm water, often the result of increased urban paving since the plant was constructed, also has legal aspects: the higher authorities object to the common practice of bypassing the STP and dumping raw sewage during periods of high flow!

## EFFECTS OF SEWAGE

Assuming we have a healthy population and no real danger of waterborne infections, why is there still great concern among ecologists (and others) about the inadequacy of sewage treatment? Essentially, it is a problem of oxygen availability. Water temperature and turbulence determine how fast oxygen can move from the atmosphere into the water. *Dissolved oxygen* (DO) in the water is used by all those aquatic organisms, from microbes to trout, that metabolize their food into $CO_2$, $H_2O$, and various small nitrogenous compounds. There is, however, just so much oxygen to go around, and an organic overload creates a desperate situation for organisms with high oxygen requirements: raw sewage teems with bacteria that feast, multiply, and use up the oxygen in the water more rapidly than it can be replaced. This, in short, is the *biological oxygen demand* (BOD), although the term is used in a more technical sense as a measure of the organic concentration in waste water. A fish, under those circumstances, suffocates because, no matter how fast it swims, it cannot get enough dissolved oxygen from the water through its gills into its blood stream. This is one cause of fish kills near sewer outfalls (Figure 20–3). Ironically, the chlorine used as a final treatment of sewage also can cause fish kills, especially when there is a malfunction in the gadget that is supposed to regulate the rate of chlorination. It has been suggested that ozone ($O_3$) bubbled through the effluent would do a safe job of disinfection, but that could add to the ozone already present in polluted air. Unless we could be sure all the ozone would combine with the organic material in the effluent, creating nontoxic compounds, it would not represent much of an improvement over the chlorination procedure.[5]

Even if the effluent is virtually free from organic material, after going through efficient primary and secondary treatment, and even if it does not contain toxic concentrations of chlorine, it still can cause problems. In many ways, these are similar to the effects of fertilizer runoff mentioned in Chapter 9, because the effluent from an STP is rich in dissolved nutrients, particularly nitrates and phosphates, and includes the unassimilated portions of such things as vitamin pills![6] Unless these are intercepted and removed by tertiary treatment, they will nourish aquatic vegetation. This is most spectacular when the effluent is dumped into an oligotrophic (nutrient poor) lake; it is much less noticeable, if it occurs at all, when the outfall is located on an estuary, already heavily laden with nutrients from other sources. In certain lakes, the waste nutrients foster the growth of blue-green algae, which fix dissolved atmospheric nitrogen into nitrates; and when these algae die, the original and additional nutrients are released, contributing to still larger algal blooms. It is the death of the algae, occurring when they run out of light or an essential nutrient, that creates a stressful situation not unlike that caused by dumping raw sewage. Bacteria, fungi, and other organisms feed on the dead algae (and on each other),

**Figure 20–3.**
*Fish kill* (Courtesy E.P.A.-Documerica)

using up the dissolved oxygen, and jeopardize fish, mayflies, and so on. The same old high BOD, low DO story! Obviously, primary and secondary treatment, without nutrient removal, may simply postpone the problem of organic overloading, rather than solving it. To protect the quality of certain fresh-water ecosystems, tertiary treatment, expensive though it is, may be necessary.

## THE DETERGENT STORY

This would seem to be the appropriate point to consider the tangled tale of detergents. It is an excellent example of runaway technology, and it also illustrates the basic problem of trading off environmental degradation for human safety or convenience.

Once upon a time, soap was the universal cleansing agent. It worked reasonably well in soft water (low in dissolved minerals), with the fat molecules (sodium sterate) combining with the dirt particles and lifting them into suspension. Usually several rinses were needed to get the laundry free from the residues. Furthermore, hard water caused problems when the mineral salts combined with the dirty soap to precipitate as a gray scum. "Spinning tub" washers made a bad situation worse, driving the scum back into the fabric being washed—hence, "tattletale gray." The water could be demineralized with various systems or softened by adding washing soda, but most housewives were delighted when *detergents* arrived on the supermarket shelves in the early 1950s. Here was one product with both a surfactant (to remove the dirt) and a sequestrant (phosphates to keep the dissolved minerals from scumming things up). Not long after, trickling filters at STPs started foaming (Figure 20–4). Sometimes even a glass of water out of the tap had a head on it. It turned out that the surfactant, alkyl benzene sulfonate (ABS), was not readily *biodegradable* and persisted in the waterways long after it left the washing machine. Chemists quickly solved that problem by substituting with linear alkylate sulfonate (LAS), which does break down after it has done its job.[7]

As you know, that was not the end of the story. It turned out that 65 percent of the phosphate in sewage could be traced back to "washday miracles." Furthermore, certain rivers and lakes were being fouled by algal "blooms and die-offs" on a larger scale than ever before. Was there a connection? The detergent industry would like us to believe that the evidence is only circumstantial, arguing that many other nutrients can cause the excessive growth of aquatic vegetation. Their spokesmen stress the safety and effectiveness of their products, stating that any substitute would be too alkaline to leave within the reach of small children.[8] The EPA has agreed, one official being quoted as saying: "When you weigh the death of a child against the possible death of a lake, there's no choice. The human health factor has to outweigh any environmental damage."[9]

Fortunately, a number of options remain open. If we are willing to spend the money, tertiary treatment will remove detergent phosphates as well as

**Figure 20 – 4.**
*Detergent foam at S.T.P.* [Courtesy E.P.A.-Documerica (Bruce McAllister)]

other nutrients that might contribute to the problems of galloping eutrophication. Also, the percentage of phosphate in detergents can be reduced greatly.[10] A product with 8.7 percent phosphate should be able to provide clean laundry in all but the hardest water. Some cities, some counties, and even some states (Connecticut, Indiana, and New York) are barring phosphates completely, but that may be both unconstitutional and unnecessary.[11] One thing is certain: the detergent story has shown quite clearly that technological progress can have ecological repercussions.[12]

## SUMMARY

Because water contaminated with 0.1 percent wastes is the largest output of a city, sewage treatment is a large, complex, and expensive business. An ideal sewage treatment plant should destroy any pathogens that might threaten human health, and it also should remove any suspended or dissolved material potentially dangerous to fish and other aquatic organisms. Suspended organic and inorganic particles can be removed by primary and secondary treatment, but tertiary treatment is required in situations where the removal of dissolved nutrients is essential. Detergents have caused further complications in sewage treatment because they have added foam, and then phosphates to sewage and to the waterways that receive the outfall of sewage treatment plants.

### Discussion Questions

1. Why is sewage such a problem?
2. What advantages accrue from the separation of storm sewers (carrying gutter runoff) from sanitary sewers (carrying other contaminated water)?
3. How can a community justify the cost of new or improved sewage treatment facilities?
4. Was the flush toilet such a good idea after all?

### Suggested Projects

1. Visit a sewage treatment plant and make a diagram of the process.
2. If you have the facilities and the competence, do a microbiological survey, culturing organisms from (a) tap water, (b) waste water, and (c) other water sources.
3. Do a class survey in order to find out which detergent brand is being used in each house for clothes washing and the percentage of phosphate it contains.

**Notes**

1. M. A. Benarde, *Our Precarious Habitat,* rev. ed., (New York: Norton 1973), pp. 130–147, deals with "sanitary sewage."
2. Some steps are being taken to treat part of the 400 million gallons now dumped untreated each day into the Hudson River by New York City. See E. Hudson, "City's Largest Sewage Plant Is Going up on the Hudson," *New York Times,* 2 September 1972.
3. "L. I. Sewers Called Vital to Protect Water Supply," *New York Times,* 4 January 1972.
4. A good, but technical, discussion can be found in L. M. Cooke, ed., *Cleaning Our Environment: The Chemical Basis for Action* (Washington, D.C.: American Chemical Society, 1969.)
5. D. Henninger, "Chlorine Kills Water Germs, But Fish Die Too. Is Ozone Better and Safer?" *New York Times,* 1972.
6. In London, seepage from sewers into drinking water supplies put "every man, woman and child . . . on the pill" (that is, on low concentrations of Enovid and related birth-control compounds). See p. 5 *Medical World News,* (July 17, 1970).
7. A good summary of the detergent story is that prepared by B. Rensberger, "Detergents: Series of Health Controversies," *New York Times,* 18 September 1971.
8. H. J. Morgens, *Phosphates in Detergents (A Case History of How Confusion and Misunderstanding Can Sweep the Country)* (Cincinnatti: Proctor & Gamble Co., 1971) 12pp.
9. "Return of the Phosphates," *Time,* (Sept. 27, 1971), p. 90.
10. "P & G Cites Effort to Curb Phosphates," *New York Times,* 10 October 1972.
11. "Phosphates Stir Dispute in Akron," *New York Times,* 23 January 1973.
12. If you really want to go to the roots of the controversy, see *Phosphates in Detergents and the Eutrophication of America's Waters* (Washington, D.C.: U.S. Govt. Printing Office, 1970), 318 pp. This publication is the hearings of the Conservation and Natural Resources Subcommittee of the congressional House Committee on Government Operations, December 15 and 16, 1969.

# 21

# Concentrated Combustion

## Key Concepts

Concentrated combustion
Toxic gases
Photochemical products
Particulates
Air pollution
Moving sources
Stationary sources
Inversion
Stagnation
Heat island
Dust dome
Global climatic fluctuations
Lines of defense
Effects on health

As shown in Chapter 12, "Sources of Energy," our patterns of energy extraction, movement, and conversion are closely related to many problems of human health and environmental quality. This can be demonstrated most clearly in cities where the aggregation of people and their machines has created the situation to be described in this chapter as *concentrated combustion*. This phrase emphasizes the simple fact that urban environments, and human lungs, are burdened with the unburnt or partially oxidized fragments of the fossil fuels we use. If oil and coal consisted only of pure carbon and if they were burned in an atmosphere of pure oxygen, the output would consist entirely of heat and $CO_2$ without the production of *toxic gases*. To the delight of the chemically-minded (and to the dismay of others), the reactions can be far more complex (Figure 21–1).[1] Some of the carbon is partially oxidized to carbon monoxide, and some enters the atmosphere as unburnt hydrocarbon fragments. Similar processes can release the sulfur contaminating many forms of fuel oil and coal. However, there are important reactions that do not directly involve the fossil fuels. At

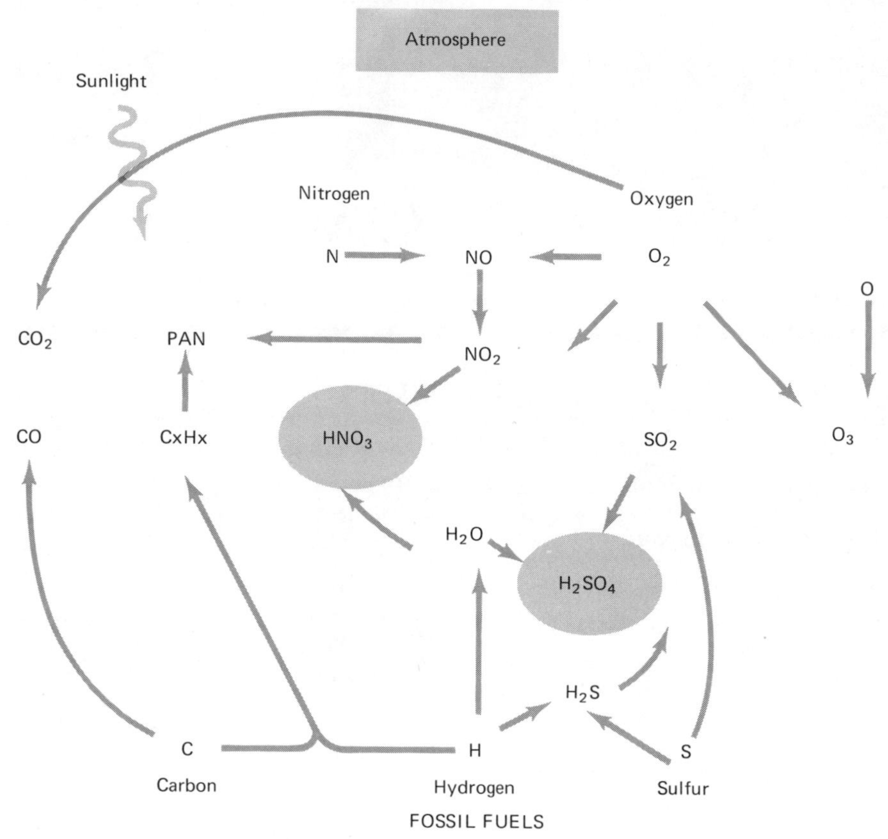


**Figure 21–1.**
*Chemical reactions creating air pollution*

high temperatures, such as those found inside the cylinder of an automobile engine, nitrogen may be oxidized to nitric oxide and then, after it leaves the exhaust, to nitrogen dioxide. In the presence of sunlight and hydrocarbon fragments, further reactions, known to be photochemical but still poorly understood, can lead to the creation of compounds such as peroxyacetyl nitrate (PAN), one of the "active ingredients" of smog. Other *photochemical products* in smog or "smaze" include ozone and aldehydes. Even droplets of water can become involved, with the result that raindrops may be dilute nitric ($HNO_3$) or sulfuric acid ($H_2SO_4$). One final category, not represented in Figure 21–1, is the catchall known as *particulates*. This includes air-borne dust (particles more than 1 micron in diameter) and smoke (generally smaller particles). Some are unburnt carbon (soot); others are the mineral residues of burnt coal (fly ash); and still others may not be combustion products at all. That latter subcategory could include asbestos fibrils (from automobile brake linings, building insulation, and the like), silica or carbonate compounds (dust blown up from bulldozed areas or farm fields), and all kinds of natural organic material (pollen, leaf fragments, and so on).

## SOURCES OF AIR POLLUTANTS

Just where in an urban area do you find the sources of all these gases and particles? You don't have to look far to find the major culprit; it's parked right outside. There are now approximately 120 million motor vehicles in the United States burning nearly 100 billion gallons of fuel each year. That works out at 11 million gallons per hour, giving you some idea of both the supply problem and the large contribution made to *air pollution* by automobiles. Other *moving sources,* airplanes, gulp 15 billion gallons of fuel (mostly lead-free kerosene) each year, but they burn it more efficiently, so their addition to air pollution is one twenty-fifth that made by ground vehicles. Automobiles are especially important as producers of carbon monoxide and also are responsible for large portions of the nitrogen oxides and hydrocarbons entering the atmosphere.[2]

*Stationary sources* of pollution include power plants, factories, incinerators, and, in fact, any building with a smokestack or a chimney. Collectively, these are the main emitters of particulates. In areas where they are permitted to burn sulfur-laden coal or oil, stationary sources, especially power plants, are also the major producers of sulfur dioxide ($SO_2$), as shown by recent estimates of air-pollutant emissions presented in Table 21–1. These numbers, although informative, should be used with some caution because they represent the national situation and each community must breathe its own particular mix of air pollutants. For example, industrial sources would be important in Gary, Indiana, but in Washington, D.C., stalled traffic would overshadow all other sources. Furthermore, weight may not be the best measure of air pollutants. Perhaps consideration should be given to the time elapsed before the pollutant is chemically transformed to a less hazardous molecule ($CO \rightarrow CO_2$) or to a more dangerous one ($SO_2 \rightarrow H_2SO_4$). Detroit would certainly be quite happy if it could be shown that carbon monoxide is oxidized to carbon dioxide so quickly that the dangers of accumulation are much less than we now fear they are.

Accumulation, or build-up, of air pollution is a very real concern. Most

**TABLE 21–1. Sources of Air Pollutants in the United States, 1970 (in millions of tons)***

| | Transportation | Power Plants | Industry | Totals |
|---|---|---|---|---|
| Carbon Monoxide (CO) | 111 | <1 | 12 | 147 |
| Hydrocarbons ($H_xC_x$) | 20 | <1 | 6 | 35 |
| Nitrogen oxides ($NO_x$) | 12 | 10 | <1 | 23 |
| Sulfur dioxide ($SO_2$) | 1 | 27 | 6 | 34 |
| Particulates | <1 | 7 | 13 | 25 |
| Total | 144 | 35 | 37 | 264† |

*Adapted from "Environmental Quality," 3rd Annual Report of the Council on Environmental Quality (Washington, D.C.: U.S. Govt. Printing Office, August 1972), p. 6.
†Includes some pollutants from space heating, incinerators, and burning dumps.

of the time we have been able to get away with atmospheric dumping. Wind blows away toxic gases; rain washes them out of the air.[3] However, a meteorological phenomenon known as an *inversion* occasionally reminds us what we are doing. A layer of warm air over a layer of cool air traps the products of combustion. This is most serious in areas where a city is located in a natural basin (for example, Los Angeles or Denver) or in a valley (for example, Donora, Pennsylvania), but a sluggish air mass may cover all the eastern seaboard states. When the period of *stagnation* lasts more than a few days, we have the makings of a national emergency[4] (Figure 21–2).

**Figure 21–2.**
*Inversion formation and break-up*

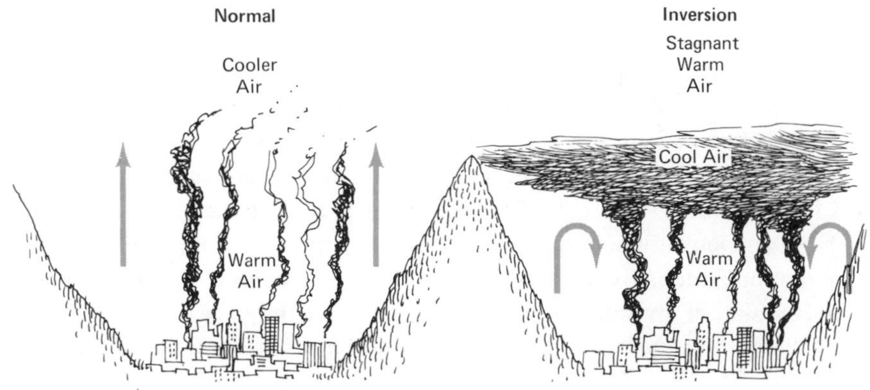

## EFFECTS ON CLIMATE

Before we consider the relationships between air pollution and human sickness, it might be a good idea to examine the effects of pollution on climate. These can be seen most clearly if we contrast urban weather with that observed in the surrounding countryside. From the viewpoint of a meteorologist, a city can be described as a *heat island* covered by a *dust dome*. These phenomena are interrelated and they, in turn, cause most of the town–country differences in humidity and precipitation (Figure 21–3).

The urban heat island is created by a combination of trapped solar energy and thermal pollution from energy conversion processes. (Generally, the waste heat is less important than the solar component, but during winter in a northern city, they may approach parity.) Asphalt "hot enough to fry an egg," walls and windows leaking heat, tall buildings blocking breezes, and air conditioners dumping water and heat on those passing by all symptomize the heat island. The urban temperature averages 1.0 to 1.5° F. higher, and may be 10 to 15° F. higher, than rural temperatures. The city has 14 percent fewer snow days and a frost-free period three to four weeks longer than that in rural areas. The relative humidity is, on the average, 6 percent lower. Finally, the hot air rising from urban areas carries with it the tons of particulate material that form the dust dome that is held over the city by surrounding cool air.

The dust screens out some of the solar ultraviolet, with the result that city dwellers receive 5 percent less ultraviolet during the summer and 30

**Figure 21–3.**

*Unique aspects of the urban climate-heat island and dust dome*

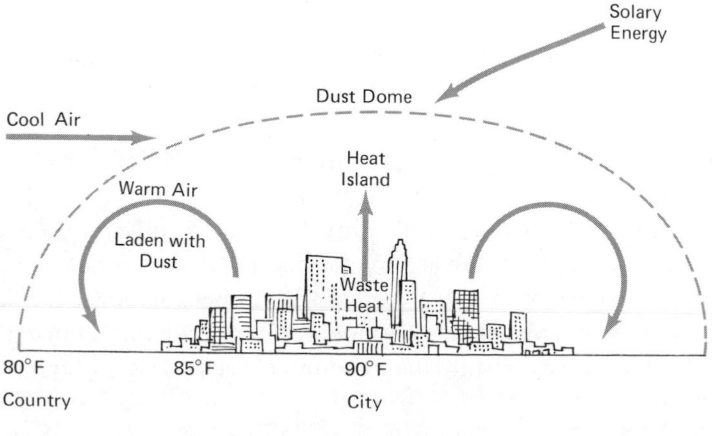

percent less during the winter. With dust particles serving as condensation nuclei, the city gets 10 percent more rainfall. You might think that would help cool things off a bit, but actually the water runs down into the storm sewers and there is little evaporative cooling. There is, however, more fog in cities, 30 percent more in summer and 100 percent more in winter, again because the dust encourages condensation. Fortunately, the fogs that once brought London to a standstill are no longer a problem there now that natural gas has generally replaced soft coal. The dust dome is, of course, a dynamic entity, particles washed down by rain or blown away by strong winds being replaced by emissions from fixed and moving sources in the city.[5]

Many of the same climatic phenomena seen in the urban environment may be at work on a global scale, but it is much more difficult to separate the effects of human activity from a tangle of natural fluctuations.[6] Let's start with the facts and then talk about where opinions begin.

*Fact 1:* There were *global climatic fluctuations* long before the advent of man and his technology. (During an ice age, average temperatures were approximately 11° F. lower than they are now.)

*Fact 2:* World temperatures drop after massive volcanic eruptions spew particulate matter high into the atmosphere. (New England experienced snowfall in August after one eruption in Indonesia.)

*Fact 3:* Solar energy is trapped in the atmosphere, especially by water vapor and carbon dioxide. (This is the so-called greenhouse effect.)

*Fact 4:* Atmospheric concentrations of $CO_2$ have risen 11 percent since the industrial revolution started the large-scale combustion of fossil fuels.

*Fact 5:* Dust from human activity in rural and urban areas also has entered the atmosphere in increasing quantities.[7]

When we try to use these facts to make predictions, we run into problems. One pollutant, $CO_2$, may make the world warmer, but this effect can be countered by another pollutant, dust, which reflects solar energy and cools the entire globe. We are conducting a very large-scale experiment with very little control over the experimental manipulations. It may turn out that pollution effects on the global climate are insignificant when compared with variations in the amount of solar energy entering the atmosphere as our planet wobbles its way around the sun. At present, however, we do not know whether pollution can melt glaciers and polar ice caps—or bring about a new Ice Age! (See Figure 21–4.)

## EFFECTS ON HEALTH

Each day, an "average American" eats about 3 pounds of food, drinks 5 pounds of liquids, and inhales 30 pounds of air. Along with the air, he gets various concentrations of the particulate material and toxic gases produced by concentrated combustion or other technological processes. Fortunately, every human is born with five *lines of defense* against dirty air. First there is the nose, which, if not congested, can function as a baffle filter. Secondly, there are the mucosa (mucus-secreting cells lining the walls of the

**Figure 21–4.**

*Possible effects of air pollution on the global climate*

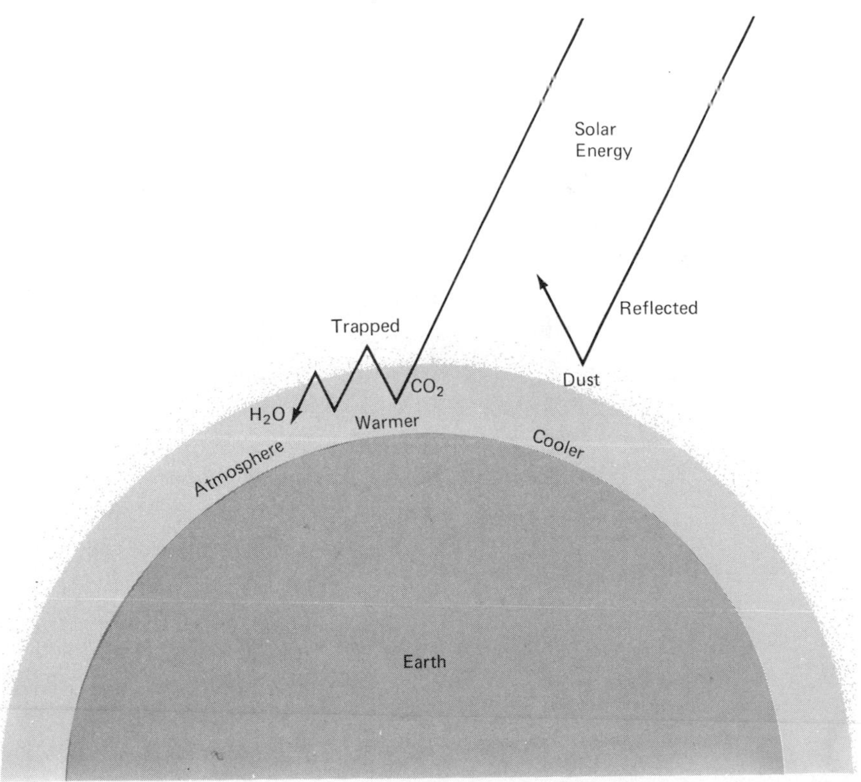

respiratory and digestive systems). These can absorb water-soluble pollutants such as $O_3$ and $SO_2$, and secrete the mucus that traps particulates. The third defense, one that can be crippled easily by chronic smoking, consists of numerous cilia, lining the trachea and bronchi. When healthy, these sweep dirt-laden mucus up to the mouth, to be expectorated or swallowed. If foreign material makes it all the way down to the aveoli (tiny sacs in the lung where gas exchange actually takes place), a fourth defense awaits in the form of a phagocyte army. These scavenging cells actually ingest the invaders. If some toxic chemical gets past the first four barriers, it still may be detoxified before doing serious damage. This final line of defense consists of complex enzyme and buffering systems, principally in the blood stream and liver[8] (Figure 21–5).

What happens when the defenses fail? This can be seen dramatically in

**Figure 21–5.**
*Structure of a healthy lung*

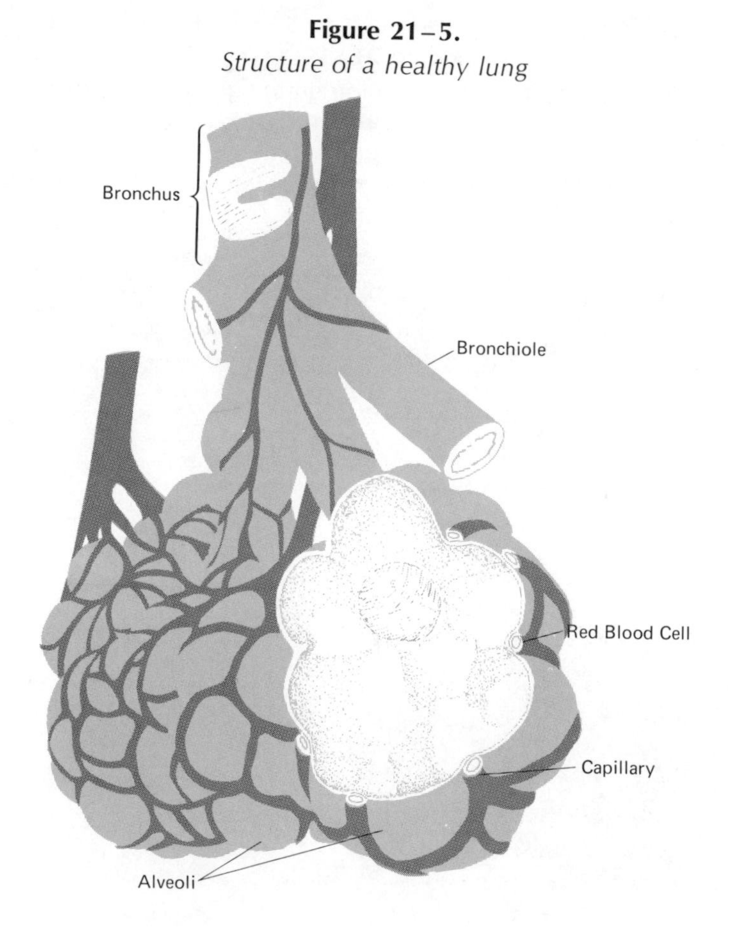

an air-pollution episode. One of the most tragic occurred in Donora, a town in the Monongahela River Valley, 28 miles south of Pittsburgh. With trains, coal boats, and several large factories, Donora has more than its share of pollution sources. Furthermore, the town is surrounded by bluffs 450 feet high or higher. When an inversion settled over the region on Tuesday, October 26, 1948, the stage was set for disaster. By October 31, smoke was so thick that people standing on the sidewalks could not see the Halloween parade going by. The bittersweet smell of $SO_2$ was noticeable, but other compounds, including $H_2S$, fluorides, chlorides, and cadmium oxide also may have been present at dangerous levels. Nearly six thousand of the fourteen thousand people living in and near Donora became sick before the inversion broke up and the air was breathable again on All Saints' Day, Monday, November 1. Normally, two people would have died that week in Donora. Instead twenty died, their ages ranging from fifty-two to eighty-four, with a mean of sixty-five. Most had already been weakened by heart and lung disease, in many cases the result of chronic exposure to lower levels of air pollution. One more day of inversion, and the death toll would have been higher. Furthermore, no one knows if those who became sick during the episode have had shorter lives as a result.[9]

This brings us to the still difficult assessment of chronic exposure to air pollution. Someone breathing dirty air may also smoke, eat too much, get nervous when honked at, and be subject to various viral or bacterial infections. Rarely can researchers find a twin brother who has had everything except the dirty air. Therefore, the correlation between illness or early death and inhalation of pollutants remains circumstantial; it is, however, convincing enough to justify serious efforts toward reducing emissions. For example, we know that CO attaches to hemoglobin, interfering with the normal transportation of oxygen to the brain. On a short term, that could cause anything from minor irritability to fatal dozing off at the wheel of a car in heavy traffic. Over longer periods, it might be a factor in mental retardation or, if the circulatory system compensates for reduced efficiency by carrying more red blood cells, it could create an overload for heart and blood vessels (Figure 21–6).

Other pollutants, the oxidants (including $O_3$, $SO_2$, $NO_2$, and PAN) have been incriminated as causal factors in minor irritation of the eyes, more serious damage to the bronchi (leading to bronchitis and asthma), and fatal emphysema (collapse of the alveoli). The latter has the dubious distinction of being the fastest growing cause of death in the United States, its incidence having increased seventeenfold between 1950 and 1966.[10] Air pollutants and cigarette smoke undoubtedly have shared the responsibility.

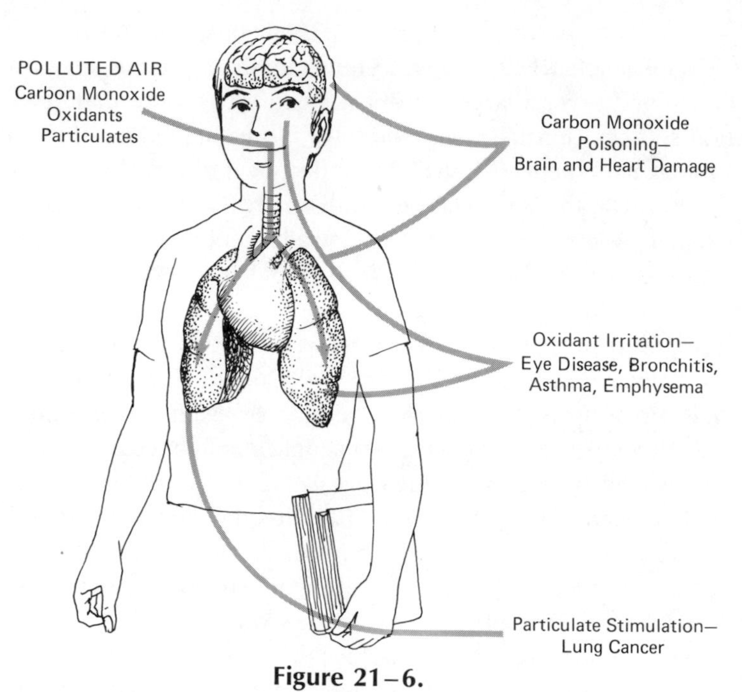


**Figure 21–6.**
*Possible effects of air pollution on human health*

There are other interactions as well. When the cilia plus mucus defenses are damaged by toxic gases, protection against pathogens causing anything from colds to pneumonia is reduced.[11]

The Surgeon General may not have come right out and said it, but "breathing can be hazardous to your health" in other ways. Air-borne coal tars, fuel fragments, radioactive particles, and asbestos fibrils may stimulate the abnormal proliferation of cells characteristic of lung cancer, although cryptic viruses also may be involved, needing only the initial irritation to turn them loose. Then there is the disturbing possibility that some air pollutants (for example, $SO_2$) may cross the placental barrier and damage a fetus during the early stages of its development. Finally, mutations in male or female gametes may be linked to air pollution, although this is perhaps the most difficult correlation of all. A chromosome damaged today may not show its flaw until a defective child is born thirty years later.[12]

One can only conclude that air pollutants from auto exhausts, smokestacks, and other sources do not improve the quality of life in an urban ecosystem. In the final six chapters of this book, we will take a forward look to examine the problems and prospects of change, with a better environment as our goal.

## SUMMARY

Fossil fuels are burnt in automobiles, homes, and power plants, directly and indirectly producing air pollutants in the forms of gases and particulates. The pollutants, together with waste heat, have a measurable effect on urban climate, which is warmer, foggier, and rainier than the surrounding countryside. There is some evidence that air pollution is also modifying world climate, but natural fluctuations, poorly understood, obscure the effects of man and his technology.

Although the human body is well equipped with defenses against airborne pollutants, there is the danger that these defenses will be overwhelmed, especially when inversion conditions trap several days' production of pollutants. Damage possibilities include carbon monoxide poisoning, emphysema, lung cancer, and birth defects.

### Discussion Questions

1. Do you consider the air of your community badly polluted?
2. What are the effects of air pollution on the urban climate?
3. Has man modified the global climate through the addition of combustion products, dust from rural areas, or other materials?
4. Which is more hazardous: (a) cigarette smoking or (b) breathing polluted air?

### Suggested Projects

1. Find out if any local agency provides an air-pollution index (see Chapter 23) and learn how the index is calculated.
2. Set out at various locations: (a) sticky slides to catch dust, pollen, and so on; (b) clean cans or jars to catch dust and rain water; and (c) mounted squares of nylon (which can be cut from discarded panty hose) to measure the fallout of acid droplets (which break the nylon fibers). With a dissecting microscope and a pH meter, some crude measures of spatial and temporal differences in air quality can be based on these simple monitoring devices.

**Notes**

1. See a nontechnical summary in A. Turk, J. Turk, and J. J. Wittes, *Ecology, Pollution, Environment* (Philadelphia: Saunders 1972), pp. 83–88; and a more technical discussion in L. M. Cooke, ed., *Cleaning Our Environment: The Chemical Basis for Action* (Washington, D.C.: American Chemical Society, 1969), pp. 23–42.
2. M. Edel, "Autos, Energy, and Pollution," *Environment,* **15**:10–17 (1973).
3. G. Likens, F. H. Bormann, and N. M. Johnson, "Acid Rain," *Environment,* **14**:33–40 (1972).
4. V. Brodine, *Air Pollution* (New York: Harcourt, 1973), includes a detailed discussion of an air-stagnation episode on p. 104.
5. Ibid., p. 72; see also W. P. Lowry, "The Climate of Cities," *Scientific American,* **217**:15–23 (1967).
6. S. F. Singer, ed., *Global Effects of Environmental Pollution* (New York: Springer-Verlag, 1970).
7. See, especially, R. A. Bryson and W. M. Wendland, "Climatic Effects of Atmospheric Pollution," in Singer, op. cit., pp. 130–138; and J. M. Mitchell, Jr., "A Preliminary Evaluation of Atmospheric Pollution As a Cause of Global Temperature Fluctuation of the Past Century," in Singer, op. cit., pp. 139–155.
8. These defenses are described in Brodine, op. cit., pp. 118–121.
9. Two good sources on Donora are Berton Roueché, "The Fog," which originally appeared in *The New Yorker;* reprinted in G. A. and R. M. Love, *Ecological Crisis* (New York: Harcourt 1970); and C. Bowen, "Donora, Pennsylvania," *The Atlantic* **226**:27–28, 32, 34 (1970).
10. R. Corman, *Air Pollution Primer* (New York: National TB and Respiratory Diseases Association, 1969) p. 71.
11. A clinical approach to these problems is represented in G. L. Waldbott, *Health Effects of Environmental Pollutants* (St. Louis: Mosby, 1973).
12. Distinction should be made between those agents that deform a fetus (teratogens) and those that damage genetic material (mutagens) in gametes or precursor cells before conception, although either process can result in the tragic birth of a defective child.

# Summary of Part IV

Because the urban environment is destined to be home for the majority of mankind, it is vital that we take advantage of any insights that the science of ecology can provide on the problems of cities. An urbanized area can be regarded as an ecosystem dominated by one species—man—and contaminated by the waste products of his technology. Every city has been created by the displacement of natural ecosystems, and it continues to modify ecosystems—those nearby by the dumping of waste and those farther away by the extraction of resources, perhaps the most important of these being water.

Although pure water and clean air enter a city, they are laden with pollutants when they leave. Efforts are made at sewage treatment plants to intercept some of the water-borne pollutants, converting them to carbon dioxide, nutrients, and solid waste. However, the preservation of air quality depends on interception at the source, be it a moving vehicle or a fixed power plant. (See Chapter 23.) Air quality also may be jeopardized by periods of stagnation during which the accumulation of toxic gases can be especially hazardous to our health, although there is evidence that chronic air pollution also is deleterious.

In short, a city is an ecosystem that has not yet evolved to the point where it efficiently recycles its waste products.

# V

# ALTERNATIVES

# 22

# A Healthy Environment

## Key Concepts

- Infectious diseases
- Virulent pathogen
- Reservoir
- Vector
- Survivorship curves
- Degenerative diseases
- Preventive medicine
- Environmental mutagens
- Genetic engineering
- Complete safety
- Early exposure
- Golden mean

Is an environment healthy when it produces sufficient quantities of nutritious food and is free from the hazards of infection or injury? Not necessarily, because human needs and values are so varied that a "perfectly healthy" environment may be so far from heaven that it seems like hell. In this chapter, health of the human mind and body will be the measure of interactions with the environment, particular emphasis being placed on modifications of the environment that change its dangers or benefits.

### THE GREAT HEALTH TRADE-OFF

In a primitive society, where personal hygiene and public sanitation are deficient or nonexistent, *infectious diseases* are the most common source of mortality. They are most apt to be lethal to infants or young children, their resistance often being lowered by climatic stress or poor nutrition.

Only the tough survive to adulthood, and even they may succumb to a *virulent pathogen* invading their tribal area for the first time. Life may not always be nasty and brutish, but it is likely to be short.

If a disease, epidemic or endemic, is studied by an ecologist, he will consider such interactions as pathogen-human, weather-host, vector-pathogen, vector-breeding sites, or alternate host-food (Figure 22–1). For example, a case of bubonic plague in Denver led to an investigation of grey

**Figure 22–1.**
*Infectious pathways*

Physical-Chemical Environment
Alternate Hosts
Man
Pathogen
Vector (e.g. mosquito)
Vector Breeding Sites
Pathogen
Human Reservoir of Infection

squirrels, the *reservoir* of the plague bacillus, and then to a program of "defleaing" the squirrels because the fleas were the *vectors* that transmitted the plague to other squirrels and to humans. Although the defleaing stations were designed to dust the squirrels with insecticidal powder, the squirrels did not cooperate; they sat in the stations and gobbled up the peanut butter bait. Not until the peanut butter was jammed into the pine cones did the scheme work, with the squirrels coming to the stations, getting dusted, then going away free of fleas but with a peanut-flavored pine cone to nibble on.[1]

Campaigns against malaria have been somewhat more elaborate. Infected humans are the reservoir for the *Plasmodium* protozoans, and *Anopheles* mosquitoes are the vectors that transmit the pathogen to those not yet infected. Infection can be prevented by various combinations of house screens, mosquito repellants, and antimalarial pills. The vectors also can be attacked with insecticides applied to house walls to kill the adults or to aquatic habitats to kill the immature stages. Unfortunately, the ugly specter of resistance has thwarted this strategy in many malarious areas. Through accelerated selection, the protozoans become resistant to chemotherapy and the mosquitoes to one or more groups of insecticides.[2] Similar drawbacks have arisen when antibiotics (for example, penicillin) were used extensively and intensively to control bacterial infections (Figure 22–2).

Generally, however, developed countries have the money, knowledge, and personnel to reduce infectious disease. *Survivorship curves* change from concave—normal to most species that produce large numbers of young with few surviving to maturity—to convex—an abnormal condition peculiar to sanitized human populations (see Figure 22–3). With most infants reaching sexual maturity and 80 percent surviving beyond their sixtieth birthday, predominant health problems become quite different from the infections that beset a primitive society. Research, prevention, and therapy all focus on diseases of middle and old age, especially breakdowns of cardiovascular systems and breakouts of cancerous cells. Essentially *degenerative,* these diseases are being attacked with the fervor and funding of earlier campaigns against infectious diseases such as typhoid and polio. What may be missing is the recognition that no easy cure or prevention is possible when dealing with a noninfectious disease that results from the interplay of many physiological and environmental factors. There is also the possibility that our cells have built-in self-destruct orders, coded through evolutionary selection, that relieve human populations of their older and less productive members. Aging is a natural process, sometimes accelerated by the stresses of modern living, and death is the inevitable end of life.

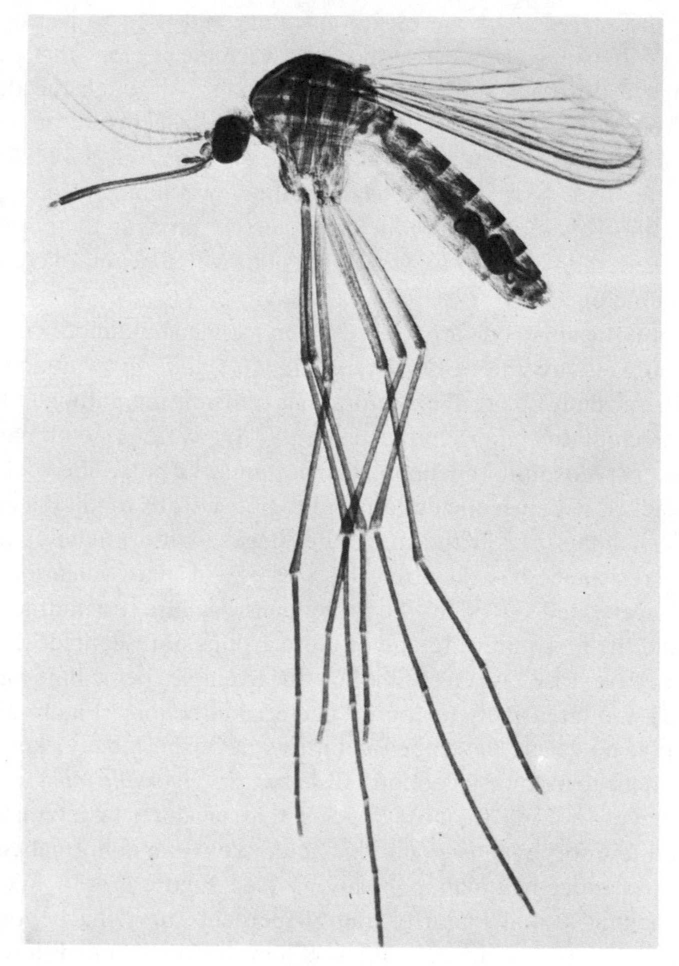

**Figure 22–2.**
Anopheles *mosquito, vector of malaria* (Courtesy Carolina Biological Supply Co.)

Ecologically speaking, this final fate is no more, or less, than a very personal contribution to recycling.[3]

## PREVENTIVE MEDICINE

Is it better to cure someone who is sick or to prevent him from getting sick? This presents a fine subject for a cost-benefit analysis, but even

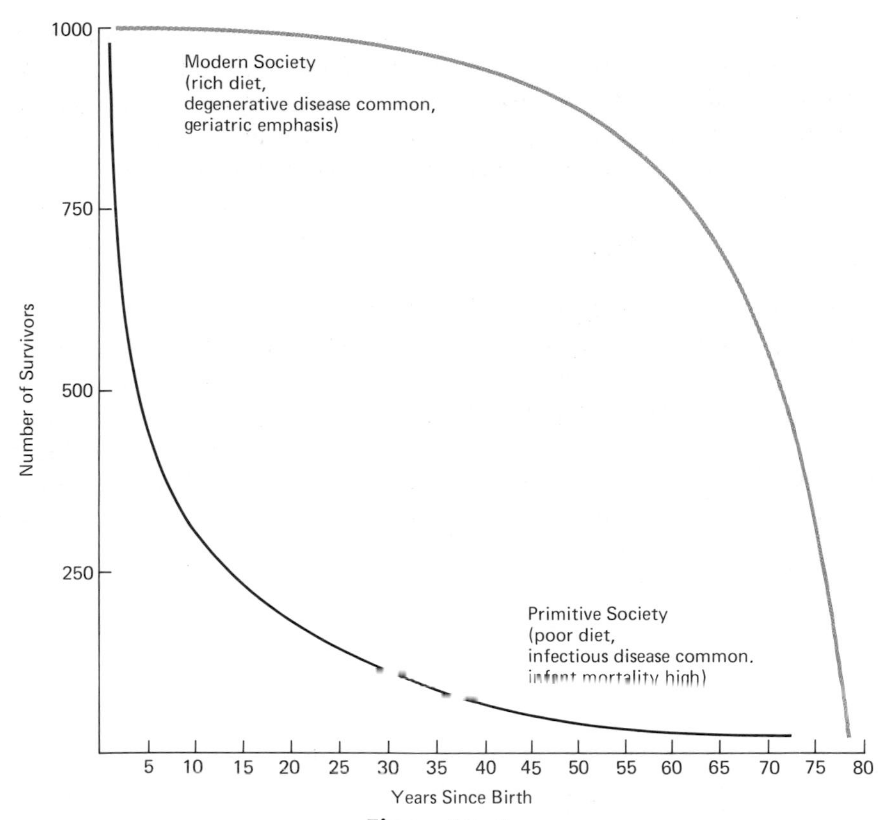


**Figure 22–3.**
*Survivorship curves*

without economic justification the modern trend has gone from cure to prevention. If you delight in historical precedents, you can go back to the early Chinese custom of paying the physician only while you remain healthy. Many health insurance plans, especially when coupled with group practice and frequent checkups by medical specialists, can be regarded as a modification of the ancient system. Yet, there are many other areas where professionals loosely grouped under the title of "Public Health" have fostered the concepts of *preventive medicine*.

The campaigns to sterilize drinking water, immunize people against contagious diseases, and control the vectors of pathogens have been quite successful in many parts of the world, contributing substantially to the population explosion by greatly reducing prereproductive (infant and child) mortality. In developed countries, the emphasis has shifted toward other preventive measures, including the use of fluoride (in toothpastes, dental applications, and drinking water) to prevent tooth decay and iodine (in table salt) to prevent the enlargement of the thyroid gland known as goiter. Efforts to reduce the incidence of emphysema and lung cancer by curtailing air pollution and cigarette smoking emphasize the fact that it is often necessary to modify both our habitat and our habits in order to protect our health.

Just how far will we go in our efforts to insure that everyone has a good chance to live a long and healthy life? We are spending billions of dollars to find the causes of cancer, but when we prove that *environmental mutagens* stimulate cancer will we be ready to spend many billions more to cleanse the environment of mutagens? Costly though such a campaign would be, it also could reduce the expense and tragedy of children born defective. Perhaps it all depends on the value we place on human life—a value that appears to approach infinity when a child is trapped in a cave and to near zero when war is being waged.

Let's consider three more examples of "preventive medicine" extrapolated from current programs. Stress, especially in urban ecosystems crowded with men and machines, as described in Chapter 19, contributes to high blood pressure, heart attacks, and cerebrovascular accidents (strokes). Can we best reduce these by tranquilizing individuals or by making the environment more serene? Or must we do both? Also related to stress, but involving many other environmental, social, and psychological factors, are the perennial problems of crime and insanity. The behavioral psychologist B. F. Skinner would have us believe that even these could be eliminated in the properly engineered social environment.[4] A world with no prisons or asylums is a tempting vision indeed, but many people may feel the price—loss of the freedom to be foolish—is too high. A final category of modification in the name of health would include changes in the quality or quantity of human populations. Programs of *genetic engineering* to improve human quality, of relocation to redistribute, and family limitation to reduce human numbers are now being considered in many nations. Some leaders make the simplistic assumption that population growth is the root of all evil and consider that birth control is the ultimate form of preventive medicine. What they do not realize is that most human problems will remain unsolved after a nation achieves ZPG. However, as shown in Chapter 3, population growth and concentration magnify many problems, so policies and techniques to reduce population impact are certainly justified (see Chapter 26).

## AVOIDANCE OF EXTREMES

There is a very real possibility that some trends toward a healthy environment may go too far. *Complete safety* and security is not a good thing—or, perhaps, it is too much of a good thing. For normal development, each individual must be exposed to certain stimuli, variations, and hazards. This need can be seen in relation to many components of our environment.

Many a mother would be surprised to learn that some "germs" are good for her children. Not only do we need intestinal flora of microorganisms to break down food and produce Vitamin K (essential to blood clotting), but we also need *early exposure* to certain viruses that will cause mild symptoms much preferable to a serious disease in later life. Mumps can cause agonizing (and possibly sterilizing) testicular swelling in the adult male, and rubella (German measles) can cause fetal deformation if a woman becomes infected during the early part of a pregnancy. Polio, in its paralytic form, is almost certainly related to improved sanitation and personal hygiene. Whenever and wherever cleanliness increases, the chances of mild cases in early childhood decrease and severe cases in the late teens or early twenties increase. Of course, we now have the live (Sabin) vaccine to replace the natural protection that used to be conferred by infections during early childhood. There is a possibility that other viruses affecting the nervous system are still at large, unchecked by either natural immunity or vaccination. This would explain many of the patterns observed in the tragic disease of multiple sclerosis.[5] In any event, it seems that a little infection at the right time is better than an overwhelming infection or no infection at all.

The *golden mean* also must apply to the food we extract from our environment (see Chapter 8). We certainly need enough protein to maintain normal growth and to repair mind and body. We also must have enough calories to sustain normal activities. Finally, we need a full range of vitamins and trace elements to keep the body chemistry in good working order.[6] However, we do not need excessive amounts. Certain vitamins and minerals can be toxic if taken in large doses. Fat, consumed directly or transformed from other foods by the body, is the greatest health hazard for many middle-aged Americans, clogging and burdening their circulatory systems. Moderation also should be the rule for any form of medication, eating, or drinking—especially for the most dangerous drug of all, alcohol (Figure 22–4).

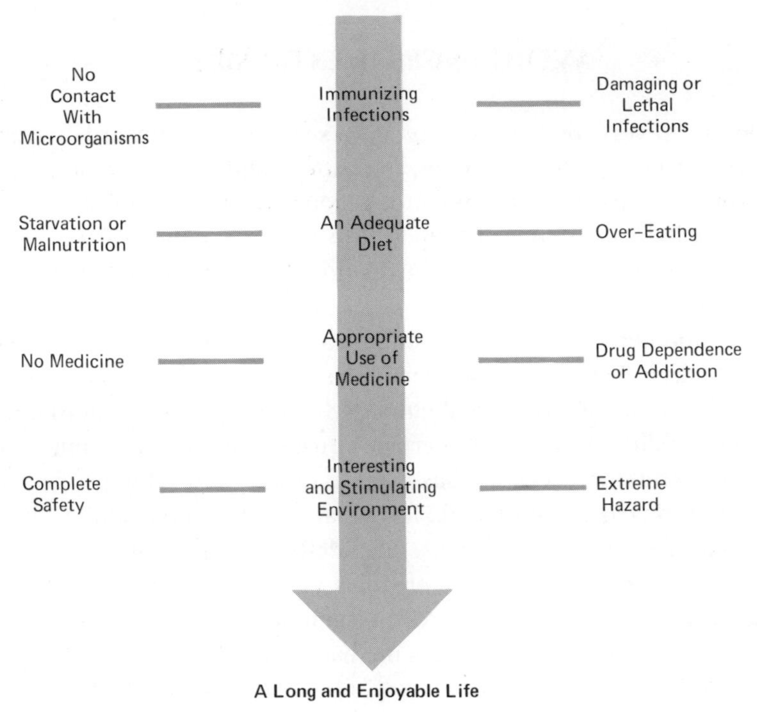


**Figure 22–4.**
*The golden mean of health*

Moving to the psychological, rather than the ecological, concept of the environment, you can see that complete safety, if equated with absolute monotony, is not a desirable goal. Many studies have shown that children and the young of many mammals need the stimulation of an interesting and diverse environment if they are to develop fully their intellectual potential.[7] Yet, stress from various combinations of noise, crowding, and competition can overwhelm the psychic defenses of individuals to the point that they break down. Another aspect is the actual frequency of physical hazards. Those individuals who are free to choose presumably try to avoid locations where they might be exposed to floods, hurricanes, or extreme droughts; they also may seek a climate with enough seasonal variation to be intellectually stimulating. It has been suggested that such an optimal climate prevails in New Haven, Connecticut, but that farfetched notion came from a Yale professor in 1915.[8]

Because there are great differences among individuals—these differences being determined by a virtually inseparable combination of genetic and cultural inheritance—it is probably impossible to define an environment that would be optimally healthy for any human. However, the principle that extremes should be avoided seems valid. Supersafety could lead to our degradation almost as swiftly as a horribly hazardous world could destroy us.

## SUMMARY

Because there are many links between individual health and environmental quality, modern preventive medicine includes programs to prevent disease by reducing environmental hazards. However, these programs must be evaluated carefully because there are disturbing possibilities that efforts to reduce dangers may create other problems, such as resistant strains of pathogens or vectors, increased incidence of drug-related diseases, and psychologically damaging monotony or sameness. We should recognize that a reduction in infectious diseases must be accompanied by an increase in degenerative diseases; we should not be so concerned with the postponement of death that we forget health is much more than the absence of terminal illness.

### Discussion Questions

1. What is your ideal description of "good health"?
2. In what ways are we paying for a great reduction in infectious diseases?
3. How far should a government go in regulating the prevention of accidents?
4. What is the origin of the phrase *golden mean?*

### Suggested Projects

1. Make an immunization chart for your class or discussion group:

| | Smallpox | DPT (diptheria, whooping cough, tetanus) | Polio | German Measles (rubella) | Mumps | Chicken Pox | Yellow Fever | Typhoid |
|---|---|---|---|---|---|---|---|---|
| Name | I* | I | I | H | O | H | O | O |
| Name | I | I | O | O | H | H | O | O |
| etc. | | | | | | | | |

*I = innoculated or vaccinated
H = had natural infection
O = no immunity

**2.** Do a student-and-parent survey of attitudes toward (a) long life, (b) good physical health, (c) good mental health, and (d) preventive medicine.

## Notes

1. A fine article on the deadly Denver squirrels is Berton Roueché, "A Small, Apprehensive Child," Annals of Medicine, *The New Yorker,* (April 10, 1971).
2. The whole quandary of relying on chemical means for malaria control is analyzed in Richard Garcia, "The Control of Malaria," *Environment,* **14**:2–9 (1972).
3. Human attitudes toward mortality are a fascinating subject, somewhat beyond the already wide scope of this book. For further insight, read psychological and philosophical writings, and then brood a bit.
4. Two intriguing and disturbing books by B. F. Skinner are *Walden Two* (New York: Macmillan, 1948), and *Beyond Freedom and Dignity* (New York: Knopf, 1971).
5. See Geoffrey Dean, "Multiple Sclerosis Problem," *Scientific American,* **223**:40–46 (1970).
6. See Earl Frieden, "The Chemical Elements of Life," *Scientific American,* **227**:52–60 (1972), and any good text on human biology.
7. See Mark Rosenzweig, Edward L. Bennett, and Marion C. Diamond, "Brain Changes in Response to Experience," *Scientific American,* **226**:22–29 (1972).
8. Huntington Ellsworth, *Civilization and Climate* (New Haven: Yale University Press, 1915).

# 23

# Nonpolluting Technology

## Key Concepts

- Uses of technology
- Monitoring
- Emission control
- Recycling
- Alternative sources of energy
- Base line
- Indices of pollution
- Sampling programs
- Catalytic converters
- Better engines
- Cleaner fuels
- Mass transit
- Recycling loops
- Contained fusion reactions
- Solar energy
- Fuel cell
- Geothermal energy
- Tidal power

Ecologists are sometimes suspected of being not only neo-Malthusians but also neo-Luddites (those who would destroy machines), fearing, and trying to prevent, technological progress. It is true that many of our environmental problems have been caused by the impact of man and machines (Chapter 4), but technology is neutral (Chapter 27) and can be put to many good uses. Applications of chemical technology that could improve the quality of our environment already have been mentioned in connection with food production (Chapter 8) and pest control (Chapter 10). Also, birth-control techniques, if safe, effective, and available, will continue to play a key role in dampening the population explosion.

In this chapter the focus is on the potential *uses of technology* in cleaning up a polluted environment. *Monitoring, emission control, recycling,* and *alternative sources of energy* are considered. This will serve to unify many of the technological solutions alluded to in Chapters 16, 17, 18, 20, and 21.

Hopefully, it will show that ecologists and engineers have a common cause in fighting pollution.

## MONITORING

Think of the weather stations that form a network over much of the earth's surface. Then consider the many environmental factors they record: precipitation, humidity, air pressure, cloud cover, wind speed and direction, and maximum and minimum temperatures. What else can they, given the appropriate gadgets, start to monitor on a worldwide basis? Particulate and radioactive fallout, vapor trails from jets, smog plumes from cities, toxic gases from transportation and industry, air-borne biocides, and even dispersing stages of pests and pathogens all could be watched or intercepted. At the UN Conference on the Human Environment (Stockholm, 1972) a step was taken in the direction of more sophisticated monitoring, with the establishment of "Earth Watch." This network of stations, many already operational, includes ten for *base-line* (natural, unpolluted atmosphere) studies in remote locations (Point Barrow, Alaska; high on the side of Mauna Loa in Hawaii; and the South Pole). Changes in $CO_2$, ozone, and dust concentrations in such isolated spots would show that pollution is affecting the entire atmosphere. One hundred other stations in various countries (ten in the United States) will monitor more localized air pollution. All 110 stations will feed their data to a central computer facility, presumably at the Environmental Secretariat in Nairobi, Kenya.[1]

Sophisticated monitoring may not permit the weatherman to do a better job of predicting rain (that requires improvements in our understanding of atmospheric physics and in our use of statistics), but it will enable him to use more meaningful *indices* of discomfort, or pollution hazard. "Alert" levels in many communities have two weak points. First, they are based on averages of observations made during the previous 24 hours, which could cause a dangerous delay in response to a rapidly worsening situation. Secondly, only easy-to-measure pollutants are monitored by many cities—those in charge arguing that all forms of air pollution usually fluctuate synchronously. This is true, but there are periods when unmeasured carbon monoxide is rising to hazardous levels while carefully monitored haze and $SO_2$ levels give no cause for concern. Even the Oak Ridge Index of air quality, which gives weight to unmeasured pollutants, could fail under such odd circumstances.[2] Despite the added expense, it would seem prudent to install, in most urban areas, a network of automatic sniffers and samplers to monitor all five major groups of air pollutants: particulates, carbon monoxide, $SO_2$, nitrogen oxides, and oxidants (ozone, PAN, and the like). When a red light starts blinking on the mayor's desk, he will be able to respond quickly by closing down or excluding the sources of pollution.

We have much further to go in the development of international and national systems for monitoring water quality. Despite the controversy over oil pollution (Chapter 18), there is no program of continuous sampling or surveillance for oceanic oil slicks. In fact, very little is known about long-term (geological) or short-term (historical) changes in the constituents of salt water. It is folly to assume that the vastness of the oceans will save them from significant changes in quality. Human contributions to fallout and runoff have become so large that they can no longer be hidden away somewhere in Davy Jones's locker.

The need for monitoring the quality of "fresh" water is even more critical. Our use, reuse, and misuse of ponds, lakes, streams, and rivers have created many situations that deserve continuous scrutiny. Unfortunately, there is no network of "water-watching" stations equivalent to those established for weather watching. However, many government agencies, at all levels, have *sampling programs* whose technicians usually return to the same locations at regular intervals. One man may be concerned only with flow, another with bacterial counts, and still another with nitrate concentration, so that much effort is duplicated. It has been suggested that a unified network of ten thousand standardized sampling stations could be based on locations in the United States now being monitored near factories, filtration plants, and sewage treatment plants.[3] Once again, there is a lag problem, because only monthly reports would be submitted. Certainly, continuous monitoring of our drinking water is desirable. At present, we may recognize a water-quality problem only when we see thousands of fish floating belly up in a reservoir.

A few words about actual monitoring techniques is appropriate at this point. Some are simple charts to estimate smoke density or containers to collect samples, but they require many man-hours (Figure 23–1). Others pump a stream of air or water through one or more testing chambers, producing virtually continuous measurements of quality. Such automatic analyzers are expensive, but many small companies are developing and marketing them—a competitive situation that should bring the cost down within the reach of the most impoverished municipality. Other techniques, lumped under the term *remote sensing,* are being developed by the National Aeronautics and Space Administration (NASA) and its contrac-

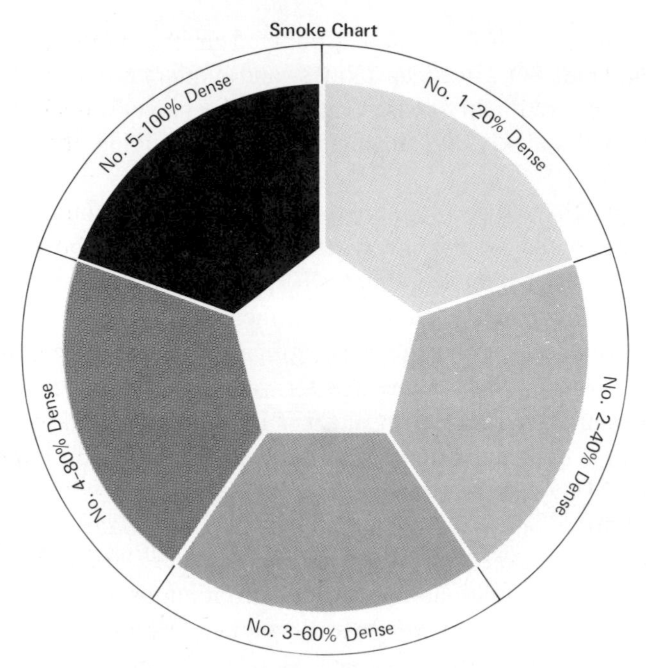


**Figure 23–1.**
*Ringelmann Chart* (Courtesy Plibico Co.)

tors, who are very anxious to bring space-age technology back to earth and to maintain the momentum of the 1960s. Orbiting satellites and high-flying planes can provide useful pictures of cloud cover, smog build-up, dust storms, and heat plumes, but their observations must be tied into those made by ground stations or else interpretation and application will be virtually impossible.

## EMISSION CONTROL

In Chapter 21, the urban sources of air pollution were listed and described, and in Chapter 20, sewage and detergents were discussed as two main components of water pollution. Here, the techniques used to prevent the escape of pollutants into the environment will be summarized briefly, leading into the next section in which the possible reuse of trapped pollutants, or other wasted resources, will be considered.

Although factories, incinerators, and power plants can produce many tons of particulates and toxic gases, these large quantities of pollutants can be intercepted in the stacks by using various combinations of baffles, scrubbers, and electrostatic precipitators. The economics of scale make it possible to justify million-dollar investments in pollution abatement for a large, fixed source. For millions of small, moving sources—motor vehicles—the economics of scale takes a different form, justifying the mass production of standardized, easily installed *catalytic converters* (Figure 23–2). These do not trap unburnt fuel fragments. Instead, they oxidize them to $CO_2$ and $H_2O$, at temperatures so low that little of the air's $N_2$ is changed to $NO_x$ although some worrisome $SO_2$ may be produced. The cost per car may still reach several hundred dollars because the catalysts are platinum and palladium, metals associated more with elegant fingers than the underside of an automobile. Further complications ensue from the fact that catalytic converters are poisoned by lead; hence, the great government pressure to make sure that lead-free gasoline will be available at every service station by 1976. There are also many efforts to replace the "infernal combustion engine" with an automotive power plant that will require less gadgetry for emission control. *Better engines* (the Wankel, steam, turbine, Diesel, and the fly wheel) and *cleaner fuels* (gas or electricity) all are being

**Figure 23–2.**
*Catalytic converter* (Courtesy Ford Motor Company)

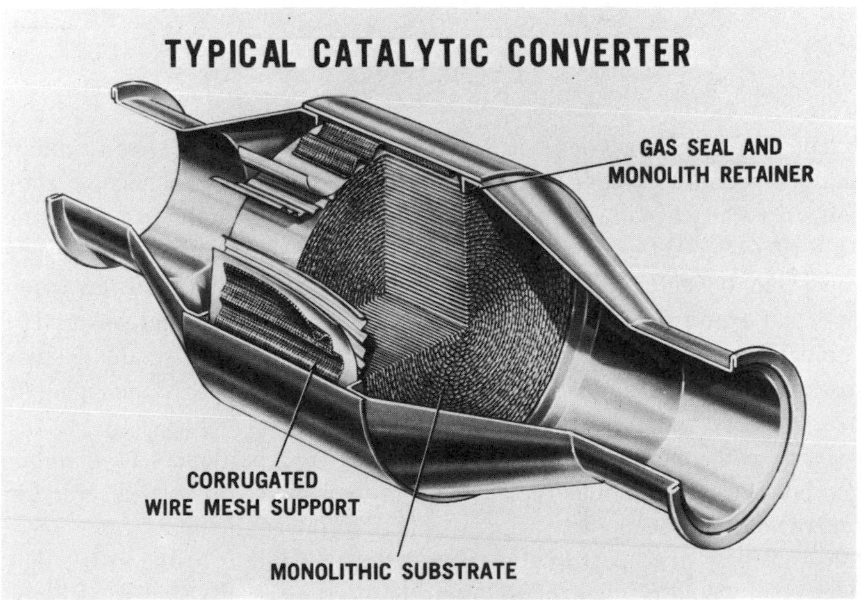

tried, but none has been greeted with wild enthusiasm by Detroit or the oil companies.[4] Fond though we are of the private vehicle, we might be wise to stop tinkering with it and make a real commitment to *mass transit* as the best way to move people without fouling the air.

Many analogous problems can be found in sewage treatment. The basic objectives are similar: removing or detoxifying hazardous materials and oxidizing organic fragments. The trickling filter bed at a sewage treatment plant is like a catalytic converter, but it relies on microorganisms to change crud into $CO_2$ and $H_2O$. Various settling tanks are used to trap inorganic particles. However, as shown in Chapter 20, the removal of particles (primary treatment) and reduction of BOD (secondary treatment) are not enough to prevent downstream blooms of algae. This is why there is a need in some areas for tertiary treatment, ion-exchange processes designed to remove dissolved nutrients. Lake Tahoe (California-Nevada) is now protected from accelerated eutrophication by a sophisticated system of chemical and physical treatments, producing a clear effluent low in nutrients. However, few communities are willing to pay for such facilities.[5] In fact, many rural and suburban areas find it cheaper to use septic tanks, even at the risk of contaminating their own well water. Furthermore, large cities next to rivers or along the coasts continue to dump raw sewage. It has been suggested that the flush toilet, like the automobile, is one of those inventions that may not have been such a good idea after all.[6]

## RECYCLING

The subject of recycling can serve as the main bridge between ecology and engineering. Ecologists are very interested in biogeochemical cycling and stress the ways in which natural ecosystems retain and reuse nutrients. This is a main difference between the natural ecosystem and the urban ecosystem (Chapter 19), because cities import food, water, and raw materials and export finished products, sewage, dirty air, and solid waste. The ecological ideal would be to close at least some of the loops, simultaneously making cities less dependent on remote sources and less damaging to nearby ecosystems.[7]

Despite the heroic efforts of many back-yard gardeners to maintain compost heaps for humus replacement in their plots, the over-all trend in recent years has been away from organic recycling. When pig farmers were told that they must pasturize garbage before feeding it to the swine they decided it would be cheaper to fatten the hogs on grain. Similarly, a loop was opened when cattle were moved from farms to feed lots because the farmer is not going to town to bring back a load of manure. He can't afford to haul it "more than a mile and a half."[8] Of course, new loops may close. Direct feeding of urea to cattle has helped cut the cost of protein. There is also the delightful possibility that shredded newspapers, suitably processed, can be substituted for straw. To the steer, it's just cellulose, whether it came from a hay field or *The New York Times*.

Paper provides many good examples of *recycling loops*. Very high quality paper, uncontaminated by glossy resins or gaudy colors, can be used to make more fine paper. Old newspapers can be bleached and used to make more newsprint or can be pressed with other fibers to make cardboard. By spraying sewage, which contains a high proportion of cellulose, on forest soils, it is even possible to accelerate the growth of trees that, in turn, can be used to make more paper.[9] This loop, which takes thirty or more years to complete, is the longest one in paper recycling, unless you include the incineration of paper, which releases $CO_2$ and eventually may be converted into cellulose by a tree and then made into paper by us.

With glass, there are also several loops, each with its own attractions. The "deposit-return" loop may be suffering from lack of governmental and public support. The convenience of one-way bottles is only one factor in their wide acceptance. Certain bottling companies have had expensive experiences with irate consumers suing after finding a mouse or roach floating in their cola. To be sure, they were able to evade punitive damages by hiring someone to consume a roach in court, thus showing that a health hazard was not involved. However, they do prefer to avoid the problem entirely by using new bottles. This involves a slightly longer loop because it is necessary to clean, dering, and smash old bottles (sorted by color), before they can be melted down to make new bottles.[10]

Although volunteer labor, as in the case of paper recycling, can make this loop close, one sometimes wonders if it is worth the effort. Perhaps the easiest out is to use ground glass as a substitute for unprocessed silica (sand) in road-building, creating a new material to be known as glasphalt.

The valuable metals are also quite amenable to recycling—not just gold, silver, and platinum, but also lead, copper, and aluminum. Most automobile batteries are salvaged for their lead. Copper is sold so easily that some enterprising types do not wait until it has reached the scrap stage but start removing wires as fast as the linemen string them up. With iron, the potential is not as great as it used to be simply because new techniques of steel-making depend less on infusions of scrap than did the old. Ironically, the use of aluminum wiring instead of copper in automobiles might make junked autos more attractive to steel foundries because copper weakens steel (Figure 23–3).

Water is the last resource to be discussed in this section on recycling. In an arid region, it would seem worthwhile to save every drop, rather than use clean water for flushing and cooling purposes. Yet, only a few communities have completed the logical loop between sewage treatment facilities and the water purification plant. Health authorities remain concerned that a virus will survive the round trip, and there are undeniable problems of flavor and odor. Water laden with energy (Chapter 17) or nutrients (Chapter 20) certainly should be considered valuable even if it cannot be restored to drinking quality. The technology of aquaculture is still embryonic, but the day may come when waste heat and nutrients accelerate the growth of algae and fish in ponds surrounding every major city.

There are some forms of waste that do not lend themselves to recycling. Radioactive waste (Chapter 16) is being produced by nuclear power plants in quantities far greater than the most imaginative nuclear engineer can put to use. Many millions will be spent devising repositories so isolated and insulated from the world that this lethal legacy never will be turned loose. ERDA already has considered the salt mines of Kansas as a safe disposal site but is now looking elsewhere.[11] Other waste, often so scrambled that it does not pay to sort it out, may end up in sanitary land fills. These are mixed blessings—better than burning, stinking, rat-breeding open dumps, but still threats to wetlands near cities in search of land, real estate, and

**Figure 23–3.**
*Recycling loops*

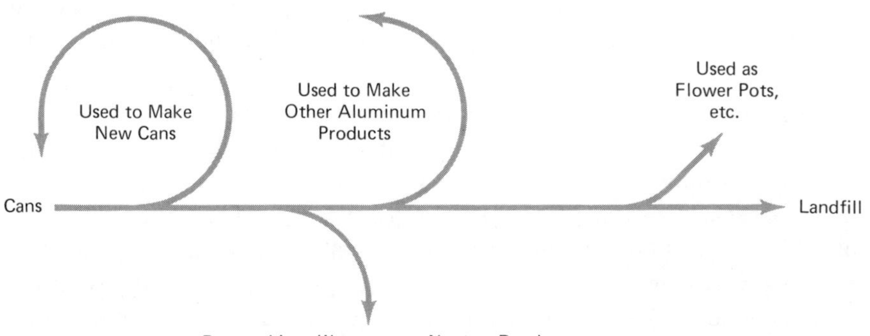

taxes. It would be illuminating if we could somehow join an archaeologist in the year 5000 probing through the foundations of a supermarket into the city dump and trying to reconstruct our life-style on the basis of the artifacts recovered: a toothpaste tube, a broken doll, a cluster of nutshells (partially fossilized), a beer bottle, and a TV set might represent the fruits of one day's dig. The archaeologist might well ask "Was that all there was?"

## ALTERNATIVE SOURCES OF ENERGY

Since the extraction, transportation, and utilization of fuel were indicated as the source of most pollution, the redirection of technology in this area is extremely important. Many technologists hope that we can harness the power of the H-bomb or the sun itself in the form of *contained fusion reactions*. Unfortunately, holding ionized gases (plasma) close enough and long enough requires vast energy inputs and near stellar-force fields. To many engineers engaged in fusion research the "magnetic bottle" has become a Holy Grail: believed in, much sought after, but elusive. If fusion power can be achieved through the compression of any combination of light isotopes (deuterium, tritium, helium 3, lithium 6, and so on), many of the problems associated with fission reactors could be avoided. There would be no danger of a "runaway reaction" and far fewer hazards from heat or radioisotope release.[12]

If a surrogate sun is so hard to make, and most of our energy is indirectly derived from sunlight, why can't we make better use of *solar energy?* We certainly can—although there are some real technical and economic obstacles. Even in the sunniest regions, some storage system would be needed to provide energy during nights and cloudy spells. To provide 1,000 megawatts (enough electricity for a city of ¾ million), 16 square miles would have to be covered (at a cost of $1.1 billion) with solar receptors (assuming 10 percent conversion efficiency).[13] A nuclear power plant providing the same amount of electricity would cost one fifth as much. Unless the costs of catching sunbeams with ground or orbiting arrays of photovoltaic cells can be greatly reduced, solar energy will just not be able to compete[14] (Figure 23–4). Perhaps we should direct our efforts toward improving existing roof-top devices that, through various heat-exchange mechanisms, gather warmth during the day and release it at night. Another possibility well worth exploring is the use of solar energy in the tropics to electrolyze $H_2O$ into $H_2$ and $O_2$, which then could be transported (in cryogenic tankers)

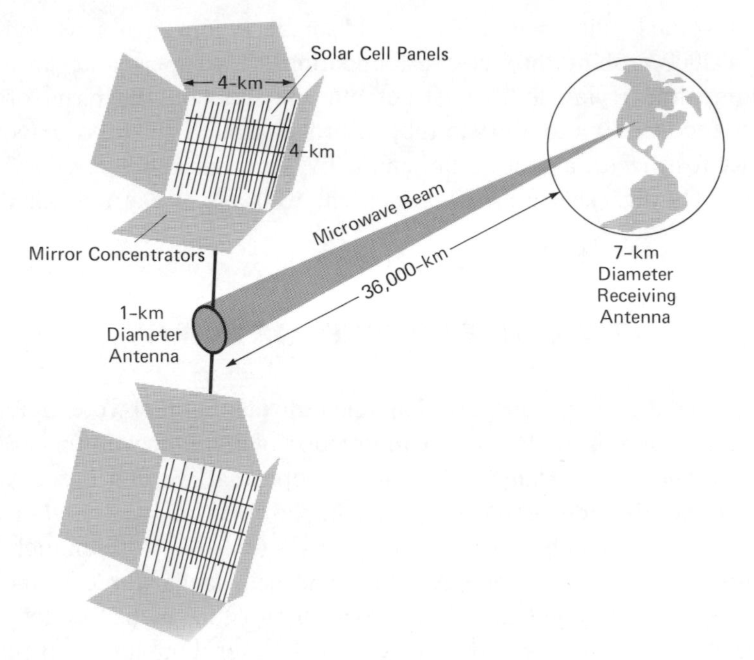


**Figure 23–4.**
*Orbiting array of solar cells*

to consuming areas where, used in *fuel cells,* it would yield clean electricity and pure water. Such technology could, of course, be based on nonsolar sources as well[15] (Figure 23–5).

Two alternatives remain: *geothermal* and *tidal power*. Both have geographic, economic, and environmental limitations but deserve consideration. Energy from the inner earth is most easily tapped in geyser areas where water is naturally percolating, going through cracks down into a zone of hot rock and coming up as steam. However, even in volcanic regions, geysers are localized and the only clusters that have been developed as power sources are in Italy, Iceland, California, Mexico, New Zealand, Japan, and the Kamchatka Peninsula of the Soviet Union.[16] In other locations, it may be possible to drill two parallel holes 20 to 25,000 feet deep, pumping water down the first and collecting steam from the second.[17] Either form of geothermal power would create pollution problems because $SO_2$, brine, and waste heat would be produced[18] and would require periodic redrilling or cleaning (Figure 23–6).

Dams across estuaries or bays can be used to harness tides, going and coming, to drive hydroelectric turbines. As coastal facilities, tidal power

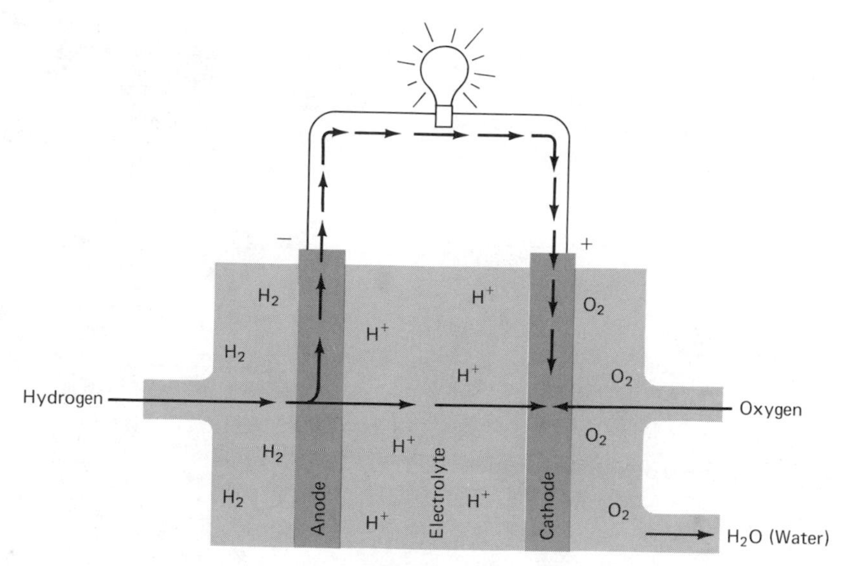


**Figure 23–5.**
*Fuel cell*

plants are near large concentrations of electricity users (Chapter 14). They also have the advantages of tapping a limitless source of energy and being pollution free,[19] however, they share with other dams (Chapter 15) the disadvantages of preventing other waterway uses (shipping, fishing, and so on) and of costing "megabucks."

Energy—especially cheap, clean energy—is simply not available to most of mankind. Perhaps technological breakthroughs will someday solve the dual problems of production and transmission, bringing low-cost power to the most isolated farmer. Ironically, this apparent blessing could be the ultimate disaster. Imagine seven billion human beings, each with the power to move mountains! Unless constrained by laws, mores, and ethics, we may complete the environmental destruction that began with the discovery of fire.

## SUMMARY

Although the proliferation of uncontrolled technology has caused many pollution problems, there are several ways in which technological innovations can help observe or prevent pollution. Monitoring devices can be used

**Figure 23–6.**
*Geothermal plant* (Courtesy New Zealand Embassy)

to measure the quality of air or water. Other equipment can help keep pollutants from entering the environment. Trapped pollutants or solid waste can be recycled into useful forms. Perhaps, most important of all, new sources of energy can be tapped or developed. If these sources are both clean and safe, they will represent real progress; however, energy from all sources must be used carefully and wisely.

### Discussion Questions

1. How is it possible for us to use technological innovations without understanding either the way they work or their impact on the environment?

2. What are some ways in which biological indicators (algae, fish, insects, and birds) can, through changes in abundance or condition, help monitor environmental quality?
3. For those commuting to work, which of the following would represent the best compromise between practicality and pollution reduction: (a) bicycles, (b) car pools, (c) buses, (d) moving sidewalks; or (e) electric trains?
4. Why have we relied on fossil fuels and failed to use other forms of energy?

## Suggested Projects

1. Get an engineer specializing in pollution abatement to talk to your class or discussion group.
2. Start a recycling center or supply an existing one. Materials most easily gathered for recycling are (a) bottles and jars, (b) newspapers and cardboard, and (c) aluminum and other valuable metals.
3. Find out as much as you can about techniques for harnessing solar energy to (a) heat homes and (b) generate electricity.

## Notes

1. Walter Sullivan, "UN Parley Endorses Air Monitoring Net," *New York Times,* 8 June 1972.
2. W. A. Thomas, L. R. Babcock, Jr., and W. D. Shults (1971) "Oak Ridge Air Quality Index" Oak Ridge National Laboratory-National Science Foundation Environmental Publication 8, 10 pp.
3. W. T. Sayers, "Water Quality Surveillance: The Federal-State Network," *Environmental Science and Technology,* **5**:114–119 (1971).
4. See the following articles from *Environment* magazine: reprinted in S. Novick and D. Cottrell, eds., *Our World in Peril: An Environment Review* (Greenwich, Conn.: Fawcett, 1971). J. Macinko, "The Tailpipe Problem," p. 345 (June 1970); W. S. Craig, "Not a Question of Size," p. 356 (June 1970); T. Aaronson, "Tempest Over a Teapot," p. 454 (October 1969); and K. Hohenemser and J. McCaull, "The Windup Car," p. 463 (June 1970). See also D. E. Cole, "The Wankel Engine," *Scientific American,* **227**:14–23 (1972).
5. L. M. Cooke, ed., *Cleaning Our Environment: The Chemical Basis for Action* (Washington, D.C.: American Chemical Society, 1969), pp. 135–137.

6. G. R. Stewart, *Not So Rich As You Think* (New York: New American Library, 1970) p. 35, has a delightful discussion of the "earth closet" as an alternative to the water closet.
7. Lewis Mumford, "The Natural History of Urbanization," *Man's Role in Changing the Face of the Earth,* ed. W. L. Thomas, Jr. (Chicago: U. of Chicago, 1957), gives a historical perspective to some of these problems.
8. Stewart, op. cit., p. 107.
9. Richard H. Wagner, *Environment and Man* (New York: Norton, 1971), p. 116.
10. B. M. Hannon, "Bottles, Cans, Energy," *Environment,* **14:**11–21 (1972).
11. "The Kansas Geologists and the AEC," *Science News,* (March 6, 1971), p. 161.
12. W. C. Gough and B. J. Eastlund, "The Prospects of Fusion Power," *Scientific American,* **224**:50–64 (1971).
13. Paul R. and Anne H. Ehrlich, *Populations, Resources, Environment,* 2nd ed. (San Francisco: Freeman, 1972), p. 65.
14. D. E. Thomsen, "Farming the Sun's Energy," *Science News,* (April 8, 1972), p. 237.
15. D. P. Gregory, "The Hydrogen Economy," *Scientific American,* **228**:13–21 (1973).
16. M. King Hubbert, "Energy Resources," *Resources and Man,* ed., Preston Cloud (San Francisco: Freeman, 1969).
17. J. N. Wilford, "New Plan Is Outlined for Tapping Geothermal Energy," *The New York Times,* 21 June 1972.
18. R. H. Gilluly, "The Earth's Heat: A New Power Source," *Science News,* (November 28, 1970) pp. 415–416.
19. Hubbert *loc. cit.*

# 24

# Environmental Modeling

## Key Concepts

Model
Simulation
Physical models
Microcosms
Biological models
Mathematical models
Hypotheses
Computer
Systems analysis
Input–output
Interface
Feedback
Real-time data
Stochastic model

*Model* is a word that has been stretched to accommodate several meanings. It can refer to a beautiful, thin girl who displays the latest fashions. Or it can be a miniature car laboriously glued together by a child (with some help from a parent). Or it can be an entire city, so well planned that it serves as a good example for all those seeking ways to improve the quality of urban life. However, even this last usage, model city, is not what ecologists refer to when they describe environmental modeling. Just what are they talking about? Because many old words are being used in new ways, this is not always easy to discern. The key concept is *simulation*. Environmental models are designed to simulate the real world. They can be grouped into three main categories: physical, biological, and mathematical.

*Physical models* are like miniature cars in that they are scaled-down replicas of the real thing. In ecology, however, they represent rivers, harbors, shore lines, or other environmental components that may be under the management of an organization such as the Corps of Engineers. These models have been useful in planning dredging, diking, and other large-scale

**Figure 24–1.**
*Harbor model* (U.S. Army Corps of Engineers photo)

operations dear to the hearts of engineers and contractors alike.[1] Less realistic physical models, often used in research and teaching, include such gadgets as wave tanks, flumes, and glorified sandboxes, which, on a small scale, demonstrate various phenomena: wave formation, sediment transport, and erosion.

Laboratory colonies of one species and *microcosms* (microecosystems) containing two or more species can be termed *biological models*. Here the environment has been scaled down and containerized but the organisms are, of course, life-sized. Confinement, as any prisoner will tell you, is unnatural and creates many problems. With laboratory cultures, accumulation of waste products and prevention of dispersal are the most troublesome sources of abnormalities, even when the organisms are provided with all their known requisites. Despite these limitations, biological models have been very useful in studying population growth, genetic shifts, and community succession.[2] You can imagine some of the possibilities for experimentation with an aquarium containing algae, algae-eating snails, and fish that eat snails, or another species that competes with the snails in eating algae. Such aquaria may never become "balanced," but starting with different combinations of organisms and providing different regimes of light, nutrition, and so on, it is possible to develop hypotheses about ecological relationships that can then be tested in the world at large.

One biological model, designed to clarify certain interactions between predator and prey, required the construction of a small universe! Actually, the "universe" was a cabinet with 252 oranges on three levels. One species of tiny mite fed on the exposed portions of the oranges and another species of mite, slightly larger, preyed on those orange-eating mites it could catch. Because one seventh of the oranges were renewed each week, a continuous game of hide-and-seek was played within the cabinet, the phytophagous mites finding and colonizing the new oranges, only to be decimated by the predators—but not before they had successfully scouted out and populated more new oranges.[3] This model approximates many real-world situations where new resources become available and are utilized by organisms that, in turn, serve to support other organisms.

## THE NATURE: COMPUTER INTERFACE

Interesting and useful though they may be, physical and biological models are now less common than *mathematical models*. In these, numbers represent populations, resources, rates of transfer, or any of the other ecological processes and environmental factors that can be quantified. Whenever possible, the mathematical models are based on hard data but, like other models, they are simulations, not to be confused with reality itself.[4] They are, in fact, sophisticated *hypotheses* that always must be tested against nature and modified if they do not fit. This is sometimes a great disappointment to those who create models (or theories), but it must be done if science is to progress.

The electronic *computer* plays a vital role in mathematical modeling. Even the simplest simulation of nature requires so many equations, transformations, and calculations that the high speed of a modern computer is essential. They also help ecological studies by storing, in their capacious memory banks, the vast quantities of data generated by environmental monitoring networks (see Chapter 23). In short, many of our attempts to describe and analyze the world around us would be doomed to frustration if we did not have computers as tools of understanding. They are, of course, no more than tools and, despite some science fiction speculation to the contrary, will remain "high-speed idiots" for many generations (computer and human).

The general term for much of the work done with mathematical models is *systems analysis.*[5] However, you must consider the background of the person using the phrase in order to understand exactly what he means by it. An engineer may be thinking of a man-made chemical processing factory, a political scientist may have in mind the governmental decision-making apparatus, but an ecologist is usually thinking of an ecosystem, defined in Chapter 2, which consists of all the organisms in a given location and the physical-chemical factors that affect them. What do all these uses of systems analysis have in common? Very likely, each has some form of the *input–output* concept. The engineer would consider the raw chemicals going in and the finished product coming out. The political scientist might take an urban problem as his starting point and then show how this led to the passing of new legislation. For the ecologist, however, the inputs would fall into such categories as solar energy, water and nutrients, and $CO_2$ for plants and $O_2$ for all organisms. The outputs might be anything from the products of decay to emigrating animals. The biggest differences are the origins of the systems being modeled. Both the engineer and the political scientist are dealing with man-made systems, but the ecologist is trying to understand a complex, natural ecosystem that has not been created by man.

It may be necessary to define a few words before we proceed:

**Interface:** the area of contact between two parts, often used to indicate linkage between the computer and auxiliary equipment

**Program:** sequence of instructions, usually written in a quasi-mathematical, shorthand computer language, such as FORTRAN

**Debugging:** removing errors of logic or instruction from the program so that the computer will do exactly what you want it to do

**Punch card:** perforated cards common in computerized billing or registration; used to feed either data or instructions into a computer

**Print out:** large sheets of paper, spewed out by a high-speed printer, which show the results of the computer's whirlwind calculations

Typically, all the machines (key punch, computer, printer, and remote terminals) are described as hardware, whereas the programs, many of which have been standardized, are called software. For environmental modeling to be useful, an ecologist must understand (or work with someone who understands) the potentials and limitations of both software and hardware.

## THREE LEVELS OF MODELING

Although mathematical models used in environmental description and analysis are now both numerous and diverse, only three will be discussed, proceeding from the simplest to the most complex. The three are population, compartment, and compartment plus feedback models. For the first, we can use the world's human population. In Figure 24–2 we have a simple graph, with five projections based on different assumptions about the year in which family size drops to the point of parental replacement. Only the

**Figure 24–2.**
*Human population growth projections* (after Figure 1-3, p. 11 in *Human Ecology*, P. R. Ehrlich, A. H. Ehrlich and John P. Holdren, San Francisco: W. H. Freeman, copyright © 1973)

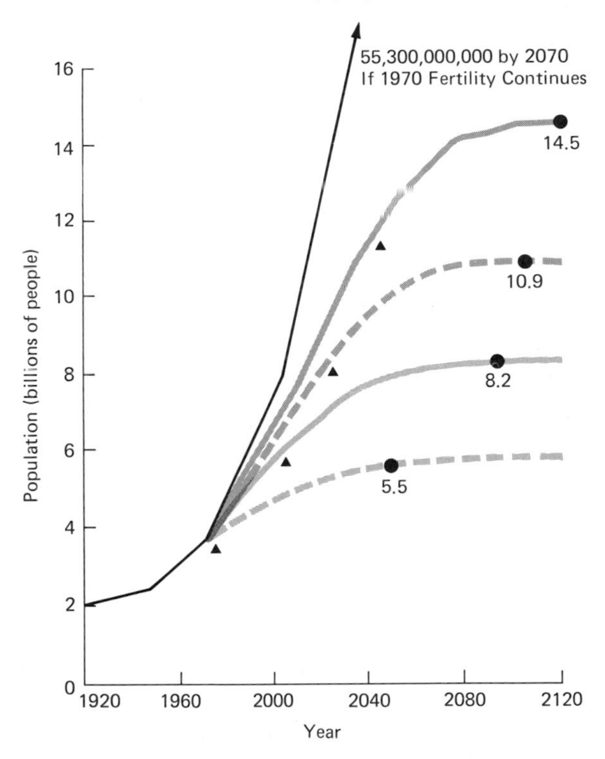

first fifty years of the graph actually describe population changes; after 1970 we are given alternative models. These models could be constructed from rather simple information on birth and death rates, or they could be refined by using knowledge of sex ratios, age distribution, age-specific rates, and desired family size.

Similar models can be used for populations of livestock or pests. For the latter, or for any natural population not considered on a worldwide basis, birth and death rates are not enough. An essential input–output is immigration-emigration; without these rates, the model is unrealistic. A population model can be refined further by building into it various constraints, such as a minimum density below which the chances of successful mating are greatly reduced or a maximum density above which resource depletion, increased disease, and related processes combine to prevent further population growth. These, however, are feedback mechanisms, best considered later in the chapter.

Compartment models are the type most commonly used in ecosystem analysis. Refer back to Figure 2–6, page 24, for a simple diagram of the food web. This could be the basis for a model of energy flow in an ecosystem, showing how much solar energy is photosynthetically fixed in green plants, how much of this stored energy is consumed by herbivores, and how much is then eaten by carnivores, with some indication of the energy transferred from each of these three compartments to detritivores. This would, of course, give you another view of the food pyramid, diagrammed in Figure 2–7. A similar, but less abstract, model of an ecosystem, based on measurements in a Georgia pond, shows the observed energy flow through phytoplankton, invertebrates, and game fish to man (Figure 24–3).

In other models at the ecosystem level, each compartment might represent all the individuals of one species or the nutrient content of an environmental component. All ecosystem models have varying degrees of intercompartmental linkage, with output from one compartment providing input for one or more compartments. Generally speaking, greater crisscrossing (interconnectivity) reduces the probability that any one compartment will expand and contract widely.

This brings us to the highest level to be discussed in this chapter: a compartment model with cybernetic *feedback* mechanisms, recognizing the fact that transfers between compartments are dynamic. If a certain minimal size is passed, further increase may become easier (this is an example of positive feedback). On the other hand, increase beyond a maximal size may exceed input availability and/or make output rates rise—that is, create negative feedback. With a model that incorporates these

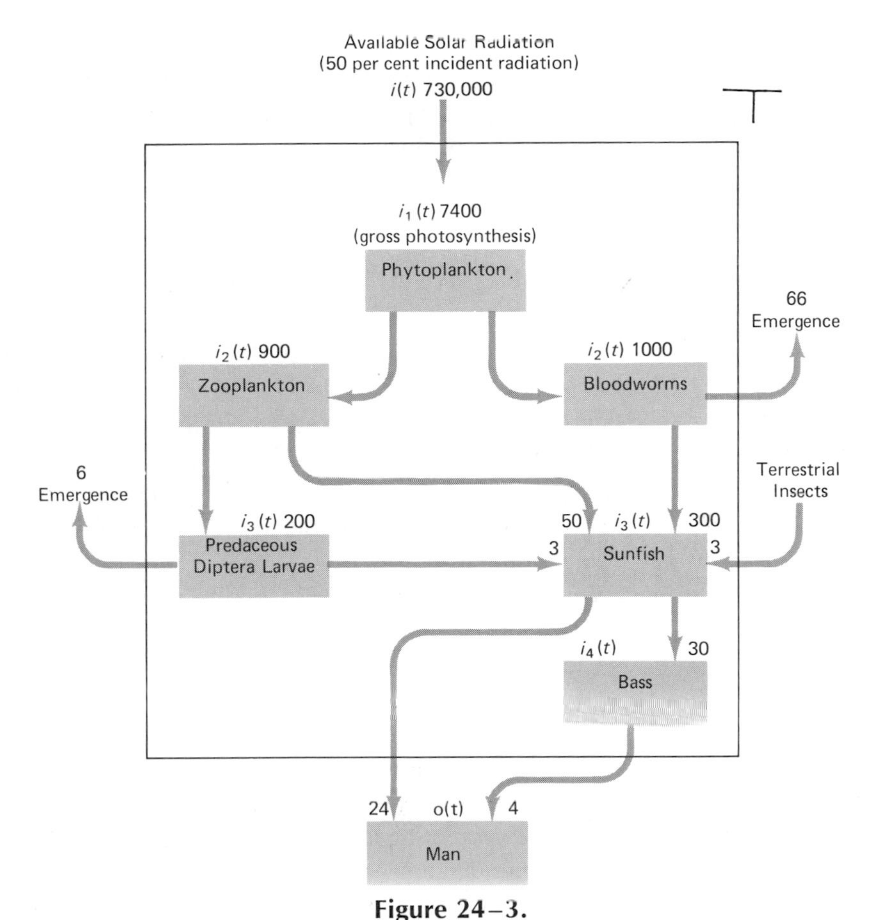


**Figure 24–3.**

*Food web in a Georgia pond* [after Eugene Odum, *Fundamentals of Ecology,* 3rd. ed. (Philadelphia: W. B. Saunders, 1971) p. 70]

dynamic interactions between compartments, we are getting much closer to reality but, programmers' nightmares that they are, they still are only approximations. Good examples of feedback models can be seen in books by J. Forrester,[6] D. Meadows,[7] and H. T. Odum.[8] The latter author, with power as a common denominator, uses electrical analog models to describe everything from ecosystems to religions! The degree of complexity achieved with compartments plus feedback can be seen in the world model developed by the Meadows group for their well-publicized Club of Rome Project. Emphasizing environmental constraints (nonrenewable energy and mineral resources, finite arable land, pollution build-up), it also has nonenvironmental components (service, industrial, and agricultural capital) that represent a unification of ecological and economic realities (to be discussed at length in Chapter 25). The main conclusion of the Meadows group was that the human compartment cannot expand without encountering various forms of negative feedback. Some ecologists would say this has occurred already; all would agree that it eventually must be true.

## USING A MODEL AS A CRYSTAL BALL

The dimension of time should be included in sophisticated models of our environment. It is relatively easy to reconstruct and model what has happened in a population, community, or ecosystem, but it becomes more difficult to describe a process as it occurs. The best approach is to form an interface between a computer and a network monitoring physical or chemical factors. With such *real-time data* input, the print-out version may represent an instant-replay model of real events. However, the most difficult task of all is prediction. You should remember this any time you see a dotted line extending into the twenty-first century (see, for example, Figure 24–2). Extrapolations such as these must, of necessity, be based on the assumptions that certain trends, already observed and measured, will continue. If the predictions do not come true, you can usually blame a "more-of-the-same" assumption built into the original program. As environmental monitoring and other forms of data acquisition are improved, it may be possible to develop self-correcting models that change their predictions as new information becomes available (computers will be learning but not thinking). At present, the best we can do is to make sure that environmental models are based on accurate data and rational assumptions. The first law of computer science is GIGO (garbage in–garbage out)!

Predictions of human population growth or behavior are especially difficult because humans hear about, and react to, models that embody warnings. We ban DDT without waiting to see how many species it really can wipe out; we stop eating swordfish before there is an epidemic of fetal deformation. We may even slow our population growth before the worst consequences of overpopulation are verified. This is one more feedback loop for the programmers to contend with, and it will continue to be important as long as humans are rational enough to say they would rather be safe than sorry.[9]

As you well know, even a meteorologist, dealing with fairly well-understood physical phenomena, has a hard time predicting tomorrow's weather. What he now does is give you odds based on a review of past weather patterns. For example, he will say there is a 20 percent chance of rain tomorrow because precipitation has occurred in one out of five weather sequences similar to those he is now following on his weather maps. What he has given you is a *stochastic model,* and this is becoming part of much environmental modeling. Rather than assume trends or rates will continue, past changes are carefully analyzed and probabilities of future departures from simple linearity are calculated. Environmental models that incorporate both cybernetic and stochastic elements can help us plan for the possibility of anything from a disastrous flood to an outbreak of the gypsy moth.

It should be obvious by now that an environmental model, although quite useful, is a very murky crystal ball. Predictions based on fragmentary data and faulty assumptions may even lead us into actions that make a bad situation worse. We should recognize the limits of computers and computer-generated models. Rather than believe that they somehow will lead us to the "Promised Land," we must decide which way we want to go, and then use new, improved models to help us decide how close we are getting to our goal.

## SUMMARY

Models—simulations of real-world systems—can be very useful in environmental analysis. Physical models are scaled-down replicas, biological models are laboratory colonies with one or more species, and mathematical models are those in which numbers represent the dimensions of environmental components or the rates of ecological processes. With modern computers, it is possible to simulate large and complex ecosystems, building on knowledge of movements into and out of a number of subcompartments. The most sophisticated models take into consideration positive and negative feedback interactions between compartments and may even give the odds for and against the continuation of observed trends in real-world situations.

### Discussion Questions

1. Do you think computers are "taking over"?
2. How many different meanings does the word *model* have?
3. What are scientific hypotheses and how are they tested?
4. In what way does a human population respond to negative feedback?
5. How much planning is being done on the basis of computer projections?

## Suggested Projects

**1.** Use data from your aquarium project (Chapter 13) to make a simple mathematical model of inputs and outputs.

**2.** Read "The Limits to Growth" by Meadows et al. or "Blueprint for Survival" by E. Goldsmith et al. and use either book as a basis for an informal (out-of-class) discussion with others who are concerned about the future.

## Notes

1. *U.S. Army Engineer Waterways Experiment Station* (Vicksburg, Miss.: Corps of Engineers, U.S. Army, undated brochure)
2. E. P. Odum, *Fundamentals of Ecology,* 3rd ed. (Philadelphia: Saunders, 1971), pp. 20–22.
3. C. B. Huffaker, K. P. Shea, and S. G. Herman, "Experimental Studies on Predation. Complex Dispersion and Levels of Food in an Acarine Predator-Prey Interaction," *Hilgardia,* **34**:305–330, (1963).
4. G. A. Mihram, *Simulation. Statistical Foundations and Methodology.* (New York: Academic 1972). A technical treatise on the subject.
5. For a brief, but sophisticated, discussion of systems analysis, see C. J. Walters, "Systems Ecology: The Systems Approach and Mathematical Models in Ecology," in Odum, op. cit., pp. 276–292. For "everything you wanted to know about systems analysis, but were afraid to ask," see B. C. Patten, *Systems Analysis and Simulation in Ecology,* vols. I and II (New York: Academic, 1971 and 1972), collections of papers showing the state of the art.
6. Jay W. Forrester, *World Dynamics* (Cambridge, Mass.: Wright-Allen Press, 1971).
7. D. H. Meadows, D. L. Meadows, J. Randers, and W. W. Behrens, III, *The Limits to Growth* (New York: Universe Books, 1972).
8. H. T. Odum, *Environment, Power, and Society* (New York: Wiley-Interscience, 1971).
9. My former colleague, J. C. Zieman, brought this uncertainty principle of human ecology models to my attention.

# 25
# Resource Allocation

## Key Concepts

- Cost and value
- Carrying capacity
- Laws of the market place
- Laws of the jungle
- Patchiness of resources
- Trade
- Renewable, nonrenewable, and land resources
- Sustained yield
- Resource substitution
- Recycling
- Biotic diversity
- Proper place
- Ecological backlash
- Equilibrium
- Law of interdependence

In this chapter we return to some of the conflicts between ecology and economics mentioned in Chapter 3. This argument is not one that can be resolved easily because both groups claim that they are being realistic. "After all," says the economist, "most decisions are based on monetary *cost and value*. The real world is one of people buying, selling, hoarding, starving, and speculating!" The ecologist will counter with a hasty disavowal that he is "antipeople." "I have not sold out to the wood-peckers, but I do think we can learn from other species. In nature, species that exceed the *carrying capacity* of their environment degrade that environment and jeopardize their own perpetuation. How can we be so sure that we are exempt from such real constraints?"[1] You might characterize the disagreement as a question of legal jurisdiction, with the economist saying "*the laws of the market place* are all-important" and the ecologist claiming that "*the laws of the jungle* take precedence."

Arguments of this sort can take many strange turns. The ecologist, although he recognizes the interdependence of living creatures, may wish the human population of each nation could be virtually self-reliant, importing no resources essential to its survival. Such populations would be living within the carrying capacities of their respective environments, with the added benefit of being immune to political-economic pressures from other nations. The astute economist is quick to point out that humans, as soon as they rise above subsistence agriculture (each cluster of farmers barely feeding themselves from the land they till), exchange rugged self-reliance for specialization and a higher standard of living. Eventually, we have one farmer, with the help of mechanization and agricultural chemicals, feeding twenty city dwellers in his nation or other nations; the city dwellers are linked to the farmer, as well as each other, through a complex network of goods and services.

The ecologist is forced to agree that *patchiness of resource availability,* a basic constraint on populations of nonhuman species, has been partially circumvented through the development of *trade*. Those to whom Allah gave sand, camels, and oil can use the oil to buy water, wheat, transistor radios, and other things they need (or want). In a similar way, stockpiling in good years has helped the human species survive and multiply even when there is a poor harvest one year. "Yes," the ecologist admits, "we have done a fair job of evening out certain resources, but what about the poor people who have no surplus products to trade or store? Shouldn't they reduce their numbers?" "Perhaps," counters the economist, "but they should also develop their resources for their own direct benefit and for trade! As a resource becomes scarce, it becomes more valuable, making it profitable to find new supplies, to develop supplies that were previously marginal, or to substitute a different resource that meets the demand. Citizens of developing countries are in a good position to improve their lot because they can insist on high prices for the raw materials needed by developed countries."

Through an examination of resource allocation, it may be possible to find ways of at least partially resolving these conflicting views. For purposes of discussion and analysis, resources will be considered in three broad categories: *renewable* (food, timber, and water); *nonrenewable* (fossil and nuclear fuels, minerals, and biotic diversity); and, in a class by itself, *land*.[2] Because land use is modified by the exploitation, transportation, or use of any resource, it underlies the entire analysis, but it is still useful to consider renewable and nonrenewable resource allocations separately.

## RENEWABLE RESOURCES

Any living species—plant or animal—can be regarded as a renewable resource because it has evolved mechanisms to perpetuate itself in spite of natural losses. Certain inanimate components of the environment are also self-renewing: fresh water, solar energy, and—to some extent—soil fertility. If ecologists were in charge, all of these renewable resources would be harvested on the basis of *sustained yield*. This concept, discussed in Chapter 6 in connection with forest management, simply means that the resource is harvested by man no more rapidly than it is replaced by nature. Common sense would seem to dictate this policy as fundamental to conservation, yet man often has found excuses for modifying it or ignoring it completely.

Take the example of forests in North America. Old forests, in which most trees are growing slowly, do not yield much in pulp or lumber, although they may be useful for recreation and as a habitat for certain species of wildlife (for example, the ivorybill). In national forests and on private land managed for maximum yield, a mix of old trees is replaced with a monoculture of fast-growing conifers. A related practice is that of clear cutting, harvesting all the trees in a given area rather than going through the forest picking out certain trees that are ready to be harvested. The economic arguments for monoculture and clear cutting are compelling: forest lands are marginally profitable, and logging (with lumberjacks, heavy equipment, and roads) is expensive, so operations must be efficient. We end up with a situation where over-all conifer growth is balanced against harvest and losses to fire, disease, or insects; however, certain species of wildlife and noncommercial trees have been greatly reduced in distribution and abundance. The letter of the sustained-yield law is followed, but the spirit may have been lost.

The tragedy of the great whales, mentioned in Chapter 4, is an example of the sustained-yield law violated in both letter and intent. The blue whale, the humpback whale, and the right whales have been driven close to extinction, and other species are under heavy pressure from the whaling fleets of Japan and the Soviet Union. This is not a natural predator-prey relationship. If it were, the whalers would have regulated their hunting efforts long before the great whales became rare. All natural predators harvest their prey on a sustained-yield basis, having instinctive restraints that prevent them from putting themselves out of business.[3]

One inanimate example, water, will complete this section. Whether used for drinking, cooling, irrigation, or the generation of hydroelectric power, water can flow no faster than it is replaced by natural precipitation. Just as we have made food crops, trees, and domestic animals grow more rapidly, so we can have more to harvest, we have tried to increase precipitation through cloud seeding and similar tricks; however, perhaps fortunately, we have had only localized success. Our principal violation of sustained yield has occurred in the southwestern United States where deep aquifers are being depleted far more rapidly than they are refilled. That cannot continue much longer. Water will be the factor that limits development throughout much of the arid West. (Refer back to Chapter 15 for a discussion of water management.)

## NONRENEWABLE RESOURCES

Scarcity of water limits the population growth of many species other than man. However, we have certain requisites that are unique. After all, no other organisms consume metallic ores, uranium, gas, or coal, and only a few bacteria can subsist on oil! The growth of modern urbanized and industrial society has been completely dependent on the availability of energy and mineral resources.[4] Yet, our attitude toward these has been much the same as our attitude toward renewable resources: "extract the rich deposits first, then shift to lower and lower concentrations until their extraction lacks economic justification, and finally try something else." The name of this final game is *resource substitution,* and it will be interesting to see how long it can be played.

To get needed fuel, we may try to shift from gas and oil fields to oil shale and tar sands where huge quantities of water will have to be imported for the extraction process. To get electricity, the proposed sequence is from fossil fuels and hydroelectric dams to "conventional" reactors, then to breeder reactors, and finally to fusion power. The shifts can get thoroughly tangled. Take, for example, those situations where oil is not used as an energy source but to make plastics and other petrochemical products that replace materials manufactured from wood (a renewable resource).

This dependence on nonrenewable resources, together with the unproven assumption that we always will be able to come up with substitutes, is more than a little worrisome. Wouldn't it be more secure to rely on renewable resources? For energy, we could capture solar power, evening out its diurnal, seasonal, and geographic availability by using $H_2$–$O_2$ fuel cells (Chapter 23). We also could try to reverse the wood-to-plastic shift. Finally, we could treat metals as a renewable resource by fully implementing the policy of *recycling*. Of course, even these changes would not bring any national population completely within the carrying capacity of its environment, but they certainly would reduce the impact of man and technology on natural ecosystems, and this would help insure continued high levels of biotic diversity.

*Biotic diversity* (the number of species sharing a given environment) is not included often in lists of nonrenewable resources, but it should be. Just as fossil fuels are deposited so slowly that they cannot be regarded as self-renewing, so also must species evolved over millions of years be considered irreplaceable. At various points in this book (especially in Chapters 7, 10, and 24), the value of diversity has been extolled. The most important reason for conserving diversity is that, in many ecosystems, it helps maintain a dynamic equilibrium that we find more compatible than wild fluctuations. However, at any level of abstraction, from the biosphere to the back yard, there are other justifications. These are value judgments, but biotic diversity, in space and through time, is considered in most cultures to be more interesting and beautiful than monotonous monoculture. This is most noticeable in cities without parks where the absence of flowers, grass, trees, and birds is painfully apparent.

## LAND USE

The legal aspects of land-use zoning are discussed in Chapter 26. Here, however, we will consider land as a resource and, unless we regain our lost gills, it may be the basic resource for the human species.[5] Three concepts: sustained yield, recycling, and carrying capacity, already mentioned in connection with other resources, will be applied to land use, together with a fourth concept, best described as "everything in its *proper place*."

Whenever and wherever land is used to produce a living resource, be it grain, fiber, fruit, wood, or meat, nutrients are removed through the harvest process. Natural processes slowly replace these lost nutrients, transferring them from unavailable forms to the water in soil where they can be utilized by plants (see Chapter 11), and we have found it necessary to accelerate the replacement processes by application of artificial fertilizers (Chapter 9). In fact, strict adherence to sustained yield in this category (nutrients harvested at a rate equal to natural replacement) would require a reduction in the world population to the one billion level. A compromise may be necessary: the management of land so that erosion, overgrazing, and overreliance on agricultural chemicals are not permitted to gradually reduce productivity, while the need for fertilizer inputs and genetic engineering to increase growth rates in response to nutrient availability is recognized. Thus, yields can be sustained over long periods.

Recycling will be of great help in achieving this goal. Manure from stockyards, dried sludge and waste water from sewage treatment plants, as well as properly composted garbage, grass cuttings, leaves, and so on can help maintain the structure, fertility, and productivity of soil. It is especially important to recycle phosphorous by such means; it is far too scarce and valuable to be used for growing unwanted algae. Recycling, in the land-use context, can take other forms: rubbish and rubble from urban areas can be used to build new parks or even ski slopes! If these projects do not destroy essential habitats for wildlife or take vital metals out of circulation, they would be quite beneficial.

The concepts of carrying capacity and everything in its proper place are intertwined and should be considered together. Ideally, any use of land should be determined not by whim, but by an honest recognition of the potentials and the limitations that characterize that particular parcel of real estate. A flood plain might be fine for agriculture but risky for housing and industry. A rocky ridge could serve as a recreational site but, because of inadequate water, it might not be a good place for a subdivision. The United States Soil Conservation Service has produced a land-capability classification that emphasizes relative suitability for cultivation as determined by fertility, drainage, slope, and rockiness.[6] Once the basic environmental constraints are accepted as givens, the way is clear for a rational zoning of land use (Figure 25–1), best exemplified by the work of Ian L. McHarg and his colleagues.[7] They take into consideration not only the physical and chemical environment but also any unique assemblages of biota, scenery, or historical sites. Subjective judgments of value make any land-use classification controversial. Nonetheless, they are a necessary antidote to unplanned, unsightly urban sprawl. Ecological guidelines are also quite useful in directing the development of emerging nations. The Institute of Ecology has provided a number of recommendations for land management in tropical lowland forests, tropical savannas, temperate grasslands, and arid regions.[8] These were transmitted to the UN Conference on the Human Environment, held in Stockholm during 1972.

You may well complain that much of this chapter seems to be professorial pussyfooting around the central question of "Who gets what?" After all, the chapter is entitled "Resource Allocation." Ecology can certainly help in maintaining sustained yield, encouraging recycling, determining carrying capacity, and developing rational patterns of land use, but can it also help in directing the distribution of resources? This is an area where both ecology and economics conjoin law and ethics.

## SOCIAL JUSTICE

A number of commentators have noted that all the passengers aboard Spaceship Earth do not have equal access to provisions. Some starve while

**Figure 25–1.**
*Land classified according to its potentialities and limitations* (U.S.D.A.-SCS photo)

others overeat. Some burn cow dung while others consume fossil fuels by the ton. Some must beg for water while others drench their lawns. These disparities occur in the same nation and are glaringly obvious on the world scene.[9] The *ecological backlash* (reaction to the predictions of overpopulation, resource depletion, and reduced quality of life) has a strong component of concern for the world's poor. How can they possibly benefit from environmental constraints on economic growth? A future with no new resources and few new jobs is grim indeed. Kenneth E. Boulding, although he is an environmentally aware economist, warns that in such a stationary economy, powerful rich people will be strongly tempted to further enrich themselves at the expense of the poor.[10]

How can economic equilibrium be attained and maintained below the carrying capacity of a nation or the entire planet without condemning most humans to perpetual poverty? A careful definition of *equilibrium* may help show the way. Environmentalists think of it as a dynamic average that persists despite great shifts in its components. With this concept in mind, you can imagine a no-growth world susceptible to many beneficial changes.

New, cheaper, and less-polluting sources of energy could be introduced, bringing "power to the people" with a minimum of undesirable side effects (Figure 25–2). Improvements in communication and transportation could increase both our knowledge of resource availability and our ability to trade surpluses, with computers accelerating the inventory, purchasing, and transportation processes. Diversion of military and space-exploration expenditures into areas of community development and public safety also would seem probable and desirable. All of these shifts are possible without an increased GNP.

However, centuries from now, economic disparities will remain even if the entire world has adopted a compromise political system (under the banner of social capitalism). These remaining disparities should serve as incentives rather than handicaps, assuming the future will be more rational than the present, with population size stabilized or reduced and technology tamed. We cannot expect a new Eden or any other form of Utopia, but we can hope for a pleasant, prosperous world, governed by wise leaders who so fully recognize the consequences of their actions that they are restrained from folly. As suggested in the last two chapters of this book, enlightened self-interest may lead us to discard the law of the jungle and the law of the market place, substituting a *law of interdependence* that will give full recognition to all the links that unite all people and make humanity part of nature.[11]

**Figure 25–2.**

*Component changes in an economy at dynamic equilibrium*

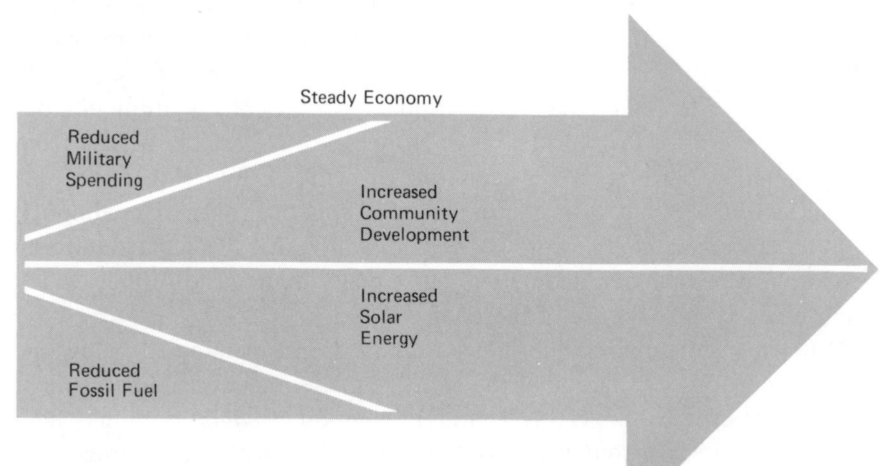

## SUMMARY

Resources, living or inanimate, renewable or nonrenewable, can be managed more wisely and distributed more fairly. While agreeing that these are worthy goals, the economist and the ecologist differ over the best means of achieving them. The economist suggests that scarcity will cause a price increase making development, trade, or substitution of new resources worthwhile. The ecologist fears that overexploitation is almost inevitable under such a system and suggests that resources should be harvested on the basis of a sustained yield, that wastes should be recycled, and that human populations should put land to appropriate uses and try to live within the carrying capacity of their environments. The more optimistic of ecologists even believe that reallocation of resources within an economy at dynamic equilibrium will achieve some degree of social justice.

### Discussion Questions

1. Who is the most realistic, the economist or the ecologist?
2. Contrast the concepts of sustained yield and resource substitution.
3. Why is biotic diversity a resource?
4. How can resources be reallocated to meet the needs of social justice?

### Suggested Projects

1. Do an opinion survey of local merchants to find out if they think environmentalists are at least partially responsible for economic problems. Here are some possible questions: (a) Is recycling more trouble than it's worth? (b) Is the high cost of energy a result of excessive caution in building refineries and power plants? (c) Should a land owner be able to do anything he wants to with his property?
2. Use almanacs or similar reference works to get data for a large chart summarizing United States imports and exports.

### Notes

1. Carrying capacity is a central concept in D. H. Meadows et al., *The Limits to Growth* (New York: Universe Books, 1972).
2. This includes the major categories covered in H. H. Landsberg, *Natural Resources for U.S. Growth—A Look Ahead to the Year 2000* (Baltimore: Resources for the Future, Johns Hopkins, 1964), which,

incidentally, assumes a population for the United States of 330 million in the year 2000.

3. Farley Mowat, *A Whale for the Killing* (Baltimore: Penguin Books, 1972), shows, with the sad story of one whale, man's distorted attitudes toward great whales and all living resources.
4. J. F. Klaff, "National Materials Policy Necessary to Conserve U.S. Resources," *Environmental Science & Technology,* **7**:912–916 (1973). An excellent summary of our requirements and the extent of recycling.
5. For further information on land use in the United States, see M. Clawson, R. B. Held, and C. H. Stoddard, *Land for the Future* (Baltimore: Resources for the Future, Johns Hopkins, 1960); or, its abridged version, M. Clawson, *Land for Americans—Trends, Prospects, and Problems* (Chicago: Rand McNally, 1963).
6. Raymond F. Dasmann, *Environmental Conservation,* 3rd ed. (New York: Wiley, 1972), p. 152, has a good land-classification scheme.
7. Ian L. McHarg, *Design with Nature* (New York: Natural History Press, 1969).
8. A. D. Hasler, ed., *Man in the Living Environment—Report of the Workshop on Global Ecological Problems* (Madison: The Institute of Ecology, University of Wisconsin Press, 1971).
9. B. Ward, *The Rich Nations and the Poor Nations* (New York: Norton, 1962).
10. Kenneth E. Boulding, "New Goals for Society," ed. S. H. Schurr *Energy, Economic Growth, and the Environment,* (Baltimore: Johns Hopkins, 1972).
11. Two of the best prescriptions for a better world are R. A. Falk, *This Endangered Planet—Prospects and Proposals for Human Survival* (New York: Vintage, 1972); and B. Ward and R. Dubos, *Only One Earth—the Care and Feeding of a Small Planet* (New York: Ballantine, 1973).

# 26

# Environmental Law

## Key Concepts

- Natural laws
- Human laws
- Zero population growth
- Land-use zoning
- Antipollution programs
- "The tragedy of the commons"
- Persuasion to coercion
- Master plan
- Protection of health
- Internalization and recycling
- Negligence, nuisance, and trespass
- Class action
- Injunctions
- Strict regulations
- New laws
- Impact statements
- Environmental bill of rights
- "Social contract"

Those suddenly aware of environmental degradation commonly respond with statements of the "there ought to be a law" variety. When they discover that laws against pollution and other forms of environmental despoilation already exist, the loudly militant of the aware cry "Sue the bastards," while the less vocal work to improve enforcement by environmental agencies. At any intensity of public response and at all levels of governmental responsibility, ecologists find themselves involved. To an ecologist, the political and legal approaches to the problems of environmental quality—entailing "nonscientific" evidence, standards, and procedures—may seem strange. Scientific theories, or *natural laws,* are based on data patiently gathered through observation and experiment. A scientist anywhere in the world can either verify or modify a natural law through his own research. However, *human laws* are (or should be) based on social needs. They are developed by legislators, enforced by the police and the judiciary, and can be broken, amended, or repealed. Natural laws transcend national boundaries, but human laws are very much a product of each national society. In the next chapter the moral neutrality of natural law will be stressed, but human laws can certainly be good or bad, depending on the extent of their benefits to citizens. Despite all this, the ecologist admits that the development and application of human laws are at least as important as understanding nature's laws in efforts to preserve and improve our environment (Figure 26–1).

Within the context of this book, ecological aspects of environmental law can be considered under three broad headings: *ZPG, land-use zoning,* and *antipollution programs*. Problems in all three areas are rooted in *"The Tragedy of the Commons,"* as the philosophical biologist Garrett Hardin has so aptly described it, with each individual seeing only the immediate benefits of his or her action, not recognizing the collective cost of resource extraction, pollutant dumping, or population increase.[1] Hardin used the analogy of farmers sharing a common pasture, each farmer seeing the profitability of adding to his own herd but failing to see that his addition would contribute to overgrazing and eventual harm to all those using the "commons." Hardin suggested that "coercion, mutually agreed upon" may be necessary to prevent such collective impacts.

**Figure 26–1.**
*Natural vs human law*

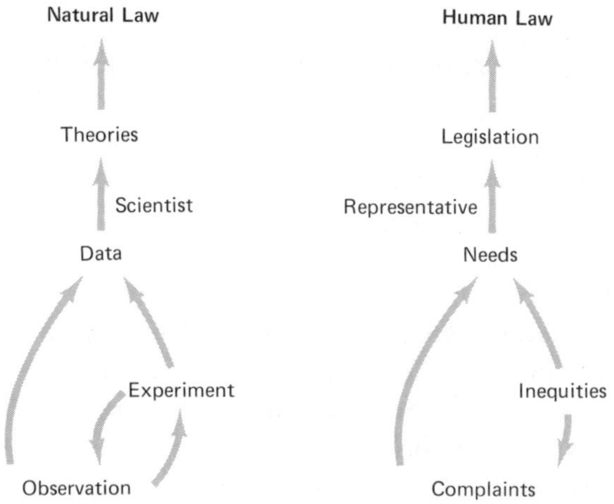

## ZPG

The ZPG organization, and those who sympathize with its aims, represents the most recent approach to the central problems of family and population limitation. Earlier in this century, the goal of Margaret Sanger was to legalize the distribution of contraceptive information and materials. Later the Planned Parenthood movement emphasized the right of parents to have "wanted children," with help being given to subfertile couples as well as to those who were "overproducers." Now, the emphasis has shifted once again, with Paul R. Ehrlich and other advocates of ZPG seeking a national population policy of "no further growth" or—better still—reduction to an as yet undetermined "optimum population."[2]

Obviously, the fact that "wanted children" contribute to population growth is the biggest obstacle to achievement of ZPG. ZPG's strategy, often misunderstood by the media (press and TV), has been to persuade couples to voluntarily limit the size of their families to two children. They do not argue that every couple should have two children, recognizing that some, for psychological or eugenic reasons, may choose to remain childless, and that others may be able to cope with more than two. The *average* number of children per couple should be 2.1, if parental replacement is the goal, the fractional surplus compensating for those who die before adulthood or never get married[3] (Figure 26–2).

In a democracy such as ours, ZPG will move from *persuasion* to *coercion* only when a majority of our elected representatives, at local, state, or federal levels, seek to implement a strong population policy. Ample precedents can be found in laws barring polygamy or restricting immigration, but it still will require great political courage to tamper with family life. Efforts already under way include those designed to truly liberate women, providing them with alternatives to motherhood. In principal, this sounds wonderful, but in practice, it may involve controversial changes toward subsidized day-care centers and even more liberalized abortion.

Although America has a long tradition of universal free education through high school, governmental policies shifting the burden of education back to parents may become popular, and income-tax reforms may further lighten the load now carried by unmarried wage earners.[4] Some individual freedom of choice will inevitably be lost through such changes, and there is a real danger that "surplus" children will be punished for being conceived

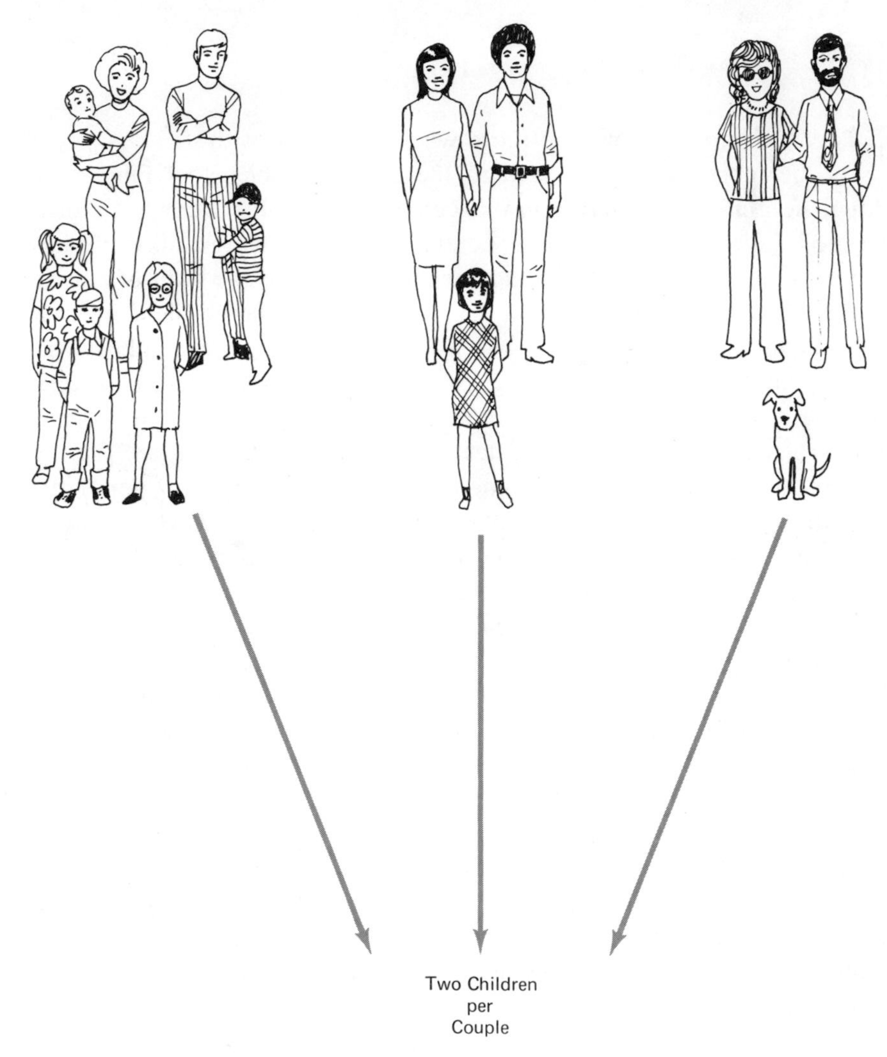


**Figure 26–2.**
*ZPG as an average replacement of parents*

by misguided, careless, or anti-ZPG parents. Central though the population problem may be in the United States and other countries, any legislation dealing with it must be wise and humane. (See Chapter 3 for background material on population growth and concentration.)

The ecologist can, like Ehrlich, advocate ZPG on TV shows or he can work with local conservation groups anxious to know if the carrying capacity of their region has been exceeded by a population increase from births and immigration. The direct contributions of an ecologist to the development of population policies or laws may not be great, but his indirect influence can be significant if he can show the effects of population pressure and the naturalness of population regulation.

## ZONING OF LAND USE

Although some ecological aspects of zoning were discussed in Chapter 25, it is appropriate to cover the legal aspects here, contrasting zoning ordinances with population policies and antipollution law. In the United States, laws whereby the government designates land usage are quite common at the county level and have, in such states as Hawaii, Vermont, and Maryland, reached the state level but have not been passed on a national scale. They are almost as controversial as those that have been proposed to achieve ZPG because zoning strikes not at our right to multiply but at our right to subdue. In all countries adhering to the free-enterprise philosophy, the right of an individual owner to do as he pleases with his land has been enshrined, although occasionally it is questioned by lonely prophets, most notably Leopold in "The Land Ethic"[5] and McHarg in *Design with Nature.*[6]

To some property owners, the greatest threat seems to be zoning in the form of a *"master plan."* The phrase is, perhaps, unfortunate, because plans indicating the most desirable patterns of land use, in a county or region anticipating growth, are not all that masterful. Such long-range plans for orderly growth are only successful if the responsible planning commission stands firm in its refusal to grant detrimental zoning variances. Court battles may result when a developer attempts to bypass the plan and trys to get a sympathetic judge to overrule the planners on the grounds that individual rights are unconstitutionally preempted by the plan. Perhaps land-use planning is somehow equated with the five-year plans of Communist and Socialist countries—even though a typical five-year plan deals with the allocation of labor and resources other than land and is designed to increase agricultural or industrial productivity. Ironically, wise zoning ordinances within the framework of a master plan may actually increase real estate values (and the local tax base) by preserving open space and preventing building on sites that are hard to supply with utilities or that are exposed to natural hazards (for example, sand dunes and flood plains). There is no objection to profits being made by real estate investors, but usage patterns should be determined more by ecological prudence and less by economic gain. This is the point at which an ecologist can be very useful by identifying potential values and hazards. There are several procedures through which a landowner can be compensated if he is told that his property is ecologically unsuitable for development. A conservation easement can be sold to those, either neighboring landowners or local government authorities, who will benefit from the constraints on development. Or the government can exercise its power of eminent domain, taking over the land and paying the owner a fair price for it.

## LAWS AGAINST POLLUTION

Because public acceptance and support has been greatest in the section of environmental law that protects against pollution, this is "where the action is!" First pause and consider the objectives of antipollution laws: preservation or restoration of environmental quality is a bit vague. *Protection of health* is somewhat more definite, yet those situations where you are trying to protect eagles from persistent pesticides, fish from hot water, or humans from some potentially hazardous physical or chemical form of pollution must be indicated. An even further clarification of objectives is necessary if you are concerned with humans in their early fetal life, the stage at which they may be most susceptible to deformation (see Chapter 22).

Ultimate goals may seem too remote and idealistic, but proximate goals—internalization of pollution costs (making environmental costs part of production costs) and recycling of wastes—can be realistic targets. With their concept of an ecosystem sustained by biogeochemical cycling, ecologists have found, *internalization and recycling* far more attractive solutions to pollution than the traditional policies of dilution and dumping. Fees or fines that increase the cost of releasing a pollutant make the value of the pollutant go up to a point where its reuse becomes both necessary and desirable. Ecologists are not likely "to kill two birds with one stone," but they are delighted when one change can lead to both resource conservation and hazard reduction.

What are some of the grounds for laws or suits against pollution? The lawyers have had to reach way back into English common law and invoke *negligence, nuisance,* or *trespass*. Victims of pollution often have had to prove that they have suffered real loss of property or direct bodily harm before they can make any claims on the polluter. Furthermore, the powers that be may decide that the polluter, by providing jobs and paying taxes, is doing more good than harm. This leads to "wrist-slapping" forms of punishment.

A slight digression may clarify some of the difficulties in dealing with an invasive pollutant. If a farmer's horse strays into a neighbor's corn field with devastating results, the farmer is clearly responsible for the damage. He cannot get off by pleading that the horse was a free agent or that he thought the fence was strong enough. Now, if the same farmer has a beehive and one of his bees stings a passing Boy Scout with fatal results, the issue is much more tricky. The boy's next of kin are going to have a hard time proving that it was the farmer's bee that killed their boy, even if there are no other beehives in the vicinity. Finally, the farmer can spray his corn field with a persistent pesticide (for example, dieldrin). Some of this poison may show up, in minute concentrations, in someone's steak in Boston and someone else's fish soup in Moscow. At present, there is no way in which the farmer can be held responsible for any consequence of his anonymous contribution to the biosphere.

Some authorities on environmental law have suggested that the concepts of nuisance and trespass must be strengthened by means of *class action,* with one individual seeking redress on behalf of all others affected by pollution in the same manner, be it ever so slight. This magnification, achieved by pooling millions of slight effects, enables courts to justify intervention and bring responsibility back to the source of pollution, although some judges have insisted that each individual represented must be claiming damages in excess of one thousand dollars. In the preceding parable, for example, the manufacturer or distributor of dieldrin would be the likely target of the suit, not the farmer using it or the agricultural extension agent who suggested that he use it.[7]

Much antipollution law is developed in a sequence that must be distressing to a strict constitutionalist who would insist that every new law be based on constitutional precedent. As in the Civil Rights movement, certain sympathetic judges have led the way, granting *injunctions* (court orders temporarily restraining activities) against polluters when convinced that the pollution represents "a clear and present danger" to human health. Injunctions have the great virtue of being quick, and they can be obtained either by private groups or government agencies concerned with environmental quality. The furor of such an action often leads to a tightened enforcement of existing laws. Officials who feel that the public really wants protection usually can find a legal basis for *strict regulation.* Bans on dumping debris in waterways can be stretched to include prohibition of thermal pollution, and edicts directed against dangerous food additives can be applied to biocide contamination (Figure 26–3).

As the dimensions of the pollution problem become more clearly defined, *new laws* are being developed at local, state, and federal levels, with a few tentative treaties on the international level (for example, against ocean dumping). Very briefly, federal laws have fallen into four categories:

1. those setting new standards for air or water quality, with guide lines and timetables for state compliance
2. those seeking to improve sewage treatment or waste processing facilities
3. those establishing new agencies to enforce standards (EPA) or monitor environmental factors (National Oceanic and Atmospheric Administration)
4. those establishing national environmental laboratories that will do research on environmental problems, including pollution, and may have a role in policy formation

The National Environmental Policy Act of 1969, signed by former President Nixon on January 1, 1970, is in a class by itself, because this law requires all federal agencies to consider and predict the consequences of

**Figure 26–3.**
*Sequences of environmental law*

Constitutional Reform
Environmental Bill of Rights—not yet agreed upon,
New Law
Usually developed over a period of several years with many hearings and committee meetings
Regulation
Strict application of existing law but only after prolonged hearings
Injunction
Quick but temporary halt

projects they fund or direct. Scrutiny of these *impact statements* has permitted citizen groups and other government agencies to impede or modify projects where the environmental costs seemed to outweigh political or economic benefits. The philosophy of impact prediction and prevention is extremely important and, hopefully, will influence corporation executives and government officials at all levels.[8] Ecological expertise can help government agencies anticipate some environmental effects of extracting oil from shale, introducing fusion power, or channelizing streams. Lawyers also can seek ecological advice on waste treatment, monitoring networks, standards for environmental quality, and research objectives of national laboratories, all likely components of forthcoming legislation.

Even with many new laws, there is still the possibility that we need an *"environmental bill of rights."* Even at the state level—for example, in New York—such constitutional modification does not lead to immediate improvement in the quality of air, water, or land. However, it does give many conservation and antipollution groups a chance to join forces at a constitutional convention. This, and the attendent publicity, are important educational processes. Perhaps a national gathering to amend the U.S. Constitution would unite the efforts of conservative and radical environmentalists.

## ADDENDA TO THE SOCIAL CONTRACT

To a nonlawyer, all these changes in environmental law may seem worthwhile but vaguely disturbing. We must recognize that we are continuing the process described by Jean Jacques Rousseau (1712–1778) in which the individual citizen surrendered to the state a certain degree of freedom, receiving in turn some form of protection. Stopping at red lights, submitting to inspection at airports, and paying social security taxes all represent recent amendments to Rousseau's *social contract.* Loving individual freedom as we do, we face some difficult decisions with regard to further amendments made necessary by growing population and runaway technology.

We agree that the "police power of the state" can be used to stop pollution; but are we quite so sure that it can, and should, be used to zone land as perpetual wilderness? Should the thwarted developer who owns the "wilderness" be able to sell conservation easements to neighbors who value his greenery or should the government step in, exercising eminent domain and pay him fair compensation for loss of value? What about peacetime rationing? Do we feel that any resources are in such short supply that government intervention is necessary to conserve them? Or are we going to let the free-market system work to the point of depletion and substitution?

Returning to the central question of population, we face the most difficult decision of all. During the next few decades Americans will, with the rest of mankind, have to agree on some acceptable forms of population control, sacrificing any real or imagined rights to unlimited procreation. If voluntary acceptance of the principles behind ZPG is not universal, some unpleasant degree of government intervention may be necessary.

## SUMMARY

Because human activities are determined as much by man-made laws as by natural laws, efforts to preserve or improve environmental quality require the collaboration of lawyers and ecologists. By describing the effects of pollution, land misuse, or population pressure, the ecologist can help justify the strict enforcement of existing laws or the development of new legislation, with the objectives of population regulation, planned growth, and protected health. Many of these goals require individual sacrifices for the common good, but they are necessary to prevent actions that, to the individual, may seem harmless, yet, through their collective impact, degrade the quality of our shared environment.

### Discussion Questions

1. Do you think the United States is ready for a national policy of ZPG? If not, what will it take to convince legislators and voters that such a policy is needed?
2. If possible, read Garrett Hardin's essay on "The Tragedy of the Commons" or his book *Exploring New Ethics for Survival* and discuss his recommendations for increased government control of individual actions.
3. Compare the movements for civil rights and environmental quality, particularly in their development of new legislation.

### Suggested Projects

1. Ask a representative from the local chapter of the ZPG organization to speak to your class or group.

**2.** Review the impact statement you prepared as a project for Chapter 4 and suggest ways in which it can be improved.

**3.** Attend a meeting of the local planning commission.

**4.** Find out which laws for air or water quality are not being properly enforced and write letters of complaint to those responsible for this enforcement.

## Notes

1. Garrett Hardin, "The Tragedy of the Commons," *Science* **162**:1243–1248 (1968); this article has been reprinted in many environmental anthologies. See also his *Exploring New Ethics for Survival (The Voyage of the Spaceship "Beagle")* (Baltimore: Penguin, 1973), a lively expansion of the original essay.
2. Various aspects of the "optimum population" question are explored in a symposium volume: S. Fred Singer, ed. *Is There an Optimum Level of Population?* (New York: A Population Council Book, McGraw-Hill, 1971).
3. Wade Greene "The Militant Malthusians," *Saturday Review,* (March 11, 1972). pp. 40–42. A good history and reasonably fair presentation of ZPG as an organization.
4. John D. Rockefeller, III, *Population and the American Future* (New York: Signet, New American Library, 1972). Mr. Rockefeller was chairman of the Commission on Population Growth and the American Future.
5. Aldo Leopold, "The Land Ethic," a chapter in *A Sand County Almanac* (New York: Sierra Club-Ballantine, 1970); pp. 237–284; first published in 1949.
6. Ian L. McHarg, *Design with Nature* (New York: Natural History Press, 1969); the book also is available in a small format, soft-cover edition (Garden City, N.Y.: Doubleday, 1971).
7. See examples of class actions in Norman J. Landau and Paul D. Rheingold, *The Environmental Law Handbook* (New York: FOE (Friends of the Earth) Ballantine, 1971).
8. Much useful information on federal efforts can be found in *Environmental Quality,* the annual reports of the Council on Environmental Quality (August 1970–1974).

# 27

# Ethics and Ecology

- Right and wrong
- Man-nature relationship
- Inclusionists
- Exclusionists
- Nature is amoral
- Reverence for life
- Peaceful coexistence
- Franciscan reverence
- Benedictine stewardship
- Evolution
- Eugenics
- Social Darwinism
- Vitalism
- Finalism
- Enlightened self-interest
- Ecological conscience
- Human and humane

Earlier in this section on alternatives, possible modifications of health policy, technology, modeling analysis, resource distribution, and environmental law were considered. Few, if any, of these alternatives will become reality unless we change our basic value systems—the concepts of *right and wrong*—by which we guide so many of our decisions and actions. At this point in the book, we have reached the outer limits of ecological applications and the ultimate question: Can ecology help us see more clearly when we are doing something right and when we are doing something wrong? (See Figure 27–1.)

This is not to be a discussion of professional ethics for ecologists, although many ecologists (including this writer) sometimes confuse facts and opinions when advising or teaching.[1] No, if there are links between

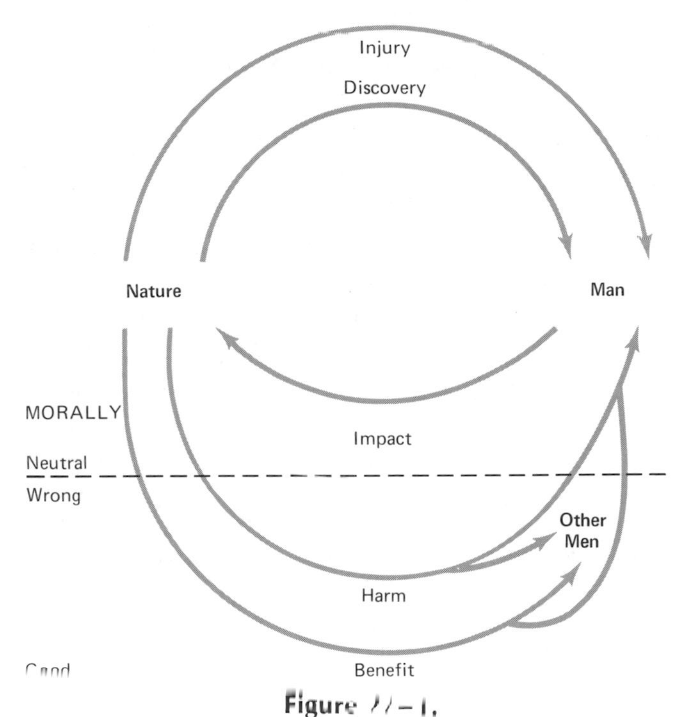


**Figure 22–1.**
*Ethical aspects of man-nature relationship*

ecology and ethics, anyone who chooses to do so can use ecological knowledge to live a bit more wisely. However, there is no promise that the life of those who are "ecologically aware" will be happier or more serene. Quite the contrary, knowledge of our personal contributions to environmental degradation and the sufferings of our fellowmen can be, and should be, profoundly disquieting.

In this chapter, the unifying thread is the *man-nature relationship*. As the Reverend Frederick Elder, in his very perceptive book, *The Crisis in Eden,*[2] has shown, most modern authors dealing with the relationship are either *inclusionists,* considering man part of nature, or *exclusionists,* claiming that man is somehow above nature. Biological scientists are usually inclusionists, although other scientists often join forces with theologians in proclaiming the exclusivity of man. After setting some ground rules on the neutrality of nature, we will consider, in this chapter how both religious traditions and scientific evidence can help us better understand our status, in or above, nature.

## THE MORAL NEUTRALITY OF NATURE

Throughout this discussion it will be assumed that *nature is amoral*—that it does not have any built-in standards of right and wrong. The tiger consuming a human is not guilty of wrong doing, even though other humans will seek him out and try to kill him. The fact that his action puts other tigers in jeopardy does not lead to a *Jungle Book* trial at which he would be convicted and punished by his animal peers. In a very real sense, the man-eating tiger is as innocent as the man-drowning river, no matter how strongly the victim and his survivors may feel about the tragedy.

Neutrality is also a characteristic of all facts, discoveries, theories, and inventions, derived through the development of natural science. Recent attempts to trace the horrors of Hiroshima back to $E = mc^2$ are dangerously misleading. Albert Einstein, the gentlest of men, knew that the Nazis could build an atomic bomb and urged that the United States do so in self-defense. Einstein deplored the use of A-bombs on Japan, especially without prior demonstration of their awesome power on some uninhabited off-shore island.[3] Einstein was not responsible for the way in which A-bombs and H-bombs have been designed, built, stockpiled, and used, these decisions have been made by government leaders in the United States and other countries in the "nuclear club." Government leaders are responsible for these weapons and citizens of each country, to the degree they are allowed, and choose, to participate in government, share the responsibility.

A similar chain of logic would show that many of the wonders and woes of modern technology can be traced to scientific discoveries, but that the credit or blame for recent applications rests with corporation executives, advertising copywriters, and the rest of us, all-too-compliant consumers. If we did away with all research on the ground that knowledge is dangerous, we would not be invited back into the Garden of Eden. Ignorance is *not* bliss, and knowledge is power—power that can be used for good or evil. This is true of ecological knowledge; it is neutral but it can be applied to help or to harm others. Anti-intellectualism, a fear of the future, and a yearning for the simple life must not be allowed to prevent us from achieving a better understanding of the world and the universe.[4]

If nature, animate or inanimate, can do us no wrong and there is nothing inherently wrong in trying to discover nature's secrets, how can we possibly harm nature? Strictly speaking, we cannot. However, the moral consequences of our impacts on nature come from their effects on ourselves and other human beings. Cruelty to animals is wrong, not because the civil rights of animals are violated, but because we debase ourselves by cruelty in any form. The real tragedy of extinction is not in the sadness of the last survivor, it is in depriving unborn humans of opportunities to know, and possibly use, the species. Pollution, like starvation, is most evil if it damages children and prevents them from reaching their full humanness. Pollution is also wrong in that pollutants are wasted resources that could have been useful rather than harmful. The somewhat moralist tone of this book and of many other ecological writings is a product of deep concern for human welfare, not some modern version of nature worship.

## RELIGIOUS ATTITUDES TOWARD NATURE

This is not the place to explore the possibility of separate natural and supernatural realms, linked only intermittently and miraculously. Rather, it is appropriate to ask if any set of religious beliefs has been helpful in guiding its adherents toward a harmonious relationship with nature? Throughout this phase of the discussion, we must remember the huge chasm that, in most lives, divides belief and practice—it is so huge that those few members of any faith successful in bridging the gap are deemed "saints."

Rousseau and others have suggested that primitive man is more attuned to nature. It is true that many tribes have totemic animals or sacred areas that they revere and protect, but their attitude toward the rest of nature often is thoroughly exploitative. Even though the Polynesians in Hawaii had little impact on the native flora and fauna, their cousins, the moa hunters of New Zealand, managed to destroy an entire avian family. The American Indian is sometimes credited with ecological wisdom. Recalling the overkills of wildlife from the Pleistocene on into the time of the Plains Indian, it seems probable that any restraint came from technological limits rather than high ideals.[5]

Turning to the great religions and philosophies of the Far East, we can find myriad writings both inside and outside their traditions claiming that the beautiful man-nature relationship, epitomized by a serene scene on a Chinese scroll, has been achieved through a somewhat mystical accumulation of Oriental wisdom. Devastated hills and congested cities in China and India show how far everyday reality has departed from the idea of ancient sages. It may even be true that the preachments of Tao and Confucius on harmony with nature were reactions to signs of environmental degradation already evident during their times (sixth and fifth centuries B.C.).[6]

The Japanese, despite their dual heritage of Shintoism (essentially nature

a

**Figure 27–2.**
**a.** *Seaside oil refinery* (Courtesy Japanese Embassy) **b.** *Cedar clear-cut and replanting on steep slope*

worship) and Buddhism have, as they readily admitted at the Stockholm meeting on the human environment, already suffered more than any other people from poisons in water, air, and food. Air pollution has caused respiratory diseases to reach epidemic proportions. Toxic metals—mercury and cadmium—have contaminated water and food, causing death and deformation. A thoroughly secularized society, giving top priority to productivity, prosperity, and progress, it has accepted pollution[7] and tolerated the overharvesting of living resources throughout the vast Pacific. Both forms of degradation could have been avoided if the Japanese government had long ago adopted a firm policy of ZPG, but it did so too late and there is now even talk of larger families to provide the next generation of workers. A stunted bonsai tree in its pot may be a thing of beauty, but it also can serve as a sad symbol of an overcrowded nation. (Figure 27–2 a, b.)

b

**Figure 27–2.** *(Continued)*

From the environmentalist viewpoint, Christianity may have the worst record of all. It is difficult for us to realize how many of our attitudes and values have been molded by the Judeo-Christian tradition. Even those who do not believe in the supernatural elements of that tradition are strongly influenced in their view of the natural world. When Karl Marx commanded his followers to "hominize" the earth, he was echoing the Biblical injunction to have dominion over the creatures of the earth. This exclusionist view of the world (something to be used by man) has led to the development, and destruction, characteristic of Western civilization.[8] There, of course, have been many unique American additions to the basic traditions of Western civilization: we have made virtues of hard work, increased production, and conspicuous consumption.

Lynn T. White, Jr., suggests in "The Historical Roots of Our Ecologic Crisis," that we should follow the example of St. Francis of Assisi or of Dr. Albert Schweitzer and develop *reverence for life*.[9] Does this mean that we should share food with pets and space with wild creatures when people are starving? The excessively rapid growth of human numbers is making it much harder to follow a policy of *peaceful coexistence* with other creatures. Pastor Richard Neuhaus has warned against extremism in the conservation movement, strongly criticizing bird lovers who appear to have no love left for their fellow human beings and elitists whose idea of a sanctuary is a private game reserve.[10] Dubos[11] also cautions against the Franciscan "talk-to-the-animals" extreme and offers St. Benedict as a better model. St. Benedict and his followers have worked to manage ecosystems for the benefit of all men. Dubos even suggests that natural ecosystems can be both wasteful and uninteresting, a heretical attitude to some conservationists, but he is correct in claiming that buildings, gardens, pastures, and parks can enhance both the diversity and beauty of landscapes. However, the dichotomy between *Franciscan reverence* and *Benedictine stewardship* is a false one. We need both Muirs to save the redwoods and Pinchots to grow pines on a sustained-yield basis, (page 8 in Chapter 1). Perhaps, then, it is not fair to attribute any modern problems to the heavy hand of Judeo-Christian tradition, because the many flaws of any civilization can be blamed on individuals who failed to choose the best and most appropriate elements of tradition to guide their efforts. It is likely that Christianity, and all great religions, contains within it enough guide lines to enable any believer to live in harmony with nature and at peace with his fellowmen.

## ETHICAL SYSTEMS BASED ON SCIENCE

Philosophers, reformers, and theologians have sought inspiration from scientific discoveries, seeing in natural law a "divine plan" or "God's Creation." However, many of these discoveries have been misunderstood or misapplied. To illustrate the dangers of misapplication that must be avoided in ecological ethics, consider how the theory of evolution has been misused to develop political and social philosophies.

To some philosophers, organic *evolution* is especially interesting because it tells us so much about our origins and appears to give clues about our destiny. Competitive interactions in a changing physical-chemical environment provide explanations for our diverse adaptations and those of other creatures. Evolutionary theory discards a whole set of creative miracles, leaving one central mystery: the origin of life. The one great flaw in using evolutionary theory as a foundation for ethical construction is the great emphasis on survival and perpetuation of genetic characteristics as measures of success in evolution. The dinosaurs didn't make it, the passenger pigeon couldn't survive, the Tasmanian natives died out—“guess they just weren't tough enough,” some might say. (See Chapter 1 for brief comments on the role of evolutionary ideas in the development of modern ecology.)

Three value systems strongly influenced by evolution are the *eugenics* movement, *Social Darwinism,* and the visions of Teilhard de Chardin. Eugenics, at its simplest, seeks to apply to mankind the principles of artificial selection, so successfully used to transform wild species into cultigens (See the “domestication” section of Chapter 8). During the 1920s, geneticists suggested that it should be possible to “improve” our species by sterilizing those known to harbor genetic defects and encouraging the “best and brightest” to have large families. A particular concern was that intellectuals, as a subgroup, were devoting too much time to cogitation, and too little to procreation, with a decline in average IQ as the projected consequence. Eugenics was given a bad reputation when embraced by Nazism with its concept of racial superiority leading to the ruthless massacre of Jews and the encouragement of Aryan stud farms designed to produce supermen. In recent years, the eugenics movement has been weakened further by the realization that each human has recessive genes that, in combination with those of his or her partner, could lead to the birth of an Einstein or an idiot. Although there is still much nonsense being written about the possibility and desirability of engineering better humans through various combinations of frozen sperm banks, egg transplants, and cloning cultures, modern eugenics can be useful when it takes the form of genetic counseling—couples with histories of hereditary defects are told the odds of their having defective offspring, letting them decide whether adoption is less risky.

Social Darwinism shares many weaknesses with the eugenics movement of the 1920s. However, a basic assumption of this evolutionary derivative is the superiority of entire groups, classes, or nations—a status presumably obtained by competitive exclusion of less acquisitive, aggressive, or "civilized" social units. This insidious philosophy can be used to rationalize a multitude of fortuitous inequities. It has a special appeal to those with wealth and privilege who, in earlier times, would have spoken of "divine right" or "Manifest Destiny." From the scientific viewpoint, both eugenics and Social Darwinism fail because they do not recognize the transitory nature of "best." A group with sickle-shaped red blood cells may be well adapted for life in a malarious region but may suffer from a high incidence of congenital anemia in another environment. When escaping from lions and catching rabbits are daily events, speed and stamina are survival characteristics, but the criteria of best change dramatically the day the first gun is brought to a territory.

Only one thinker has managed to circumvent the transitory best in his application of evolution to ethics, and he did so by assuming that all mankind is evolving toward some mystical omega point. Teilhard de Chardin, a Jesuit priest and qualified paleontologist with a special interest in human evolution, saw hopeful patterns in the record of life on earth, with the human species well along on a journey toward oneness with God.[12] Critics of Teilhard fault him for seeing more in nature than can be demonstrated empirically—his philosophy contains elements of both *vitalism* (an inner force guiding life) and *finalism* (life headed toward a goal). George Gaylord Simpson, a famous evolutionist, concedes that writings such as those of Teilhard "may have rendered a real service" persuading "wishful thinkers that evolution is, after all, consonant with their emotions and prejudices"; however, Simpson concludes that sugar coating is no remedy, and we must take the uncoated truth: evolution does not always lead onward and upward.[13]

Are there some precautions to be followed if we are to avoid some of the mistakes so often associated with "evolutionary insights?" First, ecological ethics should not be selfish. Any applications of ecological knowledge that seem to justify a stratified status quo or a narrowly profitable change should be suspect. Secondly, there is no need for anthropomorphic or sentimental views of nature, even when we see nature in the form of a beautiful or intelligent creature. By romanticizing everything from the mating behavior of ducks to the precarious lives of predator and prey, nature books and films may lead us to do the right things—but for very wrong reasons. "They are what they are, we are what we are" and "we are all in this together" are more objective statements. Finally, ecology may be subversive by making us aware of unsuspected effects and links, but it is not mysterious. Evolutionary theory can help us understand adaptations over long periods, but ecology can clarify the day-to-day operations of ecosystems, both those we manage and those we would like to preserve. Both forms of knowledge, to be useful, do not need to be falsely endowed with mystical, sentimental, or other unjustified values because they simply show how man is definitely included in nature.

## OUR RESPONSIBILITY

If an ethical system partially based on ecological knowledge is to avoid being elitist and racist or sentimental and mystical, it must maintain a high degree of objectivity and rationality. Perhaps the most realistic path to follow is one of *enlightened self-interest* because we are often on our best behavior when we realize what we do is ultimately for our own good. United States programs of aid to other countries, from the Marshall Plan to the Peace Corps, were motivated not by charity, but by the hope that aid would lead to trade or prevent war. Similarly, ecological programs may involve immediate sacrifice as an investment in our long-range benefit.

Paradoxically, one of the most important ways in which a group of humans can perpetuate themselves, and their culture, is to restrain their reproduction, keeping their numbers below the carrying capacity of their environment. This is in direct contradiction to certain evolutionary ethos that seem to endorse indefinite multiplication of one group, first at the expense of other groups, and finally at the expense of the environment. To be sure, minority groups would like to become majority groups, and majorities want to maintain their status, but an ecological ethos would recognize the dangers of competitive exclusion, especially as it reduces the diversity, stability, and strength of the human species. The value of diversity is also recognized at the ecosystem level, with full awareness of the costs inherent in simplification through monoculture or pollution stress.

Thus, our responsibility must extend beyond individuals and groups—and even beyond the human species. Even those who do not believe that God has given us the world to use wisely and well can see how great an impact we have on the environment. A concern for self-protection enhanced by some sense of obligation to our descendents should make us want to soften the impact. This sense of individual and collective responsibility for population limitation, resource conservation, and the preservation of environmental quality characterizes the ecological ethos of many recent authors. A biochemist speaks of our goal as "the survival and improvement in the quality of life for the human species in keeping with the potentialities that can already be seen to exist, and in keeping with the constraints imposed by the total ecosystem."[14] A theologian writes that "an ecological perspective can inform" (not monopolize) "our ethical judgments as to the realistic possibilities and limits of human growth and action in attaining a rich and meaningful life for mankind."[15] Whatever their motives and goals, these authors have a common concern for the welfare of all mankind.

Changing our values, behavior, and life-style in response to revelations of evolutionary or ecological studies will not be easy. However, ecological research can show us how we depend on the environment and on each other. All ecological knowledge concerns interrelationships and demonstrates interdependence. We can use such knowledge to help in the formation of an "*ecological conscience*," as Aldo Leopold called it in "The Land Ethic."[16] It will enable us to decide if our actions are harmful to other people or to ourselves. As our ecological conscience grows, we will be

**Figure 27–3.**
*All that can be expected!* (Courtesy Philip B. Stanton)

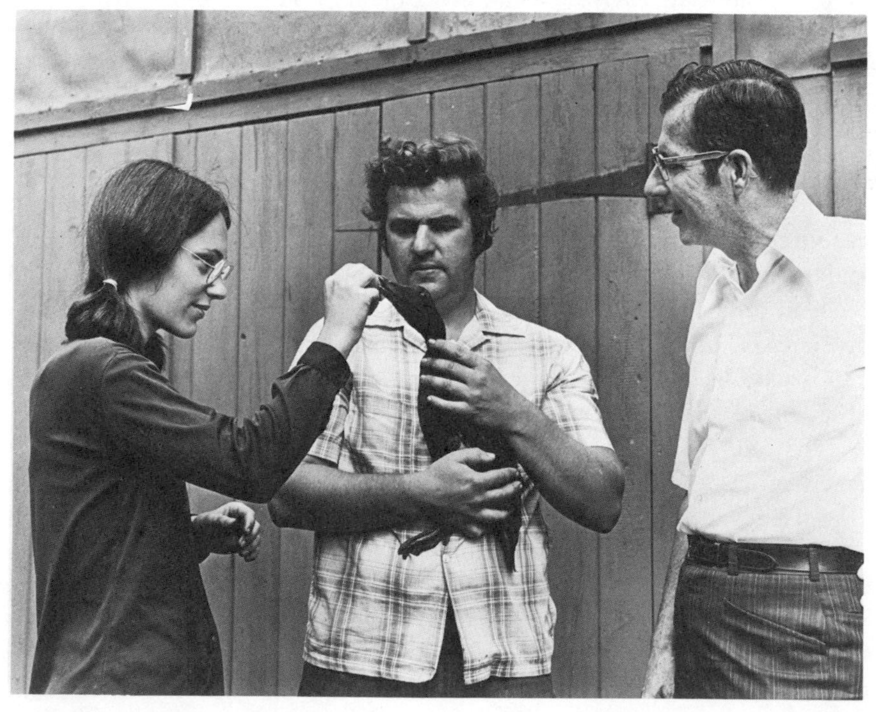

more ready to ask if our demands for power, comfort, and convenience may not be demeaning each of us and our common environment. Often the wrong attributable to each individual is slight, but collectively these lead to wasted resources, a degraded environment, and a reduction in the quality of life.[17]

To conclude this book let's consider a girl on a beach, cleaning an oil-smeared bird. Her actions may not stem from an ecological conscience or enlightened self-interest and, at that moment, she may not be concerned with the welfare of all mankind, but she is being both *human and humane*. Perhaps that is all that can, and should be, expected of us. (Figure 27–3.)

## SUMMARY

Although nature is morally neutral and knowledge derived from studies of nature retains that neutrality, knowledge can be applied in helpful or harmful ways. Knowledge of ecological relationships can be used by individuals trying to decide if their actions will be beneficial or dangerous to other people. Particularly important in such decision making is the recognition that man is part of nature and yet has special responsibilities in both the preservation and the management of living resources. The theory of organic evolution also stresses the unity of man with nature, but it has been misused by those seeking to prove the superiority of individuals, groups, or the human species. Ecological knowledge, ethically applied, can lead to the development of an ecological conscience to govern forming values and decisions based on enlightened self-interest, with the full awareness that every individual action may have far-reaching and long-range effects.

### Discussion Questions

1. If we can't, in an ethical sense, hurt nature, why can't we do anything we want to with natural resources?
2. If you feel a reverence for life, does it extend beyond pets, intelligent mammals, and beautiful birds to include insects, snakes, and other less popular creatures?
3. How do both evolutionary and ecological insights stress man's oneness with nature?
4. How, in using ecological knowledge, can we avoid the misapplications that have followed other discoveries or inventions?

### Suggested Project

Write a statement, not to be handed in as part of your course work, in which you summarize ways in which your understanding of nature will help you work toward a world that is good for you, your fellow humans (living and unborn), and all life.

### Notes

1. Geoffrey L. Kesteven, "Ethics and Ecology," *Ceres,* **2**:53–56 (1969), deals mainly with the responsibility of scientists in environmental preservation.
2. Frederick Elder, *Crisis in Eden, A Religious Study of Man and Environment* (Nashville, Tenn.: Abingdon, 1970).
3. See Virgil G. Hinshaw, Jr., "Einstein's Social Philosophy," *Albert Einstein: Philosopher-Scientist,* ed. Paul Arthur Schlipp (LaSalle, Ill.: Open Court, 1970), pp. 649–661.
4. Alvin Toffler, *Future Shock* (New York: Bantam, 1970), deals with some aspects of "future fear" in Part 5, "The Limits of Adaptability."
5. Daniel A. Guthrie, "Primitive Man's Relationship to Nature," *BioScience,* **21**:721–723 (1971), debunks the ecological example of the "red man."
6. This point is made by Yi-Fu Tuan, "Our Treatment of the Environment in Ideal and Actuality," *American Science,* **58**:244–249 (1970); reprinted in Robert Leo Smith, ed., *The Ecology of Man: An Ecosystem Approach* (New York: Harper, 1972), pp. 167–171.
7. A few Buddhist monks have reacted to this by formally cursing polluters! *Time,* (Dec. 28, 1970), p. 40.
8. This is recognized, and endorsed, by a Jesuit priest, James Schall, who considers ecology "heretical." See "Environment," *Time,* (Aug. 23, 1971), pp. 29–30.
9. Lynn T. White, Jr., "The Historical Roots of Our Ecologic Crisis," *Science,* **155**:1203–1207 (1967); this article has been reprinted in many ecology anthologies.
10. Richard Neuhaus, *In Defense of People: Ecology and the Seduction of Radicalism* (New York: Macmillan, 1971).
11. René Dubos, "Conservation, Stewardship, and the Human Heart," *Audubon,* **74**:20–28 (1972); this article is incorporated in his book *A God Within* (New York: Scribners, 1972).

12. Teilhard de Chardin, *The Phenomenon of Man* (New York: Harper, 1961); and *The Future of Man* (New York: Harper, 1964).
13. George Gaylord Simpson, *The Meaning of Evolution, A Study of the History of Life and of Its Significance for Man,* rev. ed. (New Haven: Yale University Press, 1967). The book was first published in 1948.
14. Van Rensselaer Potter, *Bioethics: Bridge to the Future* (Englewood Cliffs, N.J.: Prentice-Hall, 1971), p. 194.
15. James C. Livingston, "The Ecological Challenge to Christian Ethics," *Christian Century,* (Dec. 1, 1971), p. 1412.
16. Aldo Leopold, "The Land Ethic," *A Sand County Almanac* (New York: Sierra Club-Ballantine, 1970), pp. 237–284.
17. See René Dubos, *So Human an Animal* (New York: Scribners, 1969).

# Summary of Part V

This final section covers some alternatives to our present set of policies and attitudes in the areas of health, technology, modeling, resources, law, and ethics. Possibilities of cooperation between ecologists and other professionals, especially doctors, engineers, computer experts, resource economists, lawyers, and those interested in ethics, are examined. However, the recurring theme, spelled out in the last chapter, is that each individual should use ecological insights to choose and support changes that will improve the quality of our environment.

It should be emphasized that the alternatives, although discussed in the specialists' groupings, are crosslinked with one another and much of the material considered earlier in the book. Thus, a mathematical model (Chapter 24) can help speed the reallocation of a resource (Chapter 25) or it can guide the campaign against a pest in an integrated control program (Chapter 10). Similarly, laws restricting emissions may simultaneously raise the cost of dumping pollutants, make recycling more attractive, and reduce health hazards in an urban ecosystem. Underlying the entire exploration of alternatives is the assumption that we are working toward a better world and are looking to the science of ecology as a source of information and inspiration.

If one guide line must be chosen, the law of interdependence should serve us best. While increasing our control over the environment, we have remained dependent on it. We, like all living creatures, are supported by a complex and extensive web of relationships. To understand, utilize, and preserve this life-support system requires the combined efforts of many citizens, scientist and nonscientist, in all nations.

# Glossary

**Abrasion:** a mechanical wearing away of rock

**Abstractions:** concepts rooted in reality but without an objective reality of their own

**Activated sludge:** treatment of waste water with pumped air or oxygen

**Adaptations:** evolved characteristics representing a species' response to environmental changes

**Agglomeration:** as used here, an urban concentration

**Alkaloids:** a nitrogenous organic compound with alkaline properties

**Alluvial:** soil deposited by flowing water

**Alveoli:** tiny air sacs in the lungs

**Aquaculture:** the rearing of aquatic organisms

**Aquifers:** underground rock formations that contain and transport water

**Amino acids:** nitrogenous building blocks for proteins

**Anaerobic digester:** a large, airless container in which microorganisms break down sewage sludge

**Antibiotics:** chemicals derived from living organisms (for example, fungi) that inhibit the growth of other organisms (for example, bacteria)

**Arthropods:** invertebrates with chitinous exteriors and jointed legs (for example, crabs, spiders, and insects)

**Asbestos fibrils:** small fragments of asbestos

**Atmosphere:** the earth's gaseous mantle

**Autecology:** ecology at the individual, population, and species levels

**Autotrophs:** organisms that can fix solar or chemical energy

**Auxins:** plant hormones (chemical messengers)

**Avian malaria:** a protozoan disease afflicting birds

**Base line:** measurement of existing conditions

**Biocide:** any chemical that is designed to kill organisms

**Biodegradable:** breaks down when exposed to organisms

**Biogeochemical cycling:** the cyclic movement of chemicals between soil, atmosphere, and organisms

**Biomass:** the weight of living organisms

**Biome:** zones, usually characterized by typical vegetation (for example, grasslands and deciduous forest), determined by climatic gradients

**Biosphere:** the layer of life covering much of our planet's surface

**Biotic diversity:** the number of species per unit area or volume

**Black lung:** a disease contracted by coal miners exposed to unfiltered air

**Blowout:** the sudden release of a substance under pressure (for example, oil off Santa Barbara)

**BOD:** biological (or biochemical) oxygen demand, a standardized measure of oxygen uptake by chemicals and microorganisms in water

**Bog:** a poorly drained area in which organic material is accumulating, often as peat

**Boom boat:** a boat especially equipped to contain and recover an oil slick

**"BP":** before the present time

**Broad spectrum:** refers to biocides that kill a wide range of organisms

**Calefaction:** the release of waste heat into the environment, especially in aquatic ecosystems

**Carnivores:** meat eaters

**Carrying capacity:** the maximum density at which a species can be maintained without degradation of its environment (this is an operational definition of the concept)

**Catalytic converters:** devices to help oxidize the unburnt fuel fragments in the exhaust fumes of an automobile engine

**Cellulose:** the carbohydrate forming the bulk of cell walls in woody plants

**Cetaceans:** whales and porpoises

**Clear cutting:** the practice of cutting or harvesting all the timber in patches or larger areas

**Climax:** the final stage of succession—a mature, but by no means immutable, ecosystem

**Coevolution:** the simultaneous evolution of two or more interacting species (for example, orchid and pollinating moth)

**Community:** plants and animals in one spatial unit (area or volume)

**Concentrated combustion:** Burning fossil fuels in cities

**Conservation:** the philosophy and policy of maintaining or guarding natural resources

**Contour plowing:** the practice of plowing around hillsides rather than up and down the slopes

**Convergence:** evolution of similar adaptations to similar environments

**Cosmic rays:** high-speed atomic particles that bombard earth from space

**Cost-benefit ratio:** an economic measure of anticipated costs over expected benefits

**Cryogenic:** pertaining to low temperatures

**Cryptozoa:** those animals that are cryptic (hidden)
**Cultigens:** plants or animals that have been domesticated
**Cybernetic:** refers to feedback control systems

**Defaunation:** destruction of animals
**Defoliation:** removal of leaves
**Desalinization:** removal of salt from sea water
**Detoxifying:** reducing the toxic characteristics of a chemical
**Detritivores:** consumers of detritus
**Detritus:** organic and inorganic debris
**Diversity:** the number of species per unit area or volume
**Domestication:** the process of bringing plants or animals under human control
**Dunes:** low, rolling rows of sand hills

**Ecocide:** used to describe defoliation campaigns in Vietnam
**Ecological backlash:** a reaction to concern about the ecological consequences of present policies
**Ecology:** the study of interrelationships between organisms and their environment (other organisms plus physical and chemical factors)
**Economic threshold:** the level above which control costs can be justified
**Ecosystem:** plants and animals considered together with their physical-chemical environment in a particular area
**Electrostatic precipitators:** devices to remove dust from stack gases
**Emphysema:** a lung disease characterized by the gradual breakdown of alveoli
**Environment:** anything that affects an organism
**Epiphytes:** plants that perch on other plants
**Equilibrium:** oscillation about an average level; and input-output parity
**Erosion:** soil movement by wind or water
**Estuaries:** where a river commingles with the tides
**Ethology:** the study of animal behavior
**Eugenics:** the practice of trying to improve the human species through selective breeding
**Eutrophication:** the enrichment of an ecosystem, usually aquatic, by nutrient inflow
**Evolution:** the theory that species have, in response to natural selection, changed through time
**Exclusionists:** those who consider man to be above nature
**Exoskeleton:** the exterior skeleton of insects and other arthropods
**Extinction:** the termination of a species

**Feedback:** jargon for any return that changes outputs; + means increasing outputs and − means reducing them

**Fertilizer:** chemical sources of plant nutrients

**Filter feeders:** those aquatic organisms (for example, clams and barnacles) that feed by filtering food particles from water

**Finalism:** the idea that evolution is directed toward an end point

**Flood plains:** low areas subject to flooding along rivers

**Food chain:** organisms linked by patterns of consumption, typically plant → herbivore → carnivore

**Food pyramid:** the concept of diminishing biomass in the plant-herbivore-carnivore system

**Food web:** organisms linked in a whole net of food chains

**Fowl pox:** A virus disease afflicting chickens and other birds

**Fuel cell:** burns $H_2$ and $O_2$ to produce electricity and $H_2O$

**Genetic engineering:** selection and crossbreeding of varieties with characteristics deemed useful to man

**Genetics:** the science of heredity

**Geochemistry:** the science of chemicals in the lithosphere

**Geothermal:** pertaining to the heat from the earth's core

**"Ghost acreage":** the concept of agricultural acreage that would be needed to produce food now provided through trade and fishing

**"Glasphalt":** a mixture of glass and tar to be used in road building

**"Gob" dam:** a dam created by coal mine wastes

**"Golden mean":** the middle way; an avoidance of extremes

**Gradients:** a gradual change over distance in physical or chemical conditions

**Green revolution:** the development of high-yielding grain varieties

**Ground cover:** in the applied sense, vegetation planted to hold soil or increase fertility

**Habitat:** the environment in which a species naturally occurs—in contrast to niche, a functional position in a community web

**Herbivores:** plant eaters

**Heterotrophic:** obtaining food from extrinsic sources

**Homeostatic:** self-regulating

**Horizons:** in this context, layers of soil

**Humus:** decayed organic material in soil

**Hydrocarbon:** a chemical that contains hydrogen and carbon

**Hydrologic cycle:** movement of water through evaporation, transpiration, atmospheric circulation, and precipitation

**Hydrology:** the study of water distribution, movement, and quality

**Hydrolysis:** chemical breakdown in the presence of water

**Hydrosphere:** the world's water

**Hydroponics:** growing plants in a nutrient solution

**Hydrostatic head:** the build-up of water pressure (for example, behind a dam)
**Hypotheses:** tentative theories put forward for testing

**Impact statements:** those documents required under the National Environmental Policy Act of 1969 for major federal actions; and any similar document
**Inclusionists:** those who consider man to be part of nature
**Integrated control:** the practice of using an appropriate mix of techniques in pest control
**Interconnectivity:** the degree of complexity in a food web
**Interdisciplinary:** drawing on the resources of many specialized disciplines
**Interface:** conjoining area of contact; and a linkage between computer and auxillary equipment
**Internalization:** the process whereby considerations (environmental, in this context) influence a decision
**Inversion:** a meteorlogical condition during which the normal gradient of lower temperature with increasing altitude is disrupted by one or more layers of stagnant warm air
**Isotopes:** forms of an element with the same atomic number but slightly different atomic weights

**Leguminous:** pertaining to the bean family
**Lianas:** climbing tropical vines
**Life zones:** a broad concept applied in this text to the ringlike zones of vegetation, and associated animals, observed at different elevations on a mountain
**Limiting factor:** as used in population dynamics, this refers to a resource first depleted by a growing population, thus inhibiting further growth; it also can refer to a factor that constrains the distribution of a population
**Lithosphere:** the solid earth
**Lodge:** in this context, used to describe grain that topples before harvest
**"Loop":** an intrauterine device for the prevention of pregnancy

**Malthusianism:** the doctrine that the human population can outgrow the agricultural land on which it depends
**Mammalian toxicity:** the degree to which a chemical poisons mammals
**Mangrove forests:** a zone of "amphibious" trees found along coasts in the tropics and subtropics
**Marshes:** wet areas with predominantly grasslike vegetation
**Marsupials:** primitive mammals with pouches (for example, opossum and kangaroo)
**Megafaunas:** large reptile, mammal, and bird species
**Meteorology:** the study of weather and the atmosphere

**Methemoglobinemia:** a disease caused by nitrite impairment of hemoglobin's oxygen transport

**Microcosm:** a small, enclosed life system (for example, an aquarium, terrarium, or test-tube culture) that can be distinguished from an open ecosystem of any size

**Microhabitats:** small places for small organisms

**"Mid-City":** a typical American urban area, with about 1,200,000 residents

**Mode of action:** the way in which a chemical poisons an organism

**Model city:** a city that sets a good example

**Monitoring:** keeping track of changing conditions, natural or unnatural

**Monoculture:** one crop grown over large areas and/or long periods

**"Mousse masses":** tarry, water-logged residues of oil spills

**Mucosa:** the mucus-secreting lining of the respiratory and gastrointestinal systems

**Multiple use:** a policy of trying to use the same resource for several different purposes

**Mutagens:** anything that causes mutations

**Mutations:** changes in hereditary material

**Natural history:** the methodical observing and recording of environmental phenomena or characteristics

**Natural selection:** the evolutionary concept that those organisms well adapted to their environment are more likely to have descendents than are those not so well adapted

**Neo-Luddites:** those who would destroy or stop technological advances, seeing them as threats to jobs and humanity

**Neo-Malthusians:** those continuing the traditions of Malthus in warning that human population growth can outstrip resources

**Niche:** the concept that a species occupies a position in the web of relationships linking it to other species—the "job" it does, in contrast to the "place" it lives (habitat)

**Nonrenewable resources:** those resources that are not self-renewing (for example, minerals, fossil fuels, and space)

**"Nutrification":** a new word used to describe the provision of nutrients for plants

**Old field:** abandoned farmland

**Oligotrophic:** A lake or pond naturally poor in nutrients

**Organic compounds:** those that contain carbon

**Overkills:** any policy of excessive killing, harvesting, or impact

**Oxidation:** occurs when a chemical combines with oxygen

**Ozone:** triplet oxygen $O_3$ (screens out ultraviolet wave lenghts in sunlight)

**PAN (peroxyacetyl nitrate):** an irritating compound formed by photochemical reactions of smog chemicals

**Parabiosphere:** organisms surviving, usually in a dormant state, at the outer limits of the biosphere
**Parasitoids:** those insects with characteristics of predator and parasite; typically, the adult lays an egg on, in, or near the host and the larva gradually consumes the host
**Particulate:** air-borne dirt
**Pathogens:** organisms that cause infectious disease
**Per capita:** per head
**Persistence:** a characteristic of biocides; having toxic residues that last long after application
**Pest:** any animal that bothers us
**Pesticides:** chemicals used to kill pests
**Petrochemical:** a chemical made from oil or coal
**Phagocyte:** white cells that consume and destroy invading microorganisms
**Pheromones:** chemicals that facilitate communication between animals
**Photoperiod:** day length (plants that respond to changes in day length are said to show photoperiodicity)
**Photosynthesis:** the process by which solar energy, water, and $CO_2$ yield carbohydrates and oxygen in green plants
**Photovoltaic cells:** devices coverting light to electricity
**Physiology:** the study of an organism's internal functioning
**Phytoplankton:** free-floating single-celled algae
**"Pill":** a hormonal mixture that suppresses ovulation
**Pinniped mammals:** seals, sea lions, and walruses
**Plankters:** free-floating organisms
**Pollinators:** animals that transfer pollen
**Pollution:** the release of waste materials into the environment
**Pollution stress:** stress imposed by dumping pollutants into the environment
**Population:** organisms of the same species in a delimited spatial unit (area or volume)
**Population equivalents:** units equating human and livestock populations, thus making possible comparisons of total consumption
**Population explosions:** rapid increases in population
**Preservation:** conscious efforts to prevent the loss of natural resources
**Preventive medicine:** the practice of disease prevention through sanitation, immunization, and regular checkups
**Producers:** those organisms (generally green plants) that have the photosynthetic machinery needed to capture and fix solar energy in chemical compounds
**Protective management:** the philosophy of preventing pest outbreaks

**Quality of life:** an as-yet-undetermined measure of the "good life"
**Quarantine:** laws and regulations to exclude pests or pathogens

**Radioisotopes:** a radioactive isotope

**Recycling:** the policy and practice of reusing waste materials

**Regolith:** unconsolidated layer of weathered rock

**Remote sensing:** use of satellites or other high-altitude platforms to obtain images or measurements of ground-level conditions

**Renewable resources:** those resources that are self-renewing (for example, food, water, and solar energy)

**Requisites:** those things needed for survival

**Resistence:** as used here, inherited characteristics that enable organisms to tolerate high doses of antibiotics or pesticides

**Rural support:** those areas of farm, forest, and so on that contribute materials to cities

**Schistosomiasis:** a disease caused by parasitic worms (flukes) that spend part of their life cycle in snails; increased by irrigation and poor sanitation

**Sedimentation:** deposit of water-borne material

**Sex lures:** chemicals emitted by one sex to attract the opposite sex

**Shelter belt:** trees planted along fields to protect crops from wind damage

**Side effect:** any undesired and/or detrimental effect

**Simulation:** in computer terminology, the mimicking of real-life events by mathematical models

**Sirenians:** dugong and manatee

**Slash and burn:** traditional agricultural practice of cutting a forest patch, burning the debris, and cultivating crops until they become unproductive

**Social contract:** an unwritten agreement whereby a citizen surrenders to the state certain freedoms in exchange for certain benefits or protections

**Social Darwinism:** the hypothesis or philosophy that certain classes, nations, or ethnic groups have qualities that make them superior to other groups and permit them to become predominant

**Solution:** a dissolved chemical

**Spaceship Earth:** the concept of earth as a spaceship with finite room, resources, and limits

**Sterilization:** in this context, the use of radiation or chemicals to make an animal incapable of producing offspring

**Stochastic:** pertaining to probablistic predictions

**STP:** sewage treatment plant (also called a waste water treatment facility)

**Succession:** the replacement of one community by another over time

**Sustained yield:** a management policy of harvesting equal to replacement

**Swamps:** wet areas characterized by diverse vegetation, including trees

**Symbiotic:** living together in mutual benefit (for example, in a lichen, the alga captures solar energy and the fungus mines or traps nutrients)

**Synecology:** ecology at the community level and above

**Synergistic:** combined effects greater than the sum of separate effects

**Systematics:** the scientific classification of organisms within an evolutionary framework

**Systems analysis:** approaching an ecosystem or system of comparable complexity with the tools of mathematical modeling, and the like

**Taxonomic:** pertaining to the classification of organisms

**Teratogens:** anything that causes fetal damage or deformation

**Territory:** in animal behavior, this refers to the area defended by an animal

**Thermal enrichment:** a euphemism for release of waste heat

**Thermal plume:** warm water diffusing into a cooler stream

**Thin shelled:** a characteristic of eggs laid by birds suffering from DDT poisoning

**Threshold dose:** the level at which effects can be detected

**Tide pools:** shore-side depressions innundated by the tides

**"Top-dog" predators:** those carnivores feeding highest in a food chain or pyramid

**Tracers:** radioactive isotopes used to determine physiological or ecological pathways

**Trade-offs:** exchanging one value for another

**"Tragedy of the Commons":** the sad fact that resources open to all are overexploited

**Trickling filter:** a bed of gravel through which waste water trickles to facilitate the oxygenation of organic material

**Trophic level:** the feeding step in the food pyramid (for example, herbivore and carnivore)

**Turbidity:** cloudiness in water

**Urban implosion:** migration to, and rapid growth of, cities

**Urea:** product of protein breakdown found in urine

**Vector:** an organism that transmits a pathogen (for example, the *Aedes* mosquito and the yellow fever virus)

**Vent:** in this context, underground atomic tests leaking radioactivity into the atmosphere

**Virulent:** very potent or dangerous

**Vitalism:** the idea that evolution is guided by an inner force

**Watershed:** that portion of landscape from which drainage supplys a waterway

**Wilderness:** a natural area little disturbed by human incursions

**Zero emission:** no release of radiation or chemicals

**ZPG:** the philosophy and policy of setting limits on human population increase

**Zoning:** laws to restrict or guide land use

**Zooplankton:** small, free-floating aquatic animals

# Index